THE EARLY
MEDIEVAL CHURCH
IN WALES

THE EARLY MEDIEVAL CHURCH IN WALES

DAVID PETTS

To Jane and Isobel

First published 2009

The History Press
The Mill, Brimscombe Port
Stroud, Gloucestershire, GL5 2QG
www.thehistorypress.co.uk

© David Petts, 2009

The right of David Petts to be identified as the Author
of this work has been asserted in accordance with the
Copyrights, Designs and Patents Act 1988.

British Library Cataloguing in Publication Data.
A catalogue record for this book is available from the British Library.

ISBN 978 0 7524 4102 3

Typesetting and origination by The History Press
Printed in Great Britain

CONTENTS

INTRODUCTION

I first discovered the archaeology of medieval Wales as an undergraduate at the University of York, when I spent time learning to excavate on two archaeological sites in Wales, the Iron Age hillfort of Castell Henllys and Dolforwyn Castle. These weeks spent amidst the mud and rain of Wales gave me the chance to discover for the first time how different the history and archaeology of that country was to that of England. Although I did not at first pursue my growing interest in the Welsh material, my doctorate in the Department of Archaeology (Reading University), which started life as an analysis of late Roman burial in England, rapidly developed into an exploration of burial and religion in early medieval Wales.

Ever since I began this work in the mid-1990s I have been growing to love the archaeology, history and country of Wales. The early medieval period, and in particular, early Christianity, has become the main subject of my research and study. Whilst I have written papers and articles about this topic, this book has given me a chance to pull my thoughts together and try and develop an overview of this important time in the history of Wales. The role played by the church in medieval Wales was central, and not surprisingly has attracted a lot of writing. Much of the popular work on the early church has been seduced by the Romantic image of the Age of the Saints; this has often been based on a fairly uncritical use of the historical and archaeological sources. Thus, in the first two chapters of the book I have tried to place the study of the early church in its historical context and then outline the broad range of sources available, highlighting their strengths and weaknesses. I then provide a broad thematic overview of the different broad issues that need to be considered, including church architecture, relics and reliquaries, death and burial and the inter-relationship of the church and landscape. I conclude with a more synthetic chapter, in which I try and bring these different themes together and tell the story of the development of the church between the end of the Romans and the death of the last of the native princes. This final section is more personal and subjective, but hopefully it will encourage other workers in the field to put forward their visions of the early church.

Inevitably this book is a product of my own academic specialisms (I am an archaeologist not an historian) and personal interests, but this work, and my other academic work which forms the basis for much of the contents, would not have been possible without the help of a large number of people, who over the last 15 years have provided information, bibliographic references, advice, images and most importantly conversation about the early medieval world. I would particularly like to extend my thanks and appreciation to the following: Tudur Davies, Toby Driver, Nancy Edwards, Helen Geake, Jeremy Knight, John Lewis, Scott Lloyd, David Longley, Neil Ludlow, Dai Morgan Evans, Ken Murphy, Tim Pestell, Aimée Pritchard, Andy Seaman, Bob Silvester, Sam Turner and Gwilym Williams. Special thanks must also go to my wife, Jane Stockdale, and mother-in-law, Ann Stockdale, for support above and beyond the call of duty in the final day of the production of this book. A special thanks must also be given to the editorial staff of The History Press; between starting this book and its completion, I've changed jobs twice, moved house twice and become a father, so I am intensely grateful to Peter Kemmis Betty, Dr Wendy Logue and Miranda Embleton-Smith, who have been tolerant to the extreme with slipping deadlines and unlikely excuses.

St David's Day, York, 2009

NB: Frequent references are made to the various carved stones recorded in a number of major corpuses and catalogues. To avoid constant repetition of the full references only the catalogue numbers are given. Numbers preceded with a letter (i.e. G56, P14, B6) refer to stones recorded in the recent volumes of the Corpus of early medieval inscribed stones and stone sculpture in Wales (Edwards 2007; Rednapp and Lewis 2007). Numbers in italics refer to stones recorded in Nash-Williams' *Early Christian Monuments of Wales* (Nash-Williams 1950).

CHAPTER ONE

THE STUDY OF THE EARLY CHURCH IN WALES

INTRODUCTION

Any explorer of the churches of Wales will soon notice some unusual features; many of the churches are dedicated to unusual saints – some, such as Teilo or Padarn are rarely found outside Wales, others, such as Cybi, are uncommon even within the Principality and some, such as Erfyl and Melangell, are known only at a single church. The observant may also notice that the names of the villages frequently begin with the element Llan (meaning church or cemetery). Some churches may contain stones bearing crudely carved inscriptions or elaborately worked interlace decoration. An examination of a map will reveal that the churchyards are often (but not always) circular or at least possess distinctively curved outlines, whilst holy wells might often be found nearby. Church guidebooks frequently link their church back to the Age of Saints, often claiming an early foundation by a named saint. Some churches have become centres for the particular flavour of Christianity that calls itself 'Celtic Christianity'. All these phenomena, saints and stones and churchyards, are linked together to create a seemingly convincing story about the earliest centuries of Christianity in Wales.

This book tries to unpick genuine history from the tapestry of myth and legend that dominates many popular versions of the early Welsh church. In its place it tries to put forward a more complex and subtle story of the development of Christianity in Wales from its earliest years following the retreat of Rome from its north-western frontiers in the early fifth century to the final conquest of the independent Welsh principalities by the English in the late thirteenth century (Davies 1982a; Davies 1987). This is primarily an archaeological study, drawing on the wide range of surviving material evidence for the early medieval church, although it also utilises the existing documentary evidence. This book is also archaeological in a wider sense. It not only uses material culture as a source of evidence, but also aims to explore the way in which architecture and objects were used by the early church, and the complex and changing interrelationship between artefacts and texts.

The archaeological evidence for the period is sparse compared with that of England or Ireland. Settlement has proved hard to identify and a relatively small number of artefacts have been recovered (Edwards and Lane 1988; Arnold and Davies 2000). One of the few types of evidence that survives in any number is stone sculpture, which is of overwhelmingly ecclesiastical origin (Edwards 2001). Ranging from roughly carved stone gravestones to elaborate carved crosses, this collection of material dominates the archaeological study of the period. The limited documentary evidence from the period is also primarily ecclesiastical (Davies 1982). Perhaps inevitably the study of the church has been one of the main themes in scholarship on early medieval Wales from AD 400–1200, particularly for the earliest part of this period (Davies 2004). Whilst this emphasis on the development of Christianity may have partly arisen out of the nature of the surviving evidence, it also reflects the key role of the Church in early medieval society. In a world in which literacy was limited and which saw the rise of increasingly sophisticated political entities with their related administrative structures, churchmen were profoundly implicated not just in religious duties and pastoral responsibilities but in the formation of the many of the key organs of power in early medieval Wales. These ranged from the compilation and administration of laws to the movement of economic wealth (Pryce 1992a; Pryce 1993). Any exploration of the history and society of early medieval Wales must have an understanding of the role of the church at its heart.

THE 'CELTIC CHURCH'

One of the dominant narratives in the study of early medieval Christianity in Britain has been that of the 'Celtic Church' (Davies 2004). Amongst many popular and academic writers on Christianity and spirituality in Wales, Ireland and Scotland the notion of a unifying 'Celtic' strand of Christianity, distinct from the Roman-influenced Anglo-Saxon Christianity propagated by St Augustine, has been a key tenet (Bradley 1999). Whilst subject to increased critical scrutiny within academia, the 'myth of the Celtic church' remains widespread in popular culture (Davies 1992).

Today, the proponents of this notion of a pan-national, unified Celtic church emphasise a number of key themes. There is a belief that the early church in Wales, Ireland, Scotland and Brittany was non-hierarchical, had an equal role for men and women in spiritual life and possessed a heightened ecological sensibility (Atherton 2002; Davies 2002). However, this is a specifically twentieth-century configuration of a myth which has proved deeply malleable over the last 800 years. The churches of early medieval Insular Britain have provided a potent source for myth, history and ideology.

In Wales, one aspect of this appropriation of the early Church was the adoption and spread of St David as the national saint. There is evidence for the promotion of David as a patron saint for the entire nation of Wales rather than the individual Welsh kingdoms from as early as the late first millennium (James 1994). The tenth century prophetic poem *Armes Prydein* contains early indications of the increasingly pre-eminent role David was taking in national consciousness (Fulton 2001; Isaac 2007). In the poem David is seen as a man who will intervene for the Welsh against the English: 'Through the prayers of David and the saints of Britain, the foreigners will be put to flight as far as the channel of Legio' (Isaac 2007).

The perceived glory of the Welsh church was also present amongst the demands of Owain Glyndŵr between 1400 and 1409. He called for the restoration of the bishopric of St Davids to its former status as a metropolitan see (Davies 1997; Williams 1979). Notably, he called for its jurisdiction to cover not just the three Welsh dioceses of Bangor, Llandaf and St Asaph, but also those of Exeter, Bath, Hereford, Worcester, Coventry and Lichfield. This was not simply a rash attempt at expanding the influence of St David's at the expense of the English, but was connected firmly to pre-existing claims that this had been the former area controlled by St David's from the time of David to Samson, his twenty-fifth successor (ibid.).

THE REFORMATION AND BEYOND

Initially, the advent of the Reformation in Wales rejected the importance of the earlier Welsh church, seeing it as being imbued with the very elements of the Catholic Church that the reformers were trying to reject. This rejection of the Welsh church took a range of forms. The Bishop of St Davids, William Barlow (d.1568) wanted to transfer his cathedral from St Davids to Carmarthen (Wyn Evans 2007). This was partly for practical reasons and mirrored the plan by Bishop Parfew to move his cathedral from St Asaph (Williams 1997). However, Barlow also had theological motivations for his plans; he desired to dismantle the link between his church from the 'ungodly ymage service [and] abhomynable ydolatrye' associated with the shrine of St David (Wright 1843).

The Reformation in Wales also saw the widespread destruction of shrines and relics, many of which may have had their origin in the early medieval period (Williams 1997; Gray 1991; Gray 2000). Amongst the most notable of these events were the seizure of the image of Derfel Gadarn, a wooden carving of the saint on his horse, which was taken from the church of Llandderfel and burnt in London (Gray Hulse 1998), the demolition of the shrine of St David (Evans 1991; Williams 2007; Wyn Evans 2007) and the destruction of the shrine of St Teilo and the associated relics at Llandaf (Williams 1991). Whilst some elements of these shrines have survived – such as the fragments of the reliquary from Gwytherin (Edwards and Gray Hulse 1994), or Derfel's wooden horse, which still stands in the church porch at Llandderfel – the destruction wrought by the Reformation and later during the Civil War undoubtedly did much harm to important early medieval material.

However, Protestant reformers soon began to see the native British churches in a more favourable light. A renewed interest in early English church history was making clear the strong role that Rome had played in the conversion of much of Anglo-Saxon England to Christianity. The mission of Augustine in AD 597 had been at the direct instigation of Pope Gregory in Rome. In contemporary records it was clear that the Roman church came into direct opposition with the insular churches. In the Synod of Whitby (AD 664), Oswald made the decision that the Northumbrian church should follow the customs of the Roman church promoted by Wilfrid and Agilbert rather than the practices advocated by the Picts and the British defended by Colman (Bede EH III.25; Eddius Stephanus 10). This became one of the defining moments in the story of the 'Celtic' church, the point at which the balance was tipped in favour of the Roman church of Augustine and marking the beginning of the end for native British traditions. Bede saw the debate as being particularly focused on the different ways in which the Roman church and other churches calculated the date of Easter, though this may partly have been due to his own interest in calculating time and dates. One of the wider underlying issues was that of authority; the Roman faction emphasising the need for the other parties to accept the authority of the Pope to make decisions about religious practice. It is important to remember though, that this debate was about practices rather than any dispute over underlying issues of doctrine. Both the British and Pictish churches were always in communion with the Roman church and there was no explicit or implicit suggestion of heresy by Wilfrid or Bede (though for an alternative view see Herren and Brown 2002).

1 Antiquarian image of stone sculpture including an early medieval example (from Llandyfaelog-fach) (Strong 1796)

For many early Protestant scholars these native churches came to be seen as bodies that stood up to Papism; they also seemed to follow practices attractive to sixteenth-century reformers, such as a rejection of clerical celibacy (Bradley 1999). Matthew Parker, Archbishop of Canterbury (1550–1629) in his *De Antiquitate Britannica Ecclesiae* (1572) strived to highlight that the earliest Christianity in England owed much to the influence of the native Christian traditions, minimising the importance of contacts with Rome and any perceived taint of Papism. Parker also supported the publication of *Apologia Ecclesiae Anglicanae* (1562) by John Jewel, Bishop of Salisbury, an early defence of Anglicanism, which also emphasised the native British contribution to the early church (Bradley 1999; Crankshaw and Gillespie 2006).

In Wales similar views were promoted by the Bishop of St Davids, Richard Davies (1505–81); in his *Address to the Welsh Nation* (*Epistol at y Cembru*) he proclaimed 'The British kept their Christianity pure and immaculate, without admixture of human imaginings. Augustine's Christianity veered rather from the matchless purity of the Gospel ...' (Bradley 1999). He was also a promoter of the translation of the Bible into Welsh, with the help of the antiquary Humphrey Llwyd (1527–68) whose *Commentarioli Britannicae descriptionis fragmentum* (1572) also emphasised the continuity and integrity of the church in Britain (Brinley Jones 2004; Williams 2004). In the seventeenth century, the work of Davies went on to influence writers such as Charles Edwards (1628–91), who wrote *Y ffydd ddi-ffuant* (*The Sincere Faith* ,1672) to some copies of which he attached the pamphlet *Hebraismorum Cambro-Brittanicorum Specimen* which drew links between Welsh and Hebrew words and phrases (Williams 1968). In a similar vein writing in the early eighteenth century Theophilus Evans (1693–1767) a Carmarthenshire clergyman wrote *Drych y Prif Oesedd* (*Mirror of the Primitive Ages*, 1716) which again highlighted the presence of Anglican principle in early British Christianity and promoted the notion that the Welsh were direct descendants of Gomer, son of Japhet, son of Noah (Jenkins 2004). These Welsh writings reflected similar moves by Scottish and Irish writers to emphasis the Protestant sympathies of the early church in Britain particularly focusing on such practices as married clergy, ascetic lifestyles and the lack of papal involvement in the succession of bishops (Bradley 1999). Some writers, such as Theophilus Evans, were equally concerned to emphasise that the early church was episcopal, despite claims to the contrary by some Presbyterians (ibid). Overall, their approaches were summed up by Thomas Burgess (1730–1791), Bishop of St Davids in his *Tract on the Origin and Independence of the Ancient British Church*: 'The church of Britain was a Protestant Church nine centuries before the days of Luther' (ibid).

THE RISE OF THE ANTIQUARIANS

In the eighteenth and nineteenth centuries, the increased interest in the early church in Wales and beyond went hand in hand with burgeoning scholarship on the textual material (Bradley 1999). Although much that was written had a keen polemical edge, it was supported by solid research. As early as the mid-seventeenth century, churchmen such as James Ussher, Archbishop of Armagh (1581–1656), were increasingly turning to original manuscript sources to support their arguments, spurring an greater scepticism of many elements of the traditional narratives relating to the spread of Christianity in Britain. Catholics as well as Protestants also became increasingly involved in new studies in hagiography, such as the Société des Bollandistes founded in Antwerp in 1607, who turned their attention to insular material.

During the eighteenth century much antiquarian research in Wales was centred on recovering the antiquity of the Welsh language and the promotion of the cults of the bard and the druid (Sweet 2004). The work of the *'Hen bersoniaid llengar'* (the old literary parsons) was of great importance. This group of scholars, who were most active in the mid-nineteenth century, had the support of Thomas Burgess and aimed to revive interest in the early history of Wales particularly through the study of manuscripts and other antiquarian material, and was heavily involved in the founding of the Welsh Manuscripts Society in 1837 (Stephens 2007). One key member was W.J. Rees (1772–1855), who prepared an edition of the *Liber Landavensis* (1840) and compiled and edited *The Lives of the Cambro-British Saints* (1853), although his scholarship was later to be heavily criticised (Lloyd 2004). Another important figure was John Williams (1811–1862) author of *Eglwys Loegr yn anymddibynol ar eglwys Rufain* (*The Church of England Independent of the Church of Rome*, 1836). Williams produced editions of *Y Gododdin, Brut y Tywysogion* and the *Annales Cambriae* as well as being the first editor of *Archaeologia Cambrensis*, the journal of the Cambrian Archaeological Association, founded in 1846 (Stephens 2007).

Work on hagiography continued apace throughout the nineteenth century and into the twentieth. Sabine Baring-Gould's (1834–1924) *Lives of the Saints* included over 3,600 individual saints' biographies including many native British saints. Baring-Gould himself had a personal interest in the history of western Britain. He was president of the Royal Institution of Cornwall during which he gave presidential addresses on the 'Early History of Cornwall' and on 'The Celtic Saints' (Colloms 2004). Another key figure was the Reverend A.W.Wade-Evans whose work on saints' lives culminated in his publication of *Vitae Sanctorum Britanniae et genealogiae* (1944). His work was driven by a pride in his Welsh background stimulated by the atmosphere at late nineteenth century Oxford:

> … when I went up to Oxford in 1893 – poor innocent that I was – pro-Germanism and 'No Popery' prevailed – Ireland was riff-raff, Wales was scorned – and I was made to realise I was only a 'Celt'. It was all this that roused me to delve into things in my own account – such is the background from which my scratching and scraping emanates.
>
> (Foster 1964)

However, despite this spur to his scholarship his judgement on many aspects of early Church history was clear-eyed and he opposed 'the modern invention of a so-called "Celtic Church" as opposed to Rome – a notion so outrageous that only modern political and ecclesiastical strife could have imagined it' (ibid.) A final important figure was Canon G.H. Doble, a Cornish clergyman and folklorist who between 1929 and 1945 compiled an extensive collection of hagiographical material related to early British saints from Cornwall and Wales (Doble 1971).

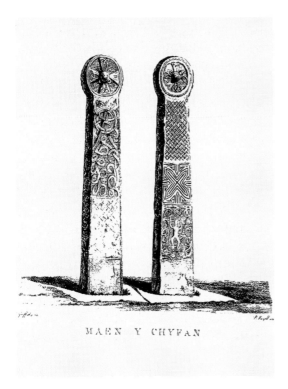

2 Maen Achwyfan by Thomas Pennant. (from Pennant 1796)

3 Etching of the Pillar of Eliseg by Alfred Clint. (Bennett 1838. © The Trustees of the British Museum)

The rise of interest in saints in the later nineteenth and early twentieth century led to a particular tendency to use a positivist understanding of the hagiographic material combined with the study of place names and church dedications to plot geographical narratives, to describe and explain the spread of saints' cults through the peripatetic wanderings of the important early church figures (e.g. Bowen 1954). This approach, despite being heavily criticised at the time and since, was and has remained extremely influential, particularly in the more popular literature (Chadwick 1959; Wooding 2007).

As well as increased interest in the documentary evidence for the early history of Wales, there was also a developing engagement with the archaeological material. Wales had a long history of antiquarian endeavour. Early scholars, such as Edward Lhuyd (1659–1707), who became keeper of the Ashmolean Museum in Oxford, recorded some early Christian sculpture. However, most were more interested in recording megalithic monuments and exploring the origins of the Welsh language. Lhuyd's *Archaeologia Britannica* (1707) was intended to consist of several volumes, but only the first appeared, a groundbreaking study of the Celtic languages. He also extensively revised the Welsh content in William Camden's *Britannia,* including some early Christian monuments leading some to call him the 'founding father of early medieval Celtic archaeology' (Sweet 2004; Edwards 2007).

A. Early Norman doorway. B. Site of Early masonry left in situ
C. Recently discovered door from Parvise to minstrels gallery. D. Entrance to Parvise
Staircase

4 Drawing of the interior of Llantwit Major church. (Halliday 1890)

INTO THE NINETEENTH CENTURY

The practice of topographic writing and illustration was slow to develop in Wales and did not result in significant work until the later eighteenth century, with the work Thomas Pennant (Fig 2) (*A Tour in Wales*, 1778–83; *The History of the Parishes of Whiteford, and Holywell* 1796), George Bennett (*The Pedestrian's Guide Through North Wales*, 1838) (Fig 3), Thomas Inglcby and John Buckler, amongst others. The latter's *Ecclesiastical, Monumental and Castellated Antiquities of North Wales* (1810) was dedicated to the important English antiquarian Sir John Colt Hoare. Colt Hoare was also a close friend of Richard Fenton (1747–1821), author of *A Historical Tour Through Pembrokeshire* (1811), and a keen excavator described as 'an iconoclastic gourmet who went through the land breaking up barrows and cracking cromlechs' (Laws 1895).

   Although much of the material recorded by these early scholars was of high medieval date, many of these antiquarians did record early medieval inscribed stones (Redknap 1998). The increased interest in the physical remains of Welsh antiquity led, in 1846, to the foundation of the Cambrian Archaeological Association, which arose directly out of the publication of the first volume of *Archaeologia Cambrensis* (Fig 4) (Moore 1998). This contained a prospectus for the future study of archaeology in Wales entitled 'On the Study and Preservation of National Antiquities' by the Reverend Harry Longueville-Jones (1806–70). The later nineteenth and early twentieth century saw the establishment of a series of further local archaeological and historical societies across Wales, such as the Powysland Club (founded 1867), the Anglesey Antiquarian and Field Society (founded 1911), and the Carmarthenshire Antiquarian Society (founded 1905). Archaeological societies in neighbouring regions, such as the Woolhope Club in Herefordshire and the Chester Archaeological and Historical Society also carried out fieldwork over the border in Wales (Silvester 1997).

   Wade-Evans wrote that 'archaeology, philology, geography, or any other auxiliary discipline that serves in some degree to uncover the past, is not history' (cited in Foster 1964). However, the value of archaeological and architectural evidence was manifest to early researchers. There was long a particular awareness of the importance of the sculptural repertoire of early medieval Wales, both in its own right and in terms of links with broadly similar Irish and Scottish traditions. Indeed the first issue of *Archaeologia Cambrensis* contained an article by John Westwood (1805–1903) on the presence of ogham stones in Wales (Westwood 1846). He proceeded to submit a series of articles on early sculpture in Wales to the journal, as well as widening his interests to include work on early hand bells (Westwood 1848). His research culminated in *Lapidarium Walliae*, a corpus of early medieval Welsh sculpture, published by the Cambrian Archaeological Association and explicitly modelled on a similar enterprise by the Royal Historical and Archaeological Association of Ireland (Fig.1e) (Westood 1876). Many of the inscriptions were also included in Emil Hübner's *Inscriptiones Britanniae Christianae* which shortly preceded it in 1876. Westwood's work was built on by Sir John Rhŷs who held the first chair in Celtic at Jesus College Oxford; again most of his output on epigraphy appearing within the pages of *Archaeologia Cambrensis*.

   Interest in the sculptural material continued into the twentieth century with the work of Romilly Allen, who contributed a key paper on early Welsh Christian art in 1899, which emphasised the links with Scotland and Wales (Allen 1899). The tendency to group the 'Celtic' sculptural material together grew in the twentieth century, perhaps reaching its apogee with R.A.S. Macalister's (1870–1950) *Corpus inscriptionum insularum Celticarum*, which aimed to contain all early inscriptions in Celtic languages or Latin, from areas deemed Celtic. Thus it contained material from Wales, Scotland, Ireland and the Isle of Man, and also 'Celtic' areas of England, such as Herefordshire, Devon, Cornwall and even Dorset (Macalister 1945). This substantial work, as the title suggests, focused only on the epigraphic material, ignoring the wider body of sculpture, and by the mid-twentieth century there was a need to improve on Westwood's *Lapidarium* (Redknap 1988). This led to the commencement on work on *Early Christian Monuments of Wales* by Victor Nash-Williams, supported by the National Museum of Wales and the University of Wales' Board of Celtic Studies (ibid). Nash-Williams, Keeper of Archaeology at the National Museum and Lecturer in Archaeology in University College Cardiff, was not himself an early medievalist or an art historian. Much of his other work was on Roman material from Wales and he excavated extensively. However, with input from R.A.S. Macalister, Sir Ifor Williams and C.A. Raleigh Radford, he was able to compile not only a substantial gazetteer, but also put in place a simple classificatory system, which although needing some adjustment, has continued to be used by scholars since the publication of the volume in 1950 (Nash-Williams' Groups 1-4).

However, not all work on the archaeological material was limited to explorations of the sculptural and epigraphic resources. Over the course of the eighteenth and nineteenth centuries other evidence was being accidentally uncovered. The growth of the railways led to a number of fortuitous discoveries, such as the finding of an inscribed stone and around 40 cist graves whilst making the Holyhead railway line at Pentrefoelas (*125*; Mascetti 2001). Coastal erosion also led to the discovery of previously unknown sites: at Tywyn-y-Capel, Llansantfraid, wind uncovered a cist grave cemetery in sand dunes (Stanley 1846). Most discoveries were fortuitous. The continuation of worship on most church sites meant that excavation was rare. One notable exception was the discovery of early foundations beneath the later medieval *eglwys y bedd* at Clynnog Fawr (Stallybrass 1914). It was only on sites that had fallen out of use that it was possible to carry out some level of coherent and extensive excavation, such as at St Justinian's Chapel, St Davids (Boake 1926), and St Patrick's Chapel, Whitesand Bay, St Davids (Badger and Grew 1925). Nonetheless the compilation of the Royal Commission for Ancient and Historic Monuments of Wales volumes particularly those for Anglesey (1937), Carmarthenshire (RCHMW 1917) and Pembrokeshire (RCHMW 1925) were valuable in bringing together the mainly architectural evidence that was not covered by the volumes of sculpture and epigraphy.

THE GROWTH OF ARCHAEOLOGY

The rate of archaeological discoveries in the second half of the twentieth century increased significantly for a series of reasons. Across the UK there was an improvement in excavation techniques. Early medieval remains in Wales are often ephemeral and lacking in easily datable material culture, but new methodologies, such as the introduction of open-plan excava-tion and single-context recording meant that it was proving easier to record early medieval remains. A number of key excavations such as Leslie Alcock's work at Dinas Powys meant that the suite of material culture diagnostic of an early medieval date was also becoming more defined (Alcock 1963).

The increased use of radiocarbon dating also meant that it was possible to provide a sci-entific date to sites that had previously been undatable due to the lack of material culture or stratigraphic relationships. The rising amount of aerial photography taking place over Wales has also led to the increased identification of potentially important early medieval sites (Howe 1996; James 1990; Musson 1994). Changes in heritage protection laws and atti-tudes towards the archaeological resource have also meant an increase amount of excavation, usually driven by development control or resource management imperatives. Although the advent of *Planning and Policy Guidance note 16 (Wales)* has had an important role in stimulat-ing excavation, it is has perhaps had less of an impact in Wales than in England due to the rural nature of much of Wales beyond the south and south-east. Finally, there have been important structural developments in the heritage sector in Wales. The establishment of the four regional archaeological units in the mid-1970s was crucial in providing a solid bed of archaeological skills combined with a detailed knowledge of their local areas. This has been essential in a country where there was relatively little active fieldwork on medieval sites being carried out by the universities. The activity of Cadw and the Royal Commission on the Ancient and Historical Monuments of Wales in carrying out large-scale survey work, both directly and through commissioned works has also continued to provide much new data, and consolidate existing information. Recent notable projects include the Historic Churches Survey, which surveyed and recorded all pre-nineteenth century churches (Evans et al 2000) and the Early Medieval Ecclesiastical Sites in North West Wales, both of which have provided significant new information about the state of the archaeological resource.

Despite the improvement in the amount of fieldwork being carried out there has still been relatively little synthetic work carried out on the archaeology of the early church out-side the realm of stone carving and epigraphy. There have been many overviews exploring specific topics, such as the carved stones (Dark 1992; Edwards 2001a, 2001b; Handley 2001; Knight 1992, 2001b; Sims-Williams 2003; Tedeschi 1995), churches (Edwards 1996, Butler 1996, Thurlby 2006; Ludlow 2001), shrines and relics (Edwards 2002), wells (Edwards 1994; Jones 1992) and burial (James 1992; Petts 2001, 2002, 2007), and important county or regional assessments of the evidence (Brook 1986; Edwards 1986; Evans 1986; Fenn 2000; Fenn and Sinclair 1990; Morgan Evans 2005). However, there have been few attempts to bring the material together and provide a wider assessment of its meaning and development and to place it in its wider context (exceptions include Thomas 1994 and Knight 1999). There has also been a greater emphasis on the earlier period, particularly the fifth to eighth centuries, the 'Age of the Saints', than on the ninth to twelfth centuries despite the fact that it is in the latter period that many key developments occurred such as the growth of the parish system, Anglo-Saxon, Viking and Norman expansion and a greater amount of documentary evi-dence (albeit limited compared with Anglo-Saxon England).

5 Drawing of the inscribed stone from Twywn.
(J.O. Westwood, *Lapidarium Walliae*, 1876)

Whilst the sculptural and particularly epigraphic material was used to explore the earliest periods of the church, there was generally little attempt to integrate the wider range of architectural and archaeological material into a narrative. Intriguingly despite the increased academic scepticism about the notion of the Celtic church and a greater deconstruction of the wider concept of Celticism (James 1999; Collis 2003), the term still appears to structure much of the academic work on the archaeology of early medieval Wales. For example, in 2004 the Society for Church Archaeology and the Society for Medieval Archaeology jointly organised a conference entitled *The Archaeology of the Early Medieval Celtic Churches* bringing together scholars from Ireland, Wales, Scotland, Brittany and south-west England. In the modern academic literature it is still more common to find articles or conference papers on the early medieval archaeology of Cornwall and Caithness side by side than on Montgomeryshire and Mercia.

This apparent lack of overlap between the 'Celtic' world and Anglo-Saxon England extends into the research interests of contemporary leading scholars, whose work may range freely across Wales, Ireland and Scotland, but rarely address the situation the other side of Offa's Dyke (cf. Handley 2001). The situation is equally true amongst Anglo-Saxonists who it seems are sometimes more aware of the current research on Merovingian France than early medieval Wales, though there are some notable exceptions (e.g. Higgitt 1986). It is rare to find a researcher whose work ranges freely beyond the 'Celtic world' and notably these scholars, such as Wendy Davies and Robert Bartlett tend to be historians rather than archaeologists, though the work of Martin Carver, who has excavated at major Anglo-Saxon and Pictish sites is also of great importance.

This is more than a simple question of academic demarcation, it has an important impact on the way in which debates about the development of early medieval Wales in general and the early medieval Welsh church in particular have developed. For example, much of the critique of the notion of Celtic Christianity has been more centred on highlighting the difference between Welsh, Irish, Scottish and Breton churches than on exploring the wider similarities and examples of parallel evolution found in Wales, England and France. In the long term this may risk leading the archaeology of early medieval Wales down a dangerously parochial path.

This book aims to cross some of the traditional disciplinary boundaries that have long been evident in the study of the early church in Britain and endeavours to understand the development of the church in Wales as a key thread in the story of the church in the 'Celtic' world, but also hopes to compare it with contemporary developments in Anglo-Saxon England and in Europe as a whole. Taking such an approach it will be seen that despite there being evidence for distinct local practices and inevitable idiosyncrasies, for the most part the church in Wales between AD 400 and 1200 followed a trajectory broadly similar to other regional churches elsewhere in Europe.

CHAPTER TWO

SOURCES FOR THE STUDY OF THE EARLY CHURCH IN WALES

INTRODUCTION

The range of available evidence for the study of the early church in Wales is not extensive, and there are distinct gaps in the record, both chronologically and regionally. Part of the challenge in exploring the data is trying to make comparisons between areas and periods where the material evidence is dissimilar. It is essential to distinguish between areas where the evidence is lacking and those where the difference tells us as much about variations in the long-term survival of artefacts and sites as about early medieval religious practice.

ARCHAEOLOGICAL EVIDENCE

The particular challenges of specific classes of archaeological evidence, such as churches and religious artefacts, will be explored in some detail in the following chapters. There are, however, two interlinked problems that cross-cut most types of archaeological data. First is the general difficulty in dating archaeological material from early medieval Wales. There is a notable lack of artefactual evidence, particularly of the type that lends itself to typological dating. Although high quality metalwork from western Britain exists, it is sadly lacking the range of objects found in sealed contexts that has formed the backbone of the archaeological chronology of the Anglo-Saxon areas of England (Youngs 1989; Redknap 2007).

Radiocarbon dating
Radiocarbon dating is the most commonly used scientific technique for dating archaeological sites. It may be used on any organic material including bone, wood and charcoal. This technique is based on the assumption that the isotope carbon 14, which is naturally taken up by all living things, decays at a known rate on death (Renfrew and Bahn 2004).

The use of radiocarbon dates is not straightforward, as the raw dates need calibration to convert them from un-calibrated radiocarbon years Before Present to calendar dates. Calibration curves are not simple lines, but contain variations within them, including wiggles and plateaux, where the relationship between un-calibrated dates BP and calendar dates is even more complex. In the period under discussion in this book there is a plateau on the calibration curve between AD 450 and AD 530 meaning that it is not possible to place many dates more accurately within this broad 80-year bracket. Radiocarbon dates are thus quoted as a range of dates rather than one date. To further complicate matters, a large number of calibration curves have been developed, so it is important to ensure that when comparing dates they are calibrated on the same curve.

The large range of error in radiocarbon dates means that if there is any degree of overlap in the given dates, it is hard to make chronological comparisons between two graves. This problem is exemplified by the series of radiocarbon dates from the post-Roman occupation at Wroxeter (Shropshire). Although these dates come from a series of layers with a clear stratigraphic relationship, this relationship is not recognisable in the radiocarbon dates (Barker 1997).

Ceramic Evidence

Very little pottery has been recovered from early medieval sites in Wales, and there are no local coarsewares. There are, however, some imported ceramics from North Africa, the Eastern Mediterranean and Gaul (Campbell 2007). Although archaeologists in Britain have broadly classified them A, B, D and E wares, they are a diverse group comprising amphorae, red tableware and stamped and wheel-thrown grey wares (Wooding 1996; Campbell 2007). In the Insular world they are known to have a mainly western distribution, including Dumnonia, Wales, Southern and Eastern Ireland and western Scotland (Thomas 1981b, Campbell 2007). Most sites only have one or two sherds, but a few, such as Dinas Powys have a much larger assemblage. It also became increasingly clear that E ware was chronologically distinct from A and B ware following Richard Warner's excavations at the royal site of Clogher, County Tyrone, where these wares were in stratigraphically distinct layers (Warner 1979).

The glossy, red A ware consists of a range of imported tableware from western Asia Minor and North Africa dating from the later fifth century to the mid-sixth century AD (Campbell 2007). The B wares were identified as amphorae, similar to those found on a wide number of Mediterranean sites and coming from Asia Minor and Tunisia and again date broadly to the late fifth to mid-sixth century (ibid). D ware seems to be of western French origin, probably developing from Late Roman finewares which belong to Rigoir's Atlantic Group of *sigillées palaéochrétiennes grises* (Rigoir et al 1973). It has a limited distribution in Britain, but is known from several sites in Wales. Its precise place of origin is not certain, but the areas around Bordeaux or the Saintonge/Touraine region are candidates. Its chronological range is not certain, beyond a broadly sixth-century date. There are hints that it may belong to a slightly later phase of trade than the East Mediterranean wares, and thus probably continues into the second half of the sixth century (Campbell 1997).

E ware has been found on over 70 British and Irish sites with a concentration in Scotland and Northern Ireland. It seems probable the vessels arrived directly from the Eastern Mediterranean rather than the pottery being shipped in the south and sent onwards. Again the exact place of origin of E ware is unclear, though close parallels have been found at Herpes, Chadenac (Charente) and Tours (Touraine), suggesting an origin in the Loire estuary area (Campbell 2007). Stratified pottery sequences from Clogher (Tyrone) (Warner 1979), Whithorn (Dumfries and Galloway) and Tours suggest a late sixth or seventh-century date (Wooding 1996).

Despite the presence of this datable ceramic material from archaeological sites, it is of limited use in dating ecclesiastical sites. Most of the known material has been recovered from secular sites such as Dinas Powys (Alcock 1963) and Hen Gastell (Campell 1996). It is rare to find imported pottery on sites related to the early church, though there are exceptions, such as the recent excavations at Llandough (Williams and Redknap 2005).

There is little evidence for ceramic material in Wales from the end of the importation of E ware in the seventh century and the appearance of imported English pottery in the eleventh and twelfth centuries. It appears that late Anglo-Saxon pottery – even that produced on the Welsh borders, such as Chester Ware – had no significant distribution in Wales, though some has been found in Monmouth and pottery with a similar fabric was recovered from the *burgh* at Rhuddlan (Clarke 1991; Owen 1994; Rutter 1988). From the later eleventh century and early twelfth century, some pottery from England, such as ceramics from Worcester and the Severn Valley, was starting to find its way into Wales, usually associated with sites of Norman activity, such as castles (e.g. Hen Domen, Ratkai 2000; Monmouth, Clarke 1991), but little of this material has been recovered away from the Welsh borders and the south of the country (Vince 1987). It is only in the later twelfth and thirteenth century that significant amounts of ceramics begin to appear on archaeological sites in Wales, including, for the first time since the Roman period, pottery actually produced in Wales, in the form of material from the Monnow Valley (Clarke 1991). It is in this period that we also begin to find ceramics associated with ecclesiastical sites again. For example, excavations at Capel Maelog recovered an assemblage of nearly 800 sherds (Courtney et al. 1990). This equated to around 5.6 sherds per square metre, which was comparable with the figure of 4.8 sherds per square metre from the church at Wharram Percy (North Yorkshire), a site of similar date (ibid). The pottery came from a range of sources, including locally produced Welsh potteries and material from the English side of the border. Other church sites at which pottery of eleventh to thirteenth-century date has been recovered include St Barruc's Chapel, where sherds of a comb and roulette-decorated jug from the Bristol Channel area were found sealed beneath the fourteenth-century paving of the chancel (Knight 1981).

The value of pottery for dating sites is not always certain. For example, although medieval pottery was recovered from excavations in and around the church at Rhossili, all the sherds were recovered from a domestic structure, possibly the priest's house, rather than the church itself (Sell 1988). Also, it is important to remember that many of the late coarse wares can be difficult to date precisely; the unglazed vessels recovered from excavations at the church at Llanelen could only date to between 1200–1350 (Kissock 1996). The final limitation in the use of ceramic evidence for dating archaeological sites is the ultimately sparse distribution of ceramic material in medieval Wales; large parts of central and upland Wales undoubtedly remained to all intents and purposes aceramic until the post-medieval period.

Stone Sculpture

Despite the relative lack of small finds, early medieval Wales is well provided with a significant body of carved stone sculpture. This material ranges from simple cross-incised stones through inscriptions in Latin, Irish and rarely Welsh, to artistically elaborate crosses. Over 600 carved stones have been discovered, over 100 since the publication of Nash-Williams' *Early Christian Monuments of Wales* in 1950 (Nash-Williams 1950; Edwards 2001). Not surprisingly, considering the importance of this corpus of material, they have attracted a great deal of research. Westwood's *Lapidarium Walliae* (1876–9) was the first corpus, but also contained earlier and later material.

The first attempt to analyse and systemise the stones appeared in 1899 with the publication of J. Romilly Allen's paper in *Archaeologia Cambrensis*. He put forward a typology for understanding the stones consisting of six main categories: (1) erect pillar or slabs with relief-carved crosses, (2) recumbent slabs with relief-carved crosses, (3) erect rectangular cross-slabs, (4) recumbent rectangular cross-slabs, (5) erect monuments in the shape of a cross (with four sub-types based on variation in the shaft), (6) hog-backed recumbent monuments or coped stones (Romilly Allen 1899). However, although he explored the formal variation in the decorations on these crosses at some length, the paper did not address the issue of dating the monuments, beyond a broad assumption that they were pre-Norman. Crucially, Allen also focused only on the stones bearing some element of ornament or design, thus excluding most of the simple, inscribed stones of fifth to seventh-century date.

The main system used for categorising these monuments is that developed by Nash-Williams for his corpus of early Christian monuments from Wales (Nash-Williams 1950; Redknap 1998). This breaks down the material into four groups, defined primarily on the basis of their form, though there is an implicit chronological element to the series.

Group 1 comprises stones with inscriptions in Latin and ogham, and are unworked or only crudely shaped (Edwards 2001). Some were inscribed in both ogham and Latin. Usually both these inscriptions carry the same message. They are mainly found in the south-west (particularly Pembrokeshire) and the north-west, though clusters are also found in Breconshire and Glamorgan.

Ogham is a simple alphabet of lines and dashes, developed primarily for use on stone, that developed in Ireland (McManus 1991). The use of ogham in Wales indicates strong links with the southern part of Ireland in the early medieval period. The inscriptions could comprise just the name of the commemorated (in the genitive; the word 'grave' or 'stone' being understood), as can be seen on a bilingual stone from Trecastle, which has inscriptions in Latin and ogham reading '(Ogham) (the stone) of Maquutrenus Salicidunus/ (Latin) (the stone) of Maccutrenus Salicidunus)' (Redknap and Lewis 2007) (Fig 6). Alternatively the name in genitive and its filiation, in Irish *maqi avi*, or *maqi mucoi*, and in Latin *fili* or *filius*, would be used. The date of the origin of ogham in Ireland is still uncertain, though linguistically it is likely to have arisen at some point between AD 100 and AD 400 (Harvey 2001). As historically attested Irish settlement in Wales did not begin until the fifth century with movement of the tribal group known as the Deisi into Dyfed, it is usually assumed that Welsh ogham stones are at least early fifth century in date, though in theory an earlier date might be possible.

Stones with inscriptions only in Latin had a wider range of epigraphic forms, including the formulae used on bilingual stones. Most had the name (in the nominative or genitive), sometimes with a filiation, and the term *Hic Iacit* (or occasionally *Hic Iacet*) meaning 'here lies'. For example, an inscription from Llanaelhaiarn reads ALIORTUS ELMETIACOS HIC IACET (*87*) (Fig 6). Other elements used include *in pace* (in peace) (e.g. SANCT(?)/INVS /SACE(?)R(dos?) / I[N] P(ace) (Sanctinus the Bishop (lies here) in peace), Bodafon; *83*) *in hoc tumulo* (in this tomb) (e.g. [A]NNICI FILIVS [H]IC IACIT TECVRI IN HOC TVMVLO (The Stone of Anniccius, son of Tecurus. He lies here in this tomb) Abercar; *41*) or the name followed by *nomine* (the person in the name of) (e.g. EQVESTRI(s) NOMINE ((The person) by the name of Equester (lies here)), Llandanwg; *279*). More complex epitaphs are also known, one stone from Penmachno has the inscription CARAVSIVS / HIC IACIT/ IN HOC CON/GERIES LA/PIDUM (Carusius lies here in this heap of stones) (*101*) (Fig 6), whilst another, also from Penmachno, reads CANTIORI(x) HIC IACIT / [V]ENEDOTIS CIVE(s) FVIT /[C]ONSOBRINO(s) // MA[G]LI /MAGISTRAT– (Cantiorix lies here. He was a citizen of Venedos [Gwynedd?] and cousin of Maglos the Magistrate) (*103*) (Fig 7). Perhaps the most elaborate is that found on the stone from Llantrisant (*33*) which reads '... iva, a most holy woman lies here, who was the very loving wife of Bivatigirnus, servant of God, bishop (?priest) and disciple of Paulinus, by race a ... docian, and an example to all his fellow citizens and relatives, both in character (and) in rule of life (as also) of wisdom (which is better) than gold and gems' (Fig 6) (RCHMW 1937, cix).

These stones with Latin epitaphs appear to derive from a widespread Late Antique epigraphic tradition found across much of France, Spain and Germany. The precise route by which these forms found their way to Wales is still not clear. The consensus had long been that the most likely contact was via Gaul (e.g. Radford 1937a, 1937b). Nash-Williams suggested a connection via Lyons and Vienne in the Rhône corridor of south-west Gaul (ECMW, 55). More recently Jeremy Knight and Charles Thomas have drawn parallels between the Insular material and the epigraphic traditions of western Gaul (e.g. Knight 1992; 1996; Thomas 1994, 1998). However, in a wide-ranging study of the Insular material in its continental context Mark Handley has clearly demonstrated that memorial formulae used in Wales and elsewhere in the west of Britain are paralleled widely throughout the Late Antique world and there is little that is diagnostically Gallic in content (Handley 2001; Handley 2003). This leaves the precise route through which the formulae found their way to Wales uncertain. Handley argues that the extent of funerary epigraphy in fourth-century Britain has been underestimated and that much of the early medieval material simply shows continuity from a pre-existing late Roman tradition.

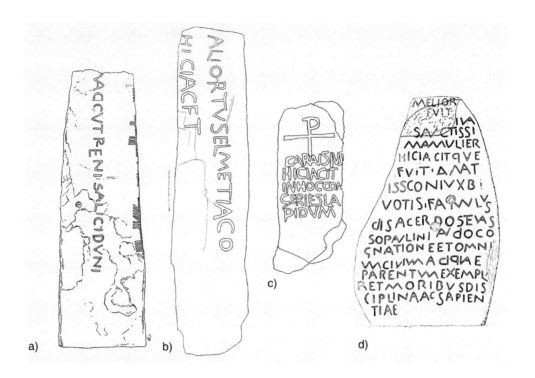

Above: 6 Early inscribed stones from Wales (not to scale). (a) Trecastle (Breconshire), (b) Llanaelhaiarn (Caernarvonshire), (c) Penmachno (Caernarvonshire), (d) Llantrisant (Angelsey)

Far left: 7 Early inscribed stone recording Cantiorix, Penmachno. (Author's photograph)

left: 8 'Palimpsest stones' (not to scale): (a) Trallwng, (Breconshire) (b) Clydai, (Pembrokeshire)

Whatever the impact of Late Antique epigraphic traditions on the Insular Latin memorials, it is clear that the ogham epigraphic tradition also had a significant influence. This can be seen most clearly in the orientation of the Latin inscription on some stones. Ogham is written vertically along an edge or corner of the stone (e.g. Bridell; *300*). Latin inscriptions are also regularly found written vertically rather than horizontally. This might occur on bilingual stones (e.g. Trallwng; B45) or on stones with only a Latin text (e.g. Llanfaelog; *9*). A small number of vertical inscriptions are known outside Wales and south-west England, most notably in Brittany, where no ogham inscriptions are found; isolated examples are even found as far as Limoges and northern Italy (Davies et al. 2000). There is thus a possibility that in some areas the use of vertical script might not be directly attributable to a desire to emulate ogham inscriptions, though as far as Wales is concerned it is the most likely explanation.

Generally, Nash-Williams' Group 1 stones carry very little ornamentation or decoration. Few have any kind of box or border line – the only examples are the stones from Llangefni and Llanfaglan (*26*, *89*). Some have a *chi-rho* symbol (a monogram derived from the initial letters of the name Christ in Greek), including stones from Penmachno and Treflys (*101*, *106*). Others bear simple crosses often in the plain ring-cross form. Crucially, in many cases where Group 1 stones carry such ornamentation; it appears that the inscription and decoration are not contemporary (e.g. Trallwng; Clydai; EMISW 1, 1345; P15) (Fig 8), and it is possible that some considerable time may have passed between the two episodes of carving (Longden 2003). These stones Nash-Williams called 'palimpsest stones' (ECMW, 18).

Nash-Williams' Group 2 consists of stones with crosses carved on them. They rarely have inscriptions, and where they do they appear in the full half-uncial hand. These carved crosses could range from the very simple (e.g. Llanddewi-Brefi; Newchurch; Corwen; Llangybi; CD10-11 CM38, *93*, *173*) (Fig 9) to more elaborate examples, some even including crucifixion scenes (e.g. Llanychaer; and possibly St Dogmael's; P49, P117) (Fig 10). Nash-Williams broadly divided these stones into three types, depending on the type of cross: (1) ring-crosses (2) linear crosses (3) outline crosses (ECMW, 20-22). The inscriptions are varied, though all are in Latin. Some simply carry a name (in the genitive) and a cross symbol (presumably indicating the Latin word *crux*) (e.g. +ARTBEU (Artbeu's cross), Merthyr Tydfil; G111). Others have two names – one in the genitive and one in the nominative (e.g +GURCI BLEDRUS (Gurci's cross, set up by Bledrus), Llangors; B29). It is usually assumed that the former is the name of the commemorated and the latter is the name of the individual responsible for erecting the monument. In some cases this is made explicit with the addition of the *fecit/erexit lapidem/crucem* (set up/erected this stone/cross). There are a small number of more extensive inscriptions, including an epitaph written in hexameters from Llanlleonfel (B34), a record of a gift of land from Llanlŷr (CD20) and invocations to prayer, such as that from Caldey Island (P6) (Fig 11). Nash-Williams recognised that there was some overlap between Group 1 and Group 2, particularly with regards to 'palimpsest stones' (ECMW, 18). This overlap has been emphasised by more recent scholars (Dark 1991) and the term Group 2 is often in practice used to refer to stones bearing a simple carved cross, but with no inscription.

Left: 9 Cross-incised stone, Llangybi
(Caernarvonshire). (Author's photograph)

Below: 10 Stone showing crucifixion, Llanychaer
(Pembrokeshire).

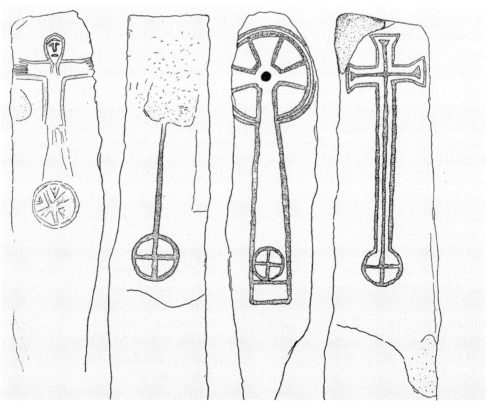

Group 3 consists of freestanding carved crosses and so-called slab crosses; they are more elaborate in style than the simpler Group 2 stones. Nash-Williams divided the Group 3 stones into two broad subgroups: (a) freestanding stone crosses or pillar-crosses (b) slab-crosses (ECMW, 27-9), although there are numerous additional miscellaneous forms. There is clear evidence of regional variation in the distribution of the sub-groups. The sculpture from North Wales is dominated by pillar crosses, with only one slab cross (from Llanrhaeadr-ym-Mochnant; *181*). This single example is notably distant from the main focus of pillar-crosses in the region which centres on the north-west.

Sculpture in the south of Wales is found mainly in Glamorgan and Pembrokeshire, with smaller clusters in Cardiganshire, Carmarthenshire and Breconshire. In Pembrokeshire and Glamorgan the proportion of pillar-crosses and slab-crosses is broadly comparable. This variation in cross types may partly reflect the different qualities of available rocks, with rocks which laminated easily providing slab shapes more available in the south of the country. However, there may be wider socio-cultural issues at play in the variation in form between the north and south; it is noticeable that stones bearing inscriptions are far more common in the south than in the north, where only three examples are known (Bardsey, Llanrhaiadr-ym-Mochant and the Pillar of Eliseg; *82, 181, 182*).

Subsumed within these wider national variations there are clear indications of more locally, regional-based clustering of cross types recognisable in cross-shape and decoration, and often demonstrating clear links with external sculptural traditions. In North Wales and spreading into Cheshire and Cumbria is a distinct group of Viking-influenced circle-headed ring-crosses from Anglesey and Flintshire, with clusters from Penmon and the Whitford/Diserth area (Edwards 1999; *37, 38, 185, 190*) (Fig 12). Wheel-headed slab-crosses, mainly found in Pembrokeshire (e.g. Penally, Carew and Nevern; P9, P73, P82), show influences from Northumbria (Fig 13). A distinct group of disk-headed slab-crosses is found focused on Glamorgan (CM10, CM12, CM19, P122, P132; G43, G51, G63, G78, G79, G83, G96) (Fig 14). Also found mainly in Glamorgan are a group of pillar-crosses distinguished by the presence of heavy mouldings on the angles of the shaft and Anglian-style cross heads. Originating in Breconshire near Builth Wells (Llanynis and Llanddewi'r cwm; B14, B39) (Fig 15) the style spread down to Glamorgan, where it appears in a more elaborate form, most spectacularly at Llandough (Nash-Williams 1950). Further west, Irish influence is clearly visible in the group of 'fretted ring-cross' slabs from St Davids (P103-5) (Fig 16). An Irish influence is also apparent in the figural depictions on a group of stones from Glamorgan (G10, G39, G52).

Although heavily decorated, some of the Group 3 stones carry inscriptions, though as noted above, these are mainly found in South Wales. The most common form is a record of the person who erected the cross, often with an invocation to pray for their own soul or the soul of another. Simple examples include that on a stone from Margam: CON/ BELIN / (po)SUIT / (h)ANC (Conbelin placed this (cross)) (G79). More elaborate is the inscription on a cross from Llantwit Major: IN NOMINE D(e)I SUMMI INCIPIT CRUX SALUATORIS QUAE PREPARAUIT SAMSONI APATI PRO ANIMA SUA [ET] PRO ANIMA IUTHAHELO REX ET ARTMALI ET TEC[AI]N + (In the name of God most high begins the Cross of the Saviour, which Abbot Samson prepared for his own soul and for the soul of King Juthahel and (for souls) of Artmail and Tecain) (G65) (Fig 17). However, two inscriptions from Ogmore and Margam in Glamorgan differ from this broad practice and instead record the donation of a plot of land, presumably to an ecclesiastical establishment (G99, G117).

Nash-Williams' Group 4 contains a range of early Romanesque monuments (47). These include a stone commemorating the foundation of a church (Llanfihangel-y-Traethu; *281*), fonts (e.g. Patrishow; B43), grave-slabs (e.g. Llanddew, ibid B13), grave-covers (e.g. ibid G114) and possible architectural fragments (e.g. Llancarfan; ibid G35). The precise criteria for inclusion in this group is unclear, and it is important to emphasise that there continued to be a tradition of sculptural monumentality in Wales in the twelfth century and onwards. Nash-Williams wrote of this group that 'the forms are mainly medieval, but in their epigraphy and decoration the monuments still preserve lingering traces of the older order' (ECMW, 47), although it is not always easy to detect anything surviving of the 'old order' in some stones in this group.

A left: 11 Stone with ogham inscription and extended Latin epitaph, Caldey Island (Pembrokeshire)

Right: 12 Maen Achwyfan, Whitchurch (Denbighshire). (Author's photograph)

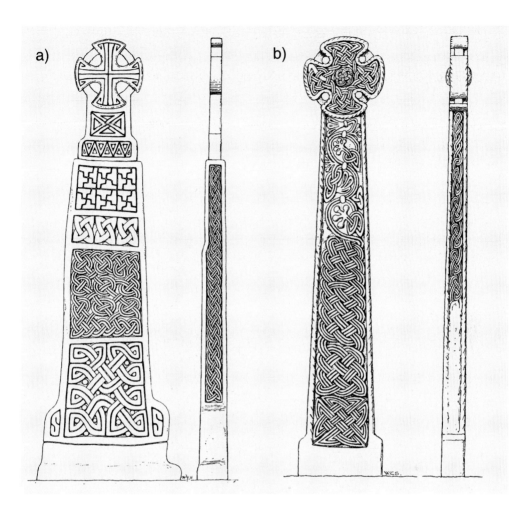

Above: 13 Circle-headed ring crosses: (a) Carew (Pembrokeshire) (b) Penally (Pembrokeshire)

Left: 14 Disk-headed slab-crosses: (a) Margam (Glamorgan) (b) Margam (Glamorgan)

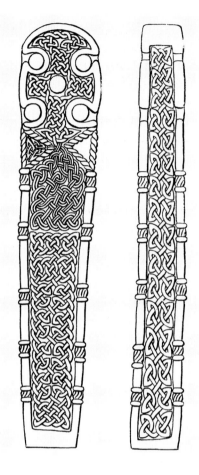

Left: 15 Pillar cross, Lanynis (Breconshire)

Below: 16 Fretted ring-crosses, St Davids (Pembrokeshire)

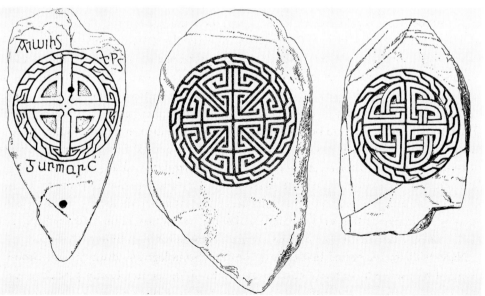

An understanding of the continuation of stone carving in Norman and later Wales is hampered by a lack of basic research. Colin Gresham's *Medieval Stone Carving in North Wales* explored the surviving grave-slabs and effigies of North Wales in the thirteenth and fourteenth centuries (Gresham 1969), but there has been no equivalent exploration of the material from southern Wales (though see Badham 1999). It also leaves the twelfth century as a poorly understood period in terms of stonework. In England, this is a period which saw widespread use of carved stone grave-slabs (e.g. Ryder 1985). It is clear that such grave-slabs were being used in Wales, with examples from Llangaffo, Llanfaglan and Newcastle-Bridgend clearly being in this tradition (*21, 90, 254*) (Figs 18–19).

Perhaps the biggest change in the sculptural traditions of Wales from the later eleventh and twelfth century was the introduction of a stone church building tradition, and the increasing impact of Romanesque art and architecture. Whilst wooden churches may have been carved and decorated, it is only with the survival of stone churches that we can recognise an architectural tradition of stone carving. There are occasional hints that some earlier structures may have incorporated some stone architectural decoration. The decorated stone shafts from Llantwit Major in Glamorgan have distinct grooves down their back, and may have supported an internal frieze or screen, although their precise date is unclear; Nash-Williams suggests a late tenth to eleventh-century date (*224*), though Malcolm Thurlby has suggested they could be as late as the twelfth century (Thurlby 2006). Generally, the Romanesque sculptural tradition finds its freest expression on stone capitals at the top of columns and around doorways, though there are a large number of Romanesque carved stone fonts (e.g. Thurlby 2006).

Dating the Sculptural Material

Nash-Williams' typology has proved influential and long-lived, and has been extended beyond Wales to describe the early stone sculpture of other areas (e.g. Radford 1975; Okasha 1993). Although based primarily on a formal analysis of the stones, Nash-Williams appears to have also used supposed date as a factor in placing particular stones into a class. For example, a group of relatively simple cross-incised stones from Llangaffo in Anglesey are in Group 4 on the basis of a supposed late date, but could equally be at home in Group 2. The decision to place stones with half-uncial inscriptions in Group 2 rather than Group 1 appears also to be based on the assumption that they post-date stones with inscriptions in ogham or capitals (Dark 1992). The distinction between Group 2 cross-inscribed stones and Group 3 cross-slabs and freestanding crosses is not always clear, whilst in general Group 3 contains a range of widely varying cross-forms, and although Nash-Williams created sub-groups, it is unclear how useful it is as an overarching category. Group 4, is clearly a hold-all category for all 'late' sculptural material, and has no defining characteristic. It is important to be extremely careful in using these groups as a way of understanding the chronology of the sculptural material. Hence, the question of the date of these sculptural groups has been largely sidestepped.

Nash-Williams suggested that each group was chronologically distinct, with Group 1 being fifth to seventh century, Group 2 seventh to ninth century, Group 3 ninth to eleventh century and Group 4 dating from the eleventh to thirteenth century. However, it is increasingly clear that there is considerable overlap between these different classes of stone. Whilst broadly speaking Group 1 is clearly chronologically earlier than Group 4, it is likely that Group 2 stones in particular had a long period of use, and may well have continued to be sculpted into the tenth century or even later (as partly recognised by Nash-Williams by his inclusion of some simple cross-incised stones in Group 4 (e.g. two stones from Merthyr Mawr, Glam., G104-5) and his acknowledgement that Group 2 stones may have continued to be used until the tenth or eleventh century (ECMW, 19-20).

There are many methods which have been used to establish a chronology for this material. Each technique has its own strengths and weaknesses and certain approaches are more suitable for analysing some types of monument than others. The most obvious method of dating stones is from the direct testimony of the inscriptions. Unfortunately very few inscriptions can be used in this way. A number bear the names of individuals, which may be related to known historical figures. The stone from Castell Dwyran carries the inscription MEMORIA VOTEPORICIS PROTICTORIS (CM3) (Fig 20a). This may be the Vortipor mentioned in Gildas' *De Excidio* (II.31), as an old man, although arguments have been put forward against accepting this identification (Sims-Williams 1990). Even assuming the man on the stone is Gildas' Vortipor, it is still not possible to obtain a precise date, as the date when Gildas himself was writing is unclear (probably the first half of the sixth century). We can thus only suggest an approximate mid/late sixth-century date for the stone, and any point between perhaps 500 and 570 is possible (Handley 2001). Another potentially datable stone comes from Llangadwaladr (*13*) and mentions King Catamanus, who may be identified with Cadfan, King of Gwynedd in the early seventh century, who died between AD 615–34 (Fig 20b). This identification is reasonably secure, but the stone is clearly different from most of the other Group 1 stones in its epigraphy, and is usually assumed to be at the end of the sequence. At the most it gives us a date of the mid-seventh century for the later stones in the group.

The only other potentially datable Group 1 inscription is the Penmachno stone which reads IN TEPO IUSTI CON (*104*). This has usually been expanded to read IN TE(M)PO(RE) IUSTI(NI) CON(SULIS) (in the time of Justinus the Consul) (Knight 1999). An alternate expansion of the inscription might be IN TE(MPORE) PO(ST) IUSTI(NI) CON(SULIS) (in the time after Justinus the Consul). The practice of dating memorial stones using the date of a consul was common across much of the Late Antique world at this period. It has been assumed that the model for the inscription came from Burgundy, where the practice of using this formula continued into the mid-seventh century. This would thus provide only a very broad date for the stone of *c.*AD 540–640. Mark Handley has recently pointed out that the formula might have been derived from Italy or North Africa, which might provide a tighter date range of *c.*AD 540–42 (Handley 2001). However, he has also noted that IUSTI could as equally be expanded as Justus or Justinian, and suggests that the possible date range of this stone could in theory be *c.*AD 328–650. Even this assumption is uncertain as an entirely different reading has also been suggested for the stone: INTEP [IDI] / IUSTI [SSI (MI)] / CON [IUX] which reads as '(The grave of) a most loving and righteous husband' clearly providing no chronological information at all (Knight 1996).

Above left: 17 Inscribed cross, Llantwit Major (Glamorgan)

Above centre: 18 Cross-marked stone, Llanfaglan (Angelsey). (Author's photograph)

Above right: 19 Cross-marked stone, Llanfaglan (Angelsey). (Author's photograph)

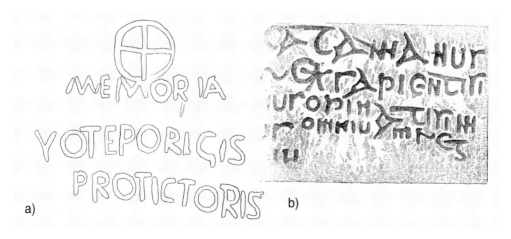

20 Inscriptions recording possibly historical identifiable individuals. (a) *Vortipo*r inscription on stone from Castell Dwyran (Carmarthenshire) (b) *Cadfan* inscription on stone from Llangadwaladr (Angelsey)

Nash-Williams suggested that a number of other Group 1 stones could be dated reasonably precisely on the basis of named individuals, such as the stone from Llandsadwrn, which records the burial of the 'blessed Saturninus and his wife' (*31*). He believed that this Saturninus was the same as the Sadwrn who founded the church and was recorded in later hagiography as the brother of St Illtud who was recorded as dying between AD 527 and 537, giving the stone an approximate date of *c.*AD 530. This approach places undue reliance on the accuracy of the later hagiographical material. As seen below, it is dangerous to use documents referring to periods which are several hundred years before the work was written. As such, it is simply not possible to use these saints' lives as a way of dating individual stones with any accuracy.

There are no Group 2 stones which refer to potentially identifiable historical individuals, but three Group 3 stones contain inscriptions that may provide some useful information. The Pillar of Eliseg near Llangollen bears an inscription that may record the erection of the stone by Cyngen, King of Powys who died in Rome in AD 854, suggesting a date for the stone of the second quarter of the ninth century. The sons of Bishop Abraham are recorded on a cross from St Davids, providing a broad date of later eleventh or early twelfth century (Edwards 2001a; G63). Finally, a cross standing at Llantwit Major carries an inscription reading 'In the Name of God the Father and of the Son and of the Holy Spirit. This cross Houelt prepared for the soul of Res his father' (Redknap and Lewis 2007). This is likely to be Hywel ap Rhys, the King of Glywsing, who is recorded in the *Brut y Tywysogion* as dying in AD 885, implying a mid/late ninth-century date for the erection of the stone.

Thus whilst it is possible to suggest a date for some stones on the basis of the individuals recorded on them, they are a tiny minority of the overall corpus. Also, in practice, the identifications are rarely secure, and often the suggested date bracket is large. Even when a more accurate date can be suggested, it is only useful in dating individual stones, and can give just a very general idea of when particular sculptural forms began or fell out of use.

An alternative way of dating stones with inscriptions is through an analysis of the language used, both in terms of its linguistic development and the type of formulae used. The Insular inscriptions of Britain have long been a source of interest for language scholars. Researchers such as Ifor Williams and Kenneth Jackson realised the potential that a close analysis of the written forms of words recorded on early medieval sculpture had for elucidating the pattern of the development in language in early medieval Britain before the widespread survival of written documentation (Jackson 1953; Williams 1972; Sims-Williams 2003). However, little of this work has been focused on providing a date for the stones themselves. The relative chronology of language change was well understood, but the stones, if dated by other means, offered a potential framework onto which an absolute chronology for linguistic developments could be hung. For a long time any attempt to date the stones on the basis of linguistic change ran a clear risk of circular argument (Handley 2001). Recently Patrick Sims-Williams has, however, attempted a major re-exploration of the linguistic material from the inscriptions in an attempt to check whether the accepted relative chronology of sound changes could be used to test the relative chronology for the stones created through an analysis of their decoration and form (Sims-Williams 2003). He was also able to adduce enough independent evidence for the absolute dating of these sound changes, that he could then suggest an approximate absolute chronology for the stone inscriptions. Encouragingly, he concluded that 'a comprehensive examination of the phonology of the Brittonic inscriptions broadly vindicates the relative chronologies that have been suggested for them on epigraphic and typological grounds' (Sims-Williams 2003).

He broke the inscriptions down into 28 period groups ranging in date from 'before *c*.540 at latest' (Period 1) to 'beginning by *c*.800 and … fully established by *c*.960.' (Period 28) (Sims-Williams 2003). The methodology used for creating these period groups means there is considerable overlap between them; for example Period 27 may begin *c*.850 but is not well established until *c*.950x.*c*1050, clearly overlapping with Period 28. Also many stones are given a range of possible periods; for example the Carew Cross is allocated to Periods 22–26. This is clearly a useful move towards developing some form of internal chronology for the early medieval inscriptions of Wales. There are some apparent limitations though; the chronological framework does not assist in distinguishing between the inscriptions dated to the fifth and early/mid-sixth century, and it is not possible to suggest a date for the first appearance of Group 1 stones. Equally, it is of less value in dating inscriptions of ninth and tenth-century date due to the high degree of overlap between the later Period groups. At a much simpler level of analysis, the presence or absence of ogham inscriptions is a useful broad indicator of date. In Ireland, the use of ogham appears to date from the fifth to seventh century, with later non-epigraphic use (McManus 1991), and thus stones with dual inscriptions are unlikely to post-date the seventh century.

Attempts have also been made to analyse the vocabulary and formulae used on inscriptions to date them. The belief in a definite Gallic link for the formulae used on the early stones meant that the Welsh chronology was tied into that of continental stones (e.g. Knight 1992, ECMW, 55; Thomas 1994; Thomas 1994). A key link was the use of the phrase HIC IACIT (HIC IACET). In his discussion of the use of this formula on the stone from Llanfaelog, Nash-Williams noted the use of this phrase on stones from both the Rhineland and southern Gaul, and suggested that the latter was a more likely model for the Welsh examples (ECMW, 55). The Gallic parallels he cited were from Lyon, dating from the mid-fifth century. Crucially, he used this to provide a chronological starting point for the Welsh use of this formula, implying a starting date of some point after *c*.AD 450 and before AD 500 (ibid.). However, as Mark Handley has shown, the use of the formula on the Lyon stones is just one example drawn from a far wider distribution of the phrase throughout Western Europe and North Africa (Handley 2001). To use the date of one small group of such stones from one cemetery in southern France to date the Welsh sequence is unjustifiable, as elsewhere the formula can be found in use in a range of contexts from the late fourth century to the thirteenth century. This cuts loose the chronology of the inscriptions on Group 1 stones from a seemingly solid mooring.

However, analysis of the range of vocabulary used on some inscriptions may be of some help in suggesting a broad date for a stone. For example, it has been suggested that the choice of words on the inscription from Llanllŷr (CD20), including the neologism *tequitus*, meaning perhaps 'area of land' or even 'monastery', is indicative of the use of a baroque style of

Latin known as 'Hisperic Latin' which is characterised by the tendency to create new words (Handley 2001a). This word is likely to have reached Wales through knowledge of the work of the *Hisperica Famina*, a classic work of Hisperic Latin, written by Isidore of Seville in the early seventh century. This gives a date before which the Llanllŷr stone is unlikely to be carved (ibid. 28).

An alternative approach to dating is through analysing the forms and variations in the forms of letters used on inscriptions. The simple nature of incised strokes used for ogham limits its value for stylistic analysis, but there is more scope for dating Latin inscriptions (Dark 1992; Harvey 2001). The types of writing used on stone might be expected to reflect the forms used on more traditional media, such as parchment and papyrus. As it is often much easier to date such documentary evidence, it makes the dating of the introduction, flowering and disappearance of certain writing styles easier to date than on stone sculpture (e.g. Bischoff 1990). Early scholars believed it was possible to date many of the Insular inscriptions this way (ECMW, 10-13). More recently many scholars have started to question how effective the study of letter form is in dating inscriptions (e.g. Dark 1991).

Group 1 stones mainly use capitals (also known as majuscules), the typical style used on Roman monumental inscriptions with the addition of a range of forms based on Roman cursive hands, know as uncial (derived from a form of capital letters adapted for non-epigraphic use) and half-uncial (derived from a hand used specifically for writing). The suite of variations found on Insular inscriptions appears to indicate a distinctive early medieval epigraphic script, incorporating elements of a late Romano-British non-official epigraphic tradition as well as Romano-British cursive traditions (Tedeschi 1991). Certain elements of this, such as the widespread use of inverted and reversed letters (particular the horizontal 'I') distinguish it from contemporary continental traditions and use of distinctive ligatures (lines connecting two letters) (ibid). This can be seen to support Handley's argument that the early medieval Insular epigraphic tradition shows strong evidence for continuity from late Romano-British practices, rather than indicating a reintroduction of it in the fifth century (Handley 2001; *contra* ECMW, 10-11).

Nash-Williams also suggested that there might have been a move to an increased use of half-uncial script over the period in question, and that this might be a way of distinguishing between earlier and later Group 1 stones (ECMW, 10-13). He suggested that as the stone from Llangadwaladr (ECMW, 13) which consisted mainly of half-uncial letters could be dated externally to *c.*AD 625 that the process of replacement of Capitals by half-uncial was well on its way by the early/mid-seventh century. He posited a possible beginning of the process in the early-mid sixth century on the basis of an external date of *c.*AD 530 for the stone from Llansadwrn (ECMW, 13), though the basis on which he established this date can be questioned. Dark, however points out that almost all of Nash-Williams' non-Capital letter forms of script on Group 1 stones may be either in Insular half-uncial and Insular minuscule (Dark 1992), which have no firm chronological date, although they appear to have been formed by the mid-seventh century. He also points out that the lack of half-uncial letters on one of the rare historically datable stones, the VORTIPOR, stone (CM3) may imply they had not achieved a *floruit* by the mid-sixth century (ibid).

However, despite recent scepticism about the efficacy of using the analysis of letter forms to date early stone inscriptions, the work of Carlos Tedeschi is restating the case for such approaches being able to supply a chronological framework. (Tedeschi 1995; 2001). He has identified four broad stylistic phases. His first phase, of fifth century, is broadly similar to late Romano-British epigraphy with traditional layout, but the use of a distinctive R with a slant-ing stroke. The next phase, belonging to the first half of the sixth century includes use of new combinations of ligature and some minuscule letters, as well as some other distinctive letter forms. The third phase dates to the second half of the sixth century, with increased use of minuscule letters and further distinctive letter forms, whilst his final phase dates to the first half of the seventh century, containing the full range of distinctive letters forms and more uncials.

Whatever the debate about the process of the transition from Capitals to half-uncial, most would accept that it had been more or less completed by the mid-late seventh century, though some Group 2 stones use Capitals (e.g. Llaneonfel; B34). Half-uncial appears to have remained the dominant epigraphic script until the eleventh century, when, following the advent of the Normans, it was replaced by a Romanesque-style script, which revived the use of Capitals, as can be seen on the fine stone from Llanfihangel-y-Traethu (*281*) (Fig 21). This example can be dated externally to the mid-twelfth century. The Romanesque style can also be seen on the pillar-stone from St Davids which bears the names of the four evangelists in plain capitals, and is probably from the twelfth century (P98). Minuscule clearly contin-ued to be used until at least the mid-eleventh century as the font from Patrishow, which has Romanesque-style decoration and can probably be dated to the late eleventh or early twelfth century, has an inscription in Hiberno-Saxon minuscules (B43) (Fig 22).

The extent to which art historical approaches can be used to date stone sculpture ranges widely depending on stone type. Group 1 stones tend to have relatively little decoration, with the repertoire limited to the use of forms of the *chi-rho* symbol and the cross, all of which were probably already being used in Britain by the fifth century, thus providing little useful chronological information (Dark 1992). Group 2 stones, with their range of cross decorations are equally difficult to date on an art historical base. Many of the crosses, whether incised, in relief, or carved in some other manner, are of a relatively simple design, and are difficult to place chronologically beyond a broad early medieval date. Some cross types, however, have clear parallels with closely-dated types used elsewhere in Britain and Ireland (Edwards 2001), some of which have been found in datable archaeological contexts, such as the cross-incised stones from a seventh-century context at Whithorn (Dumfries and Galloway) (Craig 1997) or in a sixth-century context at Tintagel in Cornwall (Nowakowski and Thomas 1990). There is nothing, however, to suggest that such simple cross stones were being used in the fifth or earlier sixth century. In Wales it is not clear how late the early medi-eval tradition of cross-incised stones merged with a twelfth and thirteenth century Norman tradition of carved stone slabs (Gresham 1968). It is noticeable that there is considerable debate over the precise date of many of these stones; Nash-Williams places two stones from Llanfaglan in the eleventh or twelfth century whereas Colin Gresham places them as late as the early fourteenth century (ECMW, 90-91; Gresham 1968).

Above left: 21 Twelfth-century inscription from Llanfihangel-y-Traethu recording foundation of a church by Wleder, mother of Odeleu

Above right: 22 Mid-eleventh century inscription on the font at Patrishow (Breconshire)

Dating through parallels in form becomes increasingly important with the Group 3 stones, which are broadly contemporary with thriving sculptural traditions in Ireland, Scotland and Anglo-Saxon England. In some cases the Welsh stones can be seen as essentially outliers of non-Welsh sculptural traditions, such as the Pillar of Eliseg, which has strong parallels to ninth-century Mercian and Northumbrian round-shafted crosses (Edwards 2001) or the Viking style crosses from Whitford and Disserth, which are part of a wider Irish Sea tradition of Hiberno-Norse sculpture, and fit into a definite eleventh-century historical context (Edwards 1999). Nonetheless, whilst in some cases it is possible to suggest quite precise dates for stones on the basis of cross-dating with datable stones elsewhere, there are potential problems. In some cases older forms may be used to deliberately hark back to earlier periods for ideological purposes. For example, sculpture from Bangor Cathedral was dated by Nash-Williams to the tenth century, whereas Malcolm Thurlby suggested that they were of later date and reflected an archaicising tendency in the artistic heritage of the region (Thurlby 2006).

Conclusions: Dating the Stones

It can be seen that the challenges of dating the early medieval stone sculpture of Wales are complex. Certain types of stone, particularly those bearing extensive sculptural decoration are more amenable to close dating on art historical grounds, than simpler crosses or unadorned inscriptions. Views on the ability to date the stones vary from extremely optimistic to wildly pessimistic. In this book the middle ground is taken; it is accepted that broadly speaking Group 1 stones date from the early/mid-fifth century to the seventh century. Whilst some are more closely datable within this range, it is still unclear how far the more detailed chronologies of Tedeschi and Sims-Williams (Tedeschi 2001; Sims-Williams 2003) will stand the test of time. Group 2 stones again probably date broadly from the mid/late sixth century into the eighth or ninth century, with some continuing to be made later, perhaps even into the tenth or eleventh century. Group 3 stones date broadly from the eighth to eleventh century and appear to fall out of use at around the same time that the tradition of building stone churches commences along with the introduction of the Romanesque artistic repertoire in the early twelfth century. It may be possible to date some stones within these groups more precisely, but many can only be placed within these broad date ranges.

As a final thought, it is important not to restrict one's thinking on the basis of Nash-Williams' Groups. They have undoubtedly been profoundly influential in the way in which scholars have analysed the material and the classifications still structure many modern overviews of the material. However, whilst clearly a useful guide to the main types of stone sculpture in early Wales, there is considerable overlap between the different groups, and Group 4 particularly does not stand up to detailed scrutiny as a distinctive class of material. It is important not to lose sight of the similarities and differences that can be found within and between the groups.

THE DOCUMENTARY EVIDENCE

Although this book is primarily a study in archaeology, reference will constantly be made to the textual and historical evidence. Indeed, one of the characteristics that distinguish early Christianity from the pagan religions practiced in Wales before the conversion is the phenomenon of literacy. Whilst literacy may have been largely restricted to the clergy, the central importance of documents in the early church is indisputable. The understanding of liturgical material, the discipline of ecclesiastical and secular life through the use of penitentials, the commemoration of the dead through inscriptions on grave stones, and by the end of the period under discussion, the recording of land-grants through charters, are all important ways in which a command of the written word was of fundamental importance to both the ecclesiastics and secular magnates of early medieval Wales. The ways in which the written word was used and the complex interrelationship between written texts and physical objects will be explored in later chapters. However, the use of documentary evidence for writing the history of the early Welsh church needs to be addressed here.

Much that has been written about the early Church in Wales has drawn heavily on material presented in the range of surviving lives of early saints. Whilst the best of this work has been alive to the complexities and challenges involved in using early medieval hagiographical material, much work can be characterised by an uncritical use of these documents. The fundamental issue that must be kept in mind at all times is that very little of this material was written at the same time as the events that were being recorded. One of the characteristics of the *Vita* of the early saints is that they are not simple historical records, and certainly not contemporary reportage. The personalities and events recorded are diffracted through the lens of the political complexities and the ideological background of the writer.

In comparison with Anglo-Saxon England, the documentary evidence for early medieval Wales is limited and relatively late in date, with most material being from the ninth century or later (Davies 1982a). Despite the late date of the documentary evidence, there has been a tendency to use it to elucidate the earlier stages of the development of the Welsh church, including attempts to reconstruct early religious and liturgical practices and also to reconstruct seemingly coherent historical narratives, usually based on the actions of named saints. Although there are these limitations, it is helpful that such documentary material that does survive is reasonably diverse in nature, including saints' lives, annalistic material, charter material, law codes and vernacular poetry.

Early Hagiography

In practice, there are few very early surviving saints' lives related to the development of the Welsh church. The earliest generally accepted *Vita* is that of St Samson, which, although written about a Welsh saint, was a product of the Breton monastery of Landévennec (Fawtier 1912; Flobert 1997). The earliest version *Vita Ia* probably dates to the eighth century. However, it is likely that there was an earlier tradition of biographical writing relating to Welsh saints, as the author identifies one of his sources for the *Vita* as the *Acta* of St Samson that had been brought overseas (presumably to Brittany from Wales) by the deacon Henoc (Poulin 1987). Other early Breton products include the *Life of St Paul Aurelian* (*Vita S. Pauli Aureliani*) (Cuissard 1883) and the *Life of St Guénolé* (*Vita S. Winwaloei*) (Latouche 1911), both written by monks from Landévennec in the late ninth century. Apart from these Breton works most of the surviving corpus of early saints' lives relating to Wales are of later date. The notable exception is the hagiographical material relating to St Germanus and a number of other fragments embedded in the *Historia Brittonum* written *c.*820/30 (Dumville 1972-4; Davies 2002).

The two *Lives of Cadog* (*Vita S. Cadoci*) by Lifris and Caradog of Llancarfan belong to the twelfth century and Rhigyfarch's *Vita S. Davidi* belongs to the later eleventh century (Davies 2002; James 1985). The twelfth century Book of Llandaf contains lives of Dyfrig (*Vita Dubricius*), Euddogwy (*Oudoceus*) and Teilo (*Teilavus*). Further saints' lives, including those of Gwynllyw (*Gundleius*), Illtud (*Iltutus*), Cybi (*Kebius*) and Padarn (*Paternus*) were contained within the vellum leaves of British Library, MS Cotton Vespasian A, xiv dating to the early thirteenth century, although containing earlier material (Wade-Evans 1944; Hughes 1958).

Most of this early hagiography is in Latin. The *Vita Sancti Gundleii* mentions in passing a 'certain British versifier, versifying in British' who composed verses in praise of the holy Gwynllyw (*VSG* 12), implying there may have been a British language hagiographic tradition. However, this does not survive, and the only material in the vernacular comes from later court poets of medieval Wales (see below).

The one key factor that links these saints' lives, whether written in Welsh or Latin, in Brittany or in Wales, is the profound influence that the political climate in which they were written has had upon their form and content. The revival of hagiographical writing in the late eleventh century in Wales parallels a similar revival in England and Ireland (Davies 2002). This can be clearly linked to the direct and indirect repercussions of the Norman Conquest. For example, Rhigyfarch's *Vita S. Dauid*, appears to have been written in the early 1090s, and was a clear attempt to assert the importance of the saint's cult, linking him to the royal dynasty in Ceredigion, and follows a visit to Saint Davids by William I in 1081, ostensibly to pray, but evidently with wider political considerations in mind. The reworking of the text of the *Vita* in the mid-twelfth century can probably be linked to the attempt by Bernard (1115–48), the Anglo-Norman Bishop of St Davids to have the see recognised as being of metropolitan status (Davies 2002). A similar process occurred with the Book of Llandaf, which was compiled around 1130 following the appointment of Bishop Urban to the Norman diocese. Urban made pleas for a metropolitan status for his see, and the writing of the book was part of the propaganda campaign connected to this.

The key ways in which these saints' lives acted to promote their respective cults was essentially by legitimising their claims to the control of churches or episcopal jurisdiction by highlighting the antiquity of these claims. This could be in done in several ways; the Book of Llandaf includes an extensive series of charters outlining the lands claimed by the church. Whilst these have clearly been massaged for propaganda purposes, it is unlikely that they are all forgeries (Davies 1979; Davies 2002).

The *Vita Cadoci* simply includes a list of what are essentially charters to the end of the story of the saint's life, highlighting the donation of land to the church of Llancarfan and outlining the circumstances of the gift. Struggles to assert national or local primacy in Wales are often played out through stories explaining how one saint was acknowledged as superior by his rival. For example, in the *Vita Cadoci* Gildas refuses to sell Cadog a 'beautiful mottled bell' instead taking it to Rome as a gift to the Pope. However, the bell will not ring, and the Pope commands Gildas to give it to Cadog proclaiming 'For two reasons will all the Britons reverence this bell, because it was owned by me, and because it has been owned by Saint Cadog' (*VSC* 27).

The fact that these saints' lives were being produced in a context of extensive jockeying for power at a local, regional and national level means they cannot be read as straightforward historical documents. They are carefully constructed narratives intended to assert contested ecclesiastical and tenurial claims. In addition, it will rapidly become clear to those who read the hagiographical material of this date that they are heavily formulaic. It has been suggested that a typical saint's life will comprise nine elements: birth, childhood, education, piety, miracles, martyrdom, *inventio* and *translatio* (Boyer 1981), and indeed most of the Welsh Lives conform to this broad patterns containing many, though not all, of these stages. The same motifs are also repeated in several saints' lives. For example, the appearance of swine in a miraculous context occurs in the *Life of St Paul Aurelian* and the *Life of St Cadog*, as well as several Irish and Scottish saints' lives (Jankulak 2003). Early medieval hagiographers have been compared with magpies in their frequent reselection and reworking of anecdotes and motifs from other sources (Clancy 2003).

Thus, early hagiography was written to a relatively strict formula with heavy borrowing of motifs and imagery, and often produced for political purposes; any use of material within these Lives must clearly be cautious and selective. However, this does not mean that they are entirely devoid of value for understanding the early medieval Welsh church. Whilst likely to be of little use for creating a coherent narrative for religious activity in the sixth century – the period they usually purport to record – they can provide useful insights into the practices and beliefs of the Welsh church in the eleventh and twelfth centuries.

Annalistic and Historical Material

There is very little straight historical or annalistic material that directly relates to the earliest centuries of the Welsh church. The works of Saint Patrick, the *Confessio* and his letter to Coroticus are from the mid-fifth century, and are obviously mainly related to the spread of Christianity in Ireland. However, some of the biographical material related to his ancestry and origin does shed some light on the state of Christianity in the later fourth or early fifth century in Britain. It is uncertain how far this material has direct relevance to Wales. Patrick's hometown *bannaven taburniaa* (*Conf.* 1) has remained elusive, and has been variously placed in north-west England and south-west England (Dark 1993; Thomas 1981a). There is equally no reason why it could not have been in southern Wales, in the Romanised area that extended from Gwent to Carmarthenshire.

More informative, is the material within the *De Excidio Britanniae* or *On the Ruin of Britain*, an exhortation by the monk Gildas to the rulers of early medieval Britain to mend their ways and return to the path of righteousness. He directly links the impact of Anglo-Saxon expansion to the religious failures of the native British rulers of Wales and south-west England. His litany of complaints is situated within a broad historical framework, placing current events in their wider context. Conventionally written around AD 540, the content of *De Excidio* demonstrates that the author has a reasonably strong awareness of recent events and key players in Wales, and his focus on moral and religious behaviour sheds light on some aspects of early Christianity in western Britain.

There is also extensive annalistic and historical material relating to Wales from both within Wales itself (including the *Annales Cambriae*, *Historia Brittonum* and the *Brut y Tywysogion*), and Ireland and Anglo-Saxon England (*Anglo-Saxon Chronicles; Bede's Ecclesiastical History*) (Davies 1982a). Often sharing material and drawing on common sources helps provide broad historical narratives for early medieval Wales. Generally, the earlier entries tend to be retrospective and often extremely schematic in form. Once the annalists begin to record contemporary events, the details often become more extensive. The extent to which this material contains data relevant to the early church varies extensively. The more discursive histories, such as Bede's *Ecclesiastical History* shed some light on relationships between the British church and the Roman-influenced Anglo-Saxon church; other material only deals with the church in passing, often recording simply the death of a bishop (e.g. the death of Bishop Daniel of Bangor *AC* sa AD 584), the sacking of a church or other major events (e.g. 'Easter is changed among the Britons on the Lord's day, Elfoddw, servant of God, emending it.' *AC* sa AD 768). It is also important to consider the context of their production. For example, the writing of

Bede, a fervent supporter of the Roman church, is permeated by negative attitudes towards the British church. The *Annales Cambriae* although using much material from northern British and Irish sources are a product of the community at St Davids, thus have a south-western bias, whilst the *Brut y Tywysogion* was compiled at a Cistercian house, probably Strata Florida, which explains the relatively higher profile of that house in the *Brut*.

Law Codes

A substantial quantity of Welsh legal material survives, both in the vernacular and in Latin. Although there are three broad groups of manuscript source, the *Llyfr Iorweth*, *Llyfr Cyfnerth* and *Llyfr Bregywyrd*, and a body of additional law, including the *Llyfr y Damweiniau*, the material is heavily interrelated in terms of form and content and is likely to have derived from a single original source (Charles-Edwards 1989; Jenkins 2000; Pryce 1993; 2000a). The different versions appear to have been derived from different areas within Wales; the Iorweth Redaction has its origin in Gwynedd, whilst the Cyfnerth Redaction probably came from the Malienydd area of mid-Wales (Pryce 2000a). There is a strong tradition that the compilation of these laws was instigated by Hywel Dda (Hywel ap Cadell) (AD 880?–950), an important tenth-century king of Gwynedd. However, all of the surviving versions of these laws from the mid-thirteenth century or later, and the extent to which they had their origins in earlier law codes is still debated (Charles-Edwards 1989; Davies 1987; Pryce 2002).

Some elements of the law books are certainly early, such as the part dealing with the 'seven bishop-houses of Dyfed' (Charles-Edwards 1970-2). At the very least, it is clear from the existence of some Welsh legal documents dating to the early-mid eleventh century, such as the *Braint Teilo*, that some form of formally collected legal material existed at this date (Davies 1974-6). Much of this earlier material appears to have been specifically related to the rights of ecclesiastical centres, particularly as they pertained to immunity and the right of sanctuary. However, whilst this earlier material is primarily ecclesiastical, most of the content of the Welsh law book was secular in content and dealt with all aspects of the medieval society, including the royal court, and covers laws dealing with inheritance, criminal damage and the settlement of disputes (Jenkins 2000). Nonetheless, the church was evidently intimately involved in many legal procedures, and the content of the laws sheds much light on the role of the church in Welsh society in the twelfth and thirteenth centuries (Pryce 1993).

Vernacular Poetry

There was a strong vernacular poetic tradition in medieval Wales. The earlier poems can be broken down into three main bodies of material which have been retrospectively attributed to known earlier figures, Aneirin, Taliesin and Llywarch Hen. The *Canu Aneirin* mainly consisted of the long saga-poem know as the *Gododdin*, though did include other works, such as the problematic *Gwarchan Maeldderw* (Isaac 2002; Klar and Sweetser 1996). The *Canu Taliesin* contained a series of poems connected to early heroic figures from northern Britain, and the *Canu Llywarch Hen*, again involved figures of a northern origin, though a subsection of this work, the *Canu Heledd*, is situated in the central Welsh marches. Often ascribed an early date (sixth century in the case of the *Canu Aneirin* and the *Canu Taliesin* and ninth century in the case of the *Canu Llywarch Hen*), there are also increasingly strong arguments that the bulk of the material may be of ninth-century or tenth-century origin or even later (Dumville 1976-8; Haycock 2007). Whatever their precise date, it is clear that they were only committed to the page at a much later date (Jackson 1969, 90; Charles-Edwards 1978). There is other early vernacular poetic material outside these corpuses, such as the *Marwnad Cynddylan* (Williams 1931-3), the *Englynion y Beddau* (the *Stanzas of the Graves*) (Jones 1967) and the *Armes Prydein* (Williams and Bromwich 1982). This combined corpus of early poetry contains relatively little direct information about the state of the early church. The *Canu Aneirin, Canu Taliesin* and *Canu Llywarch Hen* are resolutely secular in content. Nonetheless, there is some scope for utilising this material, particularly for place-names.

The court poets of the Welsh kingdoms (the *Gogynfeirdd*) in the eleventh to thirteenth centuries wrote lyrics with a far greater religious content (McKenna 1991). Key texts include three poems written in honour of saints: *Canu Cadfan* by Llywelyn Fardd, *Canu Tysilio* by Cynddelw Brydydd Mawr and *Canu Dewi* by Gwynfardd Brycheiniog (Jones and Owen 2003; McKenna 1996). These poems draw inspiration from both hagiography and secular traditions of eulogy. The *Canu Cadfan* and *Canu Tysilio* particularly contain much praise for the key churches of Cadfan at Tywyn (Merioneth) and Tysilio (Meifod), and contain useful information about these ecclesiastical establishments and give a wider sense of the physical importance of churches and relics as symbols of the cult of named saints. Other *gogynfeirdd* poems also make regular references to religious practice, particularly in a range of distinct poetic genres, including the *marwysgafn* (deathbed elegy) and the *awdl I Dduw* (ode to God) (McKenna 1991, xi). Mostly focusing on issues such as the resurrection and reconciliation, they often use a range of images that can give us some indicators of contemporary practice, such as the reference to burial in a churchyard in the *Awdl a gant Einion ap Gwalchamai I Dduw* (The Poem that Einion ap Gwalchmai sang to God):

> Before the time comes that is without assistance
> The messengers of death as guides
> Before I have a cold grave, let it be to my Lord
> That I pay compensation, graciously, generously,
> With ready contrition to my Jesus
> Propriety having been commended to me
> Before tears come falling upon the cheeks,
> Before churchyard ground, which is no dishonour.
> (ed. and trans. McKenna 1991)

The poem also contains references to the ideal of burial on Ynys Enlli (Bardsey Island) and monastic observance (McKenna 1991).

Charter Evidence

The final major class of contemporary documentary evidence that helps to shed some light on the early church in Wales are charters. These are documents recording the movement of property rights from one party to another (Davies 1982, 201-2). Written in Latin, they have a broadly standard format, consisting of a description of the transaction, a witness list, a religious sanction and sometimes a boundary clause describing the physical location of the property. These are also sometimes supplemented with a narrative description of the events leading to the transfer of the property (ibid.). Compared with the large corpus of surviving Anglo-Saxon charters, the evidence from first millennium Wales is relatively limited. The earliest examples are a group placed at the end of the 'Vespasian' recension of the *Vita Cadoci* which dates to around 1200, though the charters themselves are thought to be from the seventh or eighth century (Davies 1982a; Davies 2003, 143-4). Another small group are found as marginal inscriptions in the Lichfield Gospels and date to between the eighth and early tenth century (Jenkins and Owen 1983). Other fragmentary or undatable examples include a poorly understood group, probably from St Davids, one from Clynnog Fawr (Caernarvonshire) and a couple from Llanelwy; both the latter examples are only known in thirteenth or fourteenth-century manuscripts, but are probably earlier (Sims-Williams 1996)

In addition to these smaller groups of charter evidences is the more substantial body of nearly 150 charters from the *Liber Landavensis* (Book of Llandaf) (Davies 2003; Davies 1978, 1979). The *Liber* was compiled in the twelfth century as part of an attempt by Bishop Urban of Llandaf to settle a boundary dispute with neighbouring bishops; it contains a selection of saints' lives, papal bulls and a corpus of charters. The charters, which claim to date from the late sixth century to the late eleventh century mainly refer to property within the Diocese of Llandaf, predominantly in Gwent and the kingdom of Ergyng in south-west Herefordshire. However, there has been much debate as to the reliability of these charters (Davies 2003, 1-6). Some scholars have seen them as forgeries or at least so heavily reworked as to be useless as evidence for earlier periods (e.g. Brooke 1986, 16-49; Dark 1994, 140-8). Others have argued that despite the evident alterations there is still an important underlying stratum of early content within the charters (e.g. Davies 1978, 1979; Sims-Williams 1991).

The material from the charters is important for an understanding of the early medieval church in several ways. They can help plot the ebb and flow of individual ecclesiastical establishments through the mapping of patterns of land donations over time and space (Davies 1978). They can also help us understand more clearly the mechanisms through which churches were able to acquire economic wealth (Davies 1978, Pryce 1992a). They provide a window on to the landscape of early medieval Wales through place-names and, crucially, the descriptions of the Welsh landscape in the boundary clauses (Coe 2002, 2004). These clauses have usually been assumed to belong to a relatively late stage in the compilation of the *Liber* (Davies 1978) – probably the eleventh or twelfth century – though some possibly from as early as the mid-ninth century (Davies 1979, 142-3). However, recent scholarship has criticised this on historical and philological grounds (Coe 2004). Coe has argued that it is possible, using a series of criteria including linguistic and orthographic variants, to develop a relative chronology of the boundary clauses, and using the different positions of the boundary clauses within the charter as a whole to move to towards creating an absolute chronology (ibid.). This has resulted in a possible seven stage chronology for the boundaries, dating from up to *c*.AD 930 (Period I) to *c*.1080 (Period VII) [completion of the Book of Llandaf] (ibid).

It was not until the later eleventh and twelfth century that the use of charters became more widespread in Wales. A key development was the foundation of Cistercian houses by the native rulers of Wales, which led to a substantial increase in the survival of charters. It is not clear whether this is due to an increase in the absolute number of charters or simply a tendency for Cistercian and other monastic orders to preserve their cartularies more carefully; doubtless it is a combination of the two factors. Major collections of charters include those from Strata Marcella, founded by Owain ap Gruffudd, prince of Southern Powys in 1170, and the Aberconwy Charters of late twelfth or thirteenth-century date (Thomas 1997; Gresham 1939; Gresham 1982-3; Insley 1999). Some of these have boundary clauses attached, elucidating the landscape of medieval Wales, including references to possible sites of religious importance. For example, a confirmation of the foundation charter of Strata Marcella dating to 1202 makes reference to a *Fontem Tessilau* (Tysilio's Well), presumably a holy well dedicated to Saint Tysilio (Thomas 1997, 176-77).

GERALD OF WALES

A final key source for an understanding of the medieval Welsh church is the writings of Gerald of Wales (Giraldus Cambrensis) (*c.*1145–1223), a churchman born to a wealthy family at Manorbier in Pembrokeshire. Although mainly of Norman stock, his mother was half-Welsh and the granddaughter of Rhys ap Tewdwr, a prince of Deheubarth in South Wales. He became Archdeacon of Brecon, but aspired to become Bishop of St Davids, like his uncle David. Despite being an important figure in the later twelfth-century church in Wales, Gerald is today better remembered for his extensive writing, particularly his *Journey through Wales* and *Description of Wales* (Thorpe 1978). The former records his travels around Wales as part of a tour taken by himself and Archbishop Baldwin to preach the Crusades in 1188, whilst the latter is a more general overview of life in twelfth-century Wales; both were written in the 1190s. In both works Gerald combines straight description with an eye for the curious and bizarre. The combination of Gerald's ecclesiastical background and his penchant for the picturesque means that his works contain many vivid descriptions the religious life of the period, such as his evocation of the celebrations of the feast day of St Eluned at her chapel in Brecon, at which the congregation danced and sang itself into a frenzy, parading around the cemetery and miming the ways in which they broke the Sabbath (*Journey* 1.2).

It is important not to treat Gerald's writings uncritically. His choice of what to record and what not to record was informed by his position as a key promoter of the twelfth-century church reforms, and as a member of the Cambro-Norman Marcher lords, not entirely at home in a Norman or Welsh socio-political milieu (Bartlett 15-54). For example, in considering his description of the activities at the chapel of St Eluned (*Journey* 1.2), it is important to remember that in his *Gemma Ecclesiastica* (*Jewel of the Church*) of 1197 Gerald quotes the Council of Toledo and St Augustine in his condemnation of singing and dancing in churches and cemeteries (*GE* 43). Gerald was not simply recording picturesque religious practices; he was implicitly condemning them.

PULLING TOGETHER THE SOURCES: ARCHAEOLOGY AND HISTORY

It is apparent that there is a wide range of material and textual sources that can be drawn on to explore the development of the early church in Wales, but they must be used critically. Neither the archaeology or history provides an objective record of early forms of religious practice; each type of evidence is subject to its own strengths and weaknesses. Any attempt to build a model of early medieval Welsh Christianity founded on this material must make allowances for their relative virtues. The greatest temptation for a scholar writing about this period is to ignore or play down chronological differences, and particularly to use evidence from later periods to illuminate earlier practices. This frequently occurs with the saints' lives, which are often used to shed light on events and practices that date to the period of their subjects, rather than the period of their composition. At its most extreme, this can lead to the development of an idealised early church that shows no change or development between the Age of the Saints in the sixth and seventh centuries and the impact of the Normans and the increasing influence of the church reforms of the eleventh and twelfth centuries.

In reality, the Welsh church clearly developed and changed in many important ways over this period; by proffering a timeless and unchanging construct of the church, we would be devaluing the innovation and vitality of the people who made up the Christian community of this period. It is not only the desire to telescope time that can be tempting; there is an equal temptation to ignore differences across space. The evidence, both archaeological and historical, is not evenly distributed across the country. Class 1 stone sculpture is not found in many areas of Wales, and is only widely found in the south-west and north-west, and to a lesser extent in Glamorgan and Breconshire. Very little stone sculpture of any type is found in central Wales and in the Marches. Equally, the documentary evidence shows great variation in its spatial distribution. Although extensive, the land described in the Llandaf charters is largely limited to the south-east of the country, with only a limited number of outliers. Once more, it is important not to ignore these differences. The conflation of evidence found in different regions can easily lead to the construction of a model for the development of Welsh Christianity that ignores the very different trajectories of the church, which varied widely according to the social and political contexts in which it developed. Whether looking at variation across time or space, we should not necessarily see such apparent 'patchiness' in the evidence as an inherent problem or weakness, but instead as a phenomenon which needs explaining and understanding. We need to be constantly aware that the underlying causes of this variation in the spread of evidence are important in themselves, and that this variation should be explored and understood rather than silently ignored or glossed over.

CHAPTER THREE

EARLY CHURCH ARCHITECTURE

The evidence for the structural remains of early churches in Wales is extremely limited. Unlike England and Ireland, there are no examples of standing, pre-Romanesque church structures (Ó Carragáin 2005; Taylor and Taylor 1965-78). It was not until the eleventh century that the practice of building ecclesiastical structures in stone started to become common in Wales. The almost complete lack of standing fabric dating to before the mid-eleventh century means that to better understand the origins and evolution of early churches we are limited to archaeological evidence, and a small quantity of textual material.

The use of archaeological data has strengths and weaknesses for exploring the genesis of Welsh church structures. Many standing churches have been through centuries of change and alteration, weathering the vicissitudes of the Reformation, the Civil War and over-zealous Victorian restorers. This have often led to the earliest phases of these structures being entirely replaced or becoming difficult to interpret. However, as we shall see, archaeological excavations are able to reveal changes in plan and construction type. It is possible to detect traces of early wooden phases of church construction that would be impossible to recognise in a standing structure. Equally, the presence of early apsidal chancels later replaced by rectangular chancels is visible through subsurface excavation, but would prove impossible to detect if the structure was still extant. Nonetheless, there are distinct limitations to understanding churches simply through excavation. Archaeology is strong at detecting changes to church structures that influence the basic plan of the church. However, standing structures frequently retain immensely important information in the scars, patches and joints visible on the church fabric, which can provide crucial information about other changes. The *in situ* preservation of carved decorative stone and sculpture can also provide crucial evidence for the structural chronology of the building and allow us to address wider issues about investment and symbolism.

THE EARLIEST CHURCHES

Churches are known in Britain from as early as the fourth century, though the identification of diagnostically Christian architecture of such an early date is not easy (Petts 2003, 51-87). After centuries of persecution, there was no agreed layout for buildings dedicated to Christian worship able to be rolled out following the Edict of Milan in AD 313, which saw the Church becoming a licit religious institution. Instead, the new congregations appropriated a range of existing architectural forms. Most commonly used was the basilica, a rectangular aisled plan, often with an apsidal end. This layout had a long history and was widely used to house a range of religious and secular activities. Although in Britain a number of basilica structures of Roman date have been identified as potential early churches, such as at Colchester and Silchester, it is hard to be absolutely certain that they are Christian in origin (Frere 1976; Crummy et al. 1993). It is likely that a range of other forms were used for fourth-century churches in Roman Britain, such as simple rectangular structures. Clearly, without additional evidence, these are potentially extremely difficult to distinguish from rectangular buildings with secular functions. One structure at which such an identification might be determined is at Icklingham in Suffolk, where a small rectangular building with a possible apsidal end is located adjacent to a small cemetery and close to a large pit containing parts of a lead tank decorated with Christian imagery (West and Plouviez 1976).

Despite these caveats, it is possible to identify a number of structures in England as Roman churches with varying degrees of certainty. However, the Roman towns of Carmarthen (*Moridunum*) and Caerwent (*Venta Silurum*) have not produced any such structural evidence for fourth-century churches (though for Caerwent see Boon 1992, fig.3). Two potential examples are however recognisable in immediately adjacent areas. The Roman town of *Viriconium* (Wroxeter in Shropshire) lies around 20 miles from the Welsh border. Following the end of occupation here in the early middle ages there was no further development, leaving the interior of the city as farmland. This has led to the excellent preservation of the occupation layers within the city walls. As a result, the site has been a focus for extensive archaeological research over recent decades. Geophysical survey has produced evidence for a possible late Roman church to the south of the Baths. This basilica-plan structure (30m x 13m) is aligned west-east and has an apsidal east end (White and Barker 1998 109-10, Pl 14). The substantial, stone-walled structure may imply a sizeable Christian congregation in the city in the fourth century.

A further possible Roman church structure, just outside Wales, can be found at Gloucester, where excavations on the site of the medieval church of St Mary de Lode recovered remains of a substantial Roman building. It was demolished and replaced in the early fifth century by another building on the same alignment. It contained a number of west-east burials, including a headless burial. They were sealed beneath a rough mortar floor. A Saxon church succeeded this structure in the ninth or tenth century. It was not possible to reconstruct the overall floor plan of the earliest phases of this sequence, but a strong argument can be made for a Christian function of the Roman structures on the basis of the presence of burials and the later Christian use of the site (Bryant 1980).

Despite the apparent lack of evidence it is still possible that late Roman church structures may be recovered from sites in Wales. In addition to the possibility of recovering church structures from Roman towns, the possibility of churches existing on military sites must not be ignored. Recent work on Roman Britain's northern frontier has resulted in the discovery of a number of possible ecclesiastical structures of late Roman date within forts, such at Vindolanda, Housesteads and South Shields (Petts 2003 75-8). Until now no similar examples have been found in Wales, but such features may survive.

WOODEN STRUCTURES

As noted above, the factor that distinguishes the archaeology of early churches in Wales from that of Anglo-Saxon England or early medieval Ireland is the lack of a clear group of pre-Romanesque stone churches. In England, where the process of conversion did not commence until the seventh century, the earliest stone churches, such as Escomb in County Durham date to the eighth century. In Ireland, where Christianity was introduced in the fifth century, stone churches were probably being built from the eighth century, although a parallel tradition of building wooden churches continued until at least the eleventh century (O'Keefe 2003 63-72; Ó Carragáin 2005). The contrast with Wales is pronounced, where both the documentary and archaeological evidence for stone churches pre-dating the twelfth century is extremely limited (Pritchard forthcoming).

Despite a wide range of documentary references to early churches and ecclesiastical sites from the range of annalistic, hagiographical and charter material, specific references to the materials from which they were built are largely lacking. One possible example is the late ninth-century poem *Etmic Dynbich,* a poem of praise to the fort of Tenby (Conran 1992, 119). It makes frequent reference to Bleidudd, presumably the poet's former patron, but now deceased. The key section comes in the fourth stanza, which has been translated as:

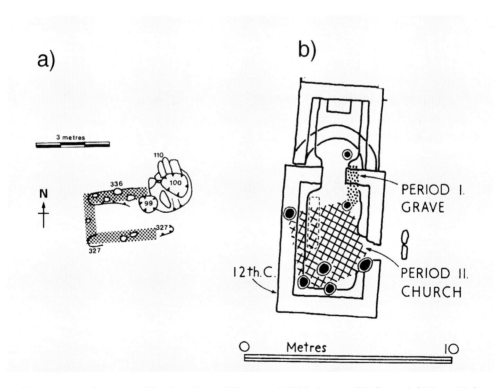

23 Early wooden churches. (a) Llanelen, Gower (Glamorgan) (Schlesinger and Walls 1997) (b) Burry Holmes (Glamorgan)

> Gay was that company that met at the Calends
> Round a generous lord, splendid and brave.
> Before he had gone to the oaken church
> From a bowl of glass gave me mead and wine
> (trans. Conran 1992)

This appears to be an explicit reference to a wooden church. However the original Old Welsh version consists of the words '*derwen lan*', which literally means 'oaken enclosure'. The term '*lan*' did indeed come to mean church, but this was an extension of its use to mean 'enclosed cemetery', which would make equal sense in this context. A more convincing reference to a wooden church structure comes from the difficult work known as the *Hisperica Famina*, a text written for learners of Latin in the seventh century (Herren 1974). Its utility as a learning aid might be doubted; the colloquys within it use a highly florid and pretentious Latin style, but it does provide vivid descriptions of a range of objects and situations. This includes references to wooden churches:

> This wooden oratory is fashioned out of candle-shaped beams;
> It has sides joined by four-fold fastenings
> The square foundations of the said temple give it stability,
> From which springs a solid beamwork of massive enclosure …
> (trans Herren 1974, lines 547-50)

The key question, however, is the origin of the text itself. Whilst clearly an Insular product, and generally assumed to be the product of an Irish scriptorium, there are still arguments for a Welsh or even Breton, provenance. However, it remains uncertain whether this passage should be seen as describing an Irish or British church. There are other textual references to wooden churches. In the *Canu Dewi Sant* by Gwynfardd Brycheiniog, written in the later twelfth century, the churches of Meidrim and Henllan (Carm.) are described as *bangeibyr*, which probably means 'high/great church', the element *ceibr* meaning beam or rafter, perhaps implying a wooden construction, though possibly only of its roof.

The archaeological evidence for wooden church building is limited to two sites in southern Wales. At Llanelen on the Gower peninsula, the remains of a simple wooden chapel have been identified (Schlesinger and Walls 1996) (Fig 23a). The ephemeral remains consist of two beam slots roughly 3m long aligned east-north-east/south-west-south. Artefactual evidence from the site, including a fragment of glass and a bead, provide a broad sixth to eighth-century date for this early structure. Just to the north-east of the structure a pit with a stone lip was found, which the excavators have suggested may have been a baptistery, though the evidence is not strong (see below).

Not far from Llanelen, just off the north-west coast of Gower lies the island of Burry Holmes. Excavation here in the 1960s revealed the remains of a medieval stone church and traces of a timber predecessor (Fig 23b). This consisted of a series of post-holes defining a small structure roughly 3.3m by 3.4m. There is no dating evidence for this structure, although the stone church that overlay it probably belongs to the twelfth century (Schlesinger and Walls 1996 109-119).

Although this archaeological evidence is limited it is possible to draw some useful conclusions about these churches. Immediately apparent is the relatively small size of the two churches. Both, at only around 3m long, are tiny in comparison with Roman and Anglo-Saxon churches; for example the nave of the church at Escomb is around 13m by 6m, whilst that at Icklingham was approximately 7m by 4m. Their size instead shows parallels with some smaller Irish churches, such as Church Island and Reask. At Church Island the stone church (8.6m by 6.5m) was preceded by a smaller wooden structure measuring only 3m by 2m (O'Kelly 1958). As at Burry Holmes, this early wooden phase was of post-hole construction. At Reask the stone church was 3.5m by 2.7m; although the evidence is less clear here, this church may also have been preceded by a wooden structure (Fanning 1981). A small wooden predecessor to a stone church was also recorded at Ardwall Island (Dumfries and Galloway), where a small post-hole structure measuring 3m by 2m underlay the larger stone church (Thomas 1967, 138-9).

It is also noticeable that although located very close to each other, they utilise different building traditions – beam slots at Llanelen and post-holes at Burry Holmes. The wooden phases from the Irish and Scottish parallels noted above are all post-hole structures. However, it is possible that at Ardwall two gullies noted on the interior of the north and east walls of the stone structure may be all that remains of an earlier wooden structure supported by beam slots, though the excavator interpreted them as features integral to the stone church (Thomas 1967, 136). The limited evidence for secular building traditions of this period, such as the halls excavated at Dinas Powys in Glamorgan suggest that they could be either built with post-holes (Dinas Powys House 1A) or may have been of drystone or turf construction (Dinas Powys House 1B) (Alcock 1963, fig.6). It is possible that there may have been chronological factors at play, with Llanelen seemingly pre-dating Burry Holmes, but with the small sample of both secular and ecclesiastical wooden architecture to draw from in Wales it is not possible to say for certain.

The reason for the lack of pre-twelfth century stone churches in Wales remains unclear. It has been suggested that this was a simple result of the relative poverty of the Welsh church (Pryce 1992a). However, even areas such as the Isle of Man, where the church is unlikely to have ever been wealthy, have produced stone and stone and turf churches (e.g. Morris 1983), and it is noticeable that there is no evidence for a Welsh tradition of dry-stone built churches to compare with Irish examples (Ó Carragáin 2005).

STONE CHURCHES

Although firm archaeological dating for the construction of stone churches is lacking, the evidence from standing buildings provides some assistance. The only church in Wales where there has been serious arguments for pre-Norman fabric is Presteigne. The Taylors date the upper part of the eastern section of the north aisle as early Norman on the basis of window form (1965, 497-99). This has been confirmed by Malcolm Thurlby who suggested that a pre-1100 date is likely (2006, 54). As the lower section of the wall must pre-date this it was suggested that it might be pre-Norman, though the Taylors made it clear this early date was highly tentative. Thurlby noted that the difference in fabric might simply be due to a different origin for the building material (ibid).

Initially identified by geophysical survey, the excavations on the small chapel at Capel Spon near Buckley (Clwyd) revealed a typical single-celled structure of late twelfth or thirteenth-century date measuring approximately 14m by 8m. The walls were of mortared ragstone with an entrance in the western gable wall (Cole and Pratt 1993). No floor levels were identified; the active erosion of the site, which was noted during excavation, had probably destroyed them. At Clynnog Fawr restoration work in the chapel of St Beuno, adjacent to the main church structure, revealed a number of earlier stone foundations within the later sixteenth-century chapel building (Fig 24). These foundations defined a rectangular structure roughly 5m by 3m in size. To the west lay a stone surface and a length of further foundations aligned north-south, whilst to the east lay what appeared to be another north-south wall foundation, presumably of a structure that ran eastwards under the east wall of the sixteenth-century building.

At Llanelen, the remains of the earlier wooden chapel were succeeded by a stone church. The structure appears to have been constructed in two stages, a simple rectangular nave (5.7m by 4.1m) succeeded by a smaller chancel (2.7m square internally) (Schlesinger and Walls 1996, 114-5). The walls of the chancel were not bonded directly onto the nave, which indicates that it was later, though there is no evidence how much time had elapsed before the church was extended. Structurally, both nave and chancel were built from local stone bonded with clay mortar. It is possible that a wooden cruck frame supported the roof, and the excavators have interpreted two slots in the north and south walls at the west end of the nave as indicators of this. Evidence for the internal organisation of space within this small structure is limited. The nave was entered through a west door and the narrow opening at the east end gave access to the chancel. This would have provided limited visibility between the two sections of the church. A similar, very narrow chancel arch can still be seen at St Illtyd, Oxwich. In the nave, traces of a stone bench were found in the south-west corner. Within the chancel there were no traces of an altar setting. Two graves were identified within the chancel area. However, these had both been badly damaged in the construction of the chancel and there is no sign that they were seen as somehow special or unusual. Evidence for the date of construction of the stone church is not certain, though it is presumably eleventh or twelfth century. It seems to have fallen out of use by the mid-thirteenth century.

At Burry Holmes, as at Llanelen, a stone church succeeded the earlier wooden church, probably in the twelfth century (Fig 25). This appears to have gone through two or possibly three distinct phases. The primary phase was a stone-walled nave (around 5.3m by 3.4m externally) with a southern door. At the east end of this was a semi-circular apse. This was seemingly not bonded into the wall of the nave and may have been added later. This was then followed by a small square-ended chancel. Communication between the nave and apse, and then chancel, again appears to have been limited to a narrow chancel arch, which was apparently never widened.

Excavation at other churches has proved less informative. Work carried out in the mid-1980s at Llanychlwydog in Pembrokeshire recovered parts of the medieval church that had preceded the current church, which is mid-nineteenth century (Murphy 1987). Like Llanelen and Burry Holmes the church was a two-celled stone structure, probably from the twelfth century. The presence of several early cross-slabs and the fact that the west wall of the medieval church appeared to cut a stone lined grave indicate that the stone church was not the first phase of Christian activity at the site. Evidence for an earlier wooden predecessor was lacking, though the trenches were limited in extent and it appears that much of the interior was cut by medieval and post-medieval burials making it unlikely that the remains of any such putative church would survive.

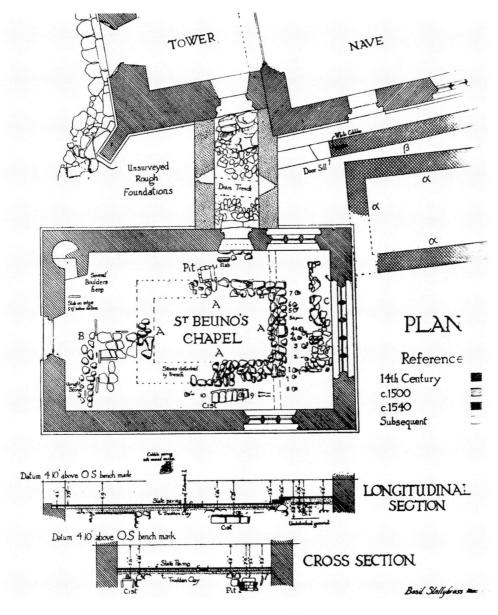

24 Early stone structure at Clynnog Fawr (Caernarvonshire). (Stallybrass 1914)

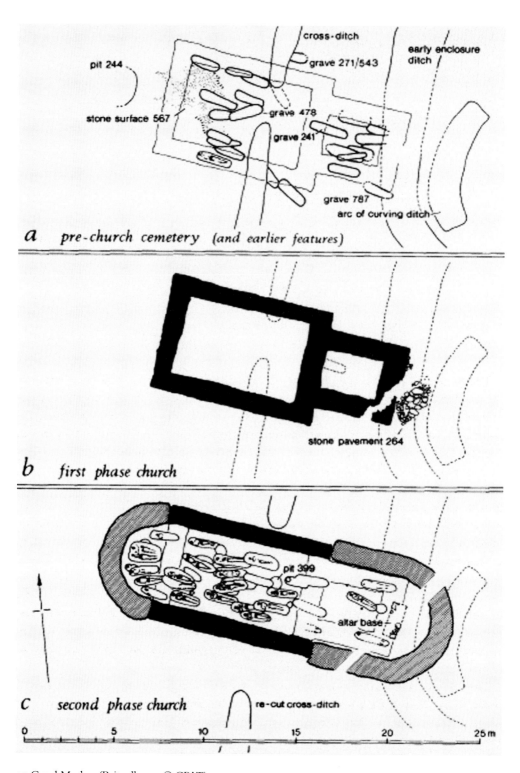

a   pre-church cemetery (and earlier features)

b   first phase church

c   second phase church

25 Capel Maelog. (Britnell 1990 © CPAT)

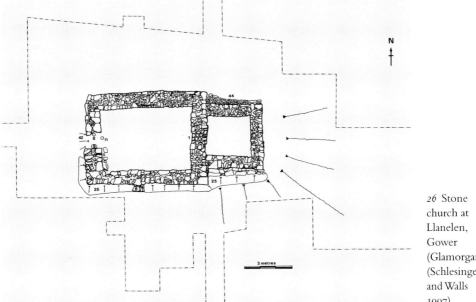

 caption:

26 Stone
church at
Llanelen,
Gower
(Glamorgan).
(Schlesinger
and Walls
1997)

The church at Capel Maelog does not appear to have been preceded by an earlier structure
(Fig 25). Despite being fully excavated using modern techniques, no traces of a wooden predecessor were recognised. Instead it appears to have been built *de novo* as a stone church at some
point in the late twelfth or early thirteenth century (Britnell 1990). The first phase of the church
was another example of a simple two-cell church structure, the nave measuring 4.4m by 6.9m
internally and the chancel roughly 4.4m square. The excavated foundations of both nave and
chancel were of local dolerite and bonded with clay. As no walls were still standing it was not
possible to be certain about the entrance, though it is probable on the basis of evidence from
the second phase that it was entered via a door in the south wall. It is not easy to assess whether
the chancel and nave were contemporary, or whether, as at Llanelen, the chancel was secondary.
Certainly there were foundations for the entire east wall of the nave, perhaps indicating a slightly
later date for the chancel. At some point, probably before the mid to later thirteenth century,
the church saw significant structural alterations. The west wall of the nave and the chancel were
demolished and replaced by apses. Although there is no direct structural or stratigraphic relationship between the two apses, the excavators argued on the basis of the similar fabric that they
were contemporary (Britnell 1990, 46). Intriguingly, it is possible that some of the stone used in
this second phase was taken from the nearby Roman fort at Castell Collen.

The use of space within the church appears to have changed significantly in this second
phase. With the disappearance of the chancel the building appears to have reverted to a
single-cell form. It is possible though that the altar may have continued to be separated from
the main body of the church by a wooden screen. This may have been based on a wooden
sill beam, or possibly a single post-hole to the west of the altar may have been related to such
a structure. It is certainly noticeable that there is a distinct gap between the burials placed in

the nave of the Phase II church and those inserted into the floor of the chancel. It is clear on the basis of the spread of a later floor surface that the west apse was also screened off, though there is no evidence for this initially. The plan of the second phase of Capel Maelog is unusual. Whereas at Burry Holmes an earlier east apse was replaced by a chancel, the reverse is the case here. The construction of a western apse is even more unusual, both in Wales and in England, certainly in such a relatively small and low status church (Spurgeon 1990, 86).

Excavations at the Chapel of St Justinian, Pembrokeshire, facing Ramsey Island, revealed a sequence of stone structures (Fig 27) (Boake 1926). Within the walls of the standing structures, the foundations of a smaller, rectangular structure were identified measuring 5m by 4m externally. This had a north door and a small number of burials were found inside it, including one elaborate cist grave covered in white quartz pebbles. There was clear evidence for earlier religious activity on site, as the cist grave overlay another grave, which was cut by the northern wall of the building. The south-east corner of the small rectangular building also overlay a further west-east aligned wall which ran westwards for over 7m. It is difficult to properly understand the structural activity at this site. One possibility is that the earliest wall is the south wall of a stone nave. Its apparent termination at the west end may be simply the location of a door in the south wall, as at Burry Holmes. The north and west walls presumably lay beneath those of the standing building. The small rectangular structure could be a chancel added to the east end of the earlier nave. The north door to the putative chancel has parallels with other two-cell aisle-less churches in Wales, such as St Thomas, Over Monnow, where there is a priest's door at the west end of the north wall of the chancel. Priests' doorways appear to become more common in the later twelfth century, so this may help date this element of the suggested sequence at St Justinian's Chapel (Thurlby 2006, 171). This suggested reconstruction would mean that the projected chancel arch would be slightly off-centre. This is paralleled at other churches in Wales, such as at St Mary, Llanfairynghornwy and Rhosili, where the chancel arches were offset to the south, and Pennant Melangell where the chancel arch is offset to the north. It seems likely that at the latter site this occurred in order to accommodate a special grave in the southern half of the chancel. Malcolm Thurlby has suggested a similar situation at Llanfairynghornwy (Thurlby 2006, 171). At St Justinian's Chapel, the unusual burial associated with the quartz pebbles would lie in a similar location. This would then mean that the unusual burial actually lay in the chancel of a two-celled stone church, rather than in the north-east corner of a small single-celled structure.

With the spread of Norman influence along the Welsh border and areas of direct Norman control in south and south-west Wales, there is a clear spread of stone structures which date to the eleventh and twelfth century on the basis of datable Romanesque-style sculptural detailing (Thurlby 2006). Crucially, apart from Presteigne, there are no cases where *in situ* Romanesque architecture is preceded by a non-Romanesque phase. Possible pre-Conquest fabric is known just over the modern border in Herefordshire at Bredwardine, which lies on the south bank of the Wye, where herringbone masonry can be seen in the north and west walls of the nave. There is also a blocked western doorway seemingly replaced by a Norman south door built in tufa (Gethyn-Jones 1979, 9; Taylor and Taylor 1965, 97). It is possible that Bredwardine may be the site named *Lann Iunabui* in the Llandaf Charters (Coplestone-Crow 1989, 42; LL 73a). Herringbone masonry is not always a clear indicator of early date. It has been noted that in

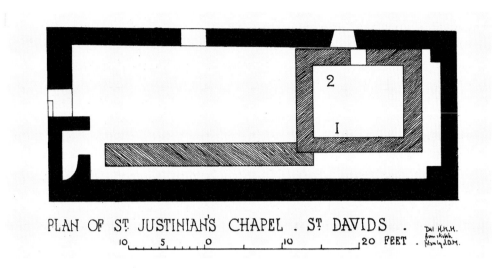

PLAN OF ST. JUSTINIAN'S CHAPEL . ST. DAVIDS .

10 5 0 10 20 FEET .

27 St Justinian's Chapel (Pembrokeshire). (Boake 1926)

Herefordshire its use tends to be confined to the extreme north and east of the county, and it is possible that it is a local or regional characteristic, although Bredwardine is the one outlier of this group (Parsons 1995). However, it is useful to note the general absence of herringbone construction in Wales itself, where it is limited to two examples in South Wales: St Peter's, Dixton, which may be an outlier of the Herefordshire group, and St Peter's, Cogan. Kilpeck, best known for its spectacular Romanesque carving, mainly dates to the mid-late twelfth century, although there are hints that the north-east corner of the structure may include earlier fabric as long-and-short work survives, usually seen as a diagnostic pre-Conquest feature.

The spread of stone architecture in the later eleventh and twelfth century forms a clear horizon in the study of the Welsh church. The reason for this new phase in ecclesiastical architecture has rarely been addressed beyond an implicit assumption that it reflects Norman influence. This fails to answer why despite being bounded by stone churches to the west and east this technique was not used before. Does it indicate merely a re-building of previously wooden structures, as at Llanelen or does it imply a major phase of constructing entirely new churches, as at Capel Maelog? The extent to which this can be answered archaeologically is limited. The tiny sample of adequately excavated churches makes it dangerous to make widespread generalisations.

It may be possible to further explore this question through the historical material. A figure frequently placed centrally in the discussion of church building is Gruffudd ap Cynan (1054/5–1137). After growing up in Ireland, the grandson of a king of Gwynedd, he returned to Wales and after an eventful series of campaigns, which included a long imprisonment in Chester, was able to seize power in Gwynedd. Evidence for his role as a catalyst in church construction is found in two sources. In an encomium on his death, the *Brut y Tywysogion* records that he died in 1137 '… after building many churches in his time and consecrating them to God …' (*BYT*). This role is outlined more extensively in the twelfth-century biography of him, the *Historia Gruffudd vab Kenan*. A translation of the Welsh text reads:

Gruffudd, on his part made great stone churches for himself in his chief places and constructed courts and [gave] banquets constantly and honourably. Wherefore he also made Gwynedd glitter then with limewashed churches like the firmament of stars

HGVK, 82

Recently, the original Latin version has been identified (Russell 2005). In this text the passage reads slightly differently: 'Gruffudd also built large churches next to his palaces which he built and established beautifully sparing no expense. What then was the result? Gwynedd, with churches and dedications like the heaven with stars' (*VGFC* 33). This version uses the word *ecclesia* for 'church' and *basilica* for 'large church'. In the passage describing his legacy to Welsh, Irish and English churches the term used is *ecclesia*, even for major ecclesiastical centres, such as Bangor and St Davids. It is uncertain as to whether it is possible to read anything into this difference in vocabulary.

However it is read, this passage seems to suggest that as well as providing stone churches in his own personal power centres, Gruffudd promoted the construction of many other churches. The Latin version contains no information about the church construction. However, the Welsh version uses the term *egleysseu kalcheit* ('lime-washed churches'). This might imply that they were primarily of stone construction. A similar phrase *eglwys wenn wyngalch ualch wynhaed* ('A white bright-chalk church, finely whitened') is used in Llywelyn Fardd's poem *Canu Cadfan* (lines 33–4) about the church at Tywyn, which was probably rebuilt in stone in the 1140s (Thurlby 2006, 224). Excavation on a church at Rhosili recovered plaster on the external wall, which might indicate that it too had a white external rendering, although the date of this plaster layer is uncertain; it may be quite late as it sealed an earlier window opening and decorative quoins (Williams et al. 1985, 82-3).

It is less clear whether Gruffudd was responsible for directly commissioning these churches, or allowing them to be built through patronage, which is recorded in his gifting of money to Welsh churches, including Holyhead, Penmon, Clynnog, Bardsey Island, Meifod, Llanarmon and Dineirth, as well as churches in Ireland and England (Evans 1990). It has also been argued that Grufudd was directly responsible for a distinct phase in church construction in Anglesey, particularly the priories at Penmon, Ynys Seriol and Abberffraw (Thurlby 2006, 191-238). Gruffudd ap Cynan was not, however, the only leader in Gwynedd who was associated with church building. His adversary Trahaearn ap Caradog (d.1081) was described in the *Brut y Twysogyon* as 'the strength of the learned and the honour and foundation of the churches' (*BYT* 1078). The description of a Gwynedd glittering with lime-washed churches is also reminiscent of a number of literary descriptions invoking the image of church construction from tenth to twelfth century sources. Around the turn of the millennium the French monk Rodolfus Glaber wrote of a massive increase in church construction 'as if the world were … cladding itself in a white mantle of churches' (France 1989, 114-7). In 1050 Bishop Hereman of Ramsbury visited the Pope; according to Goscelin of Saint-Bertin he told him of 'England being filled everywhere with churches which daily were being added to anew in new places, about the distribution of innumerable ornaments and bells in oratories' (Migne 1880, col.32).

28 Penmon
Priory (Anglesey),
(Author's
photograph)

This means that it is important to be wary when attributing the rapid spread of stone church building in Gwynedd specifically to Gruffudd. The notion of supporting and encouraging the church is associated with earlier Venedotian rulers, and links into a wider rhetoric of church building in the eleventh and twelfth centuries. The mention of lime-washed churches only appears in the Welsh version of the *Historia Gruffudd vab Cynan*, and is not found in the earlier Latin text. Nonetheless, whether stimulated by Gruffudd ap Cynan, Trahaearn or other North Welsh rulers it is clear from an analysis of the standing architecture that there was a major phase of church construction in early to mid-twelfth century Anglesey. Architecturally the most important twelfth-century church on Anglesey is that at Penmon (Fig 28). The church was originally a *clas*, though by the early thirteenth century it had become an Augustinian priory. The church is cruciform in plan with an aisleless nave. There is a simple chancel arch, and a more elaborate arch on the west arch of the tower decorated with chevrons and carved capitals depicting animal and human figures. The south transept has chevron-decorated arcading on two walls, presumably a similar scheme could be found in the north transept before it was reconstructed. The fabric is mainly twelfth century in date, though the chancel was rebuilt in the thirteenth century, and the north transept and part of the south transept underwent reconstruction in the mid-nineteenth century. The precise date of construction is still debated; Thurlby posits a date of 1100–1120 for the earliest phases (Thurlby 2006, 206), and links the construction of the nave and transepts to the patronage of Gruffudd ap Cynan. Others prefer a later date (RCHAMW 1937; Radford 1961). The stone tower may predate the other elements of the building (ibid). It has been suggested that the original chancel may have been a stone-vaulted chamber, but did not contain the main altar, which is likely to have stood beneath the tower.

A short distance across the water on the island of Ynys Seriol lie the remains of another early stone church. This church consisted of a central tower standing between a western nave (no longer extant) and a once barrel-vaulted chancel. The tower is very similar in form to that at Penmon (Hughes 1930). Following Thurlby's dating, this would place it c. 1100–1120 (Thurlby 2006, 213). He also draws constructional parallels between the vault at Ynys Seirol and the south doorway at the small single-celled stone church at Capel Lligwy only 15km away. Accordingly, it is possible that there were substantial stone churches at both Penmon and Ynys Seriol and feasibly a smaller stone chapel at Capel Lligwy. It is thus possible that other stone churches on the island may also have an early twelfth-century date. It is still unclear, however, whether Grufudd was responsible for both the earlier phase at Penmon and Ynys Seriol or simply the new nave and transept at Penmon. Nonetheless, even if not responsible for the initial phase of stone church construction on Anglesey, he was clearly a significant patron of churches on the island. This is probably reflected in the west nave arch at Aberffraw, which lay close to the site of a major royal centre (Johnstone 1997). Stylistic links make it likely that construction at Penmynydd and Llanbabo (both Anglesey) were also contemporary to the main period of construction at Penmon (Thurlby 2006, 218-9).

CHURCH LAYOUT

Most of the churches from the eleventh and twelfth centuries are relatively simple in plan, consisting of either a single cell or having a two-cell plan with nave and chancel. However, some churches were more architecturally complex, with the addition of towers, naves and central transepts. The addition of aisles can be seen at churches associated with both Norman and native Welsh patronage. St Woolos, Newport, granted by William Rufus to Gloucester Abbey, has a five-bay nave with aisles and a clerestory dating to c. 1125–50; it is possible that an *eglwys y bedd* once stood to the west of the main tower (Knight and Wood 2006). At Caerleon traces of a clerestory and the western bay of a south nave of twelfth-century date can also be seen (Newman 2000). In native Welsh territory, the mid-twelfth century reconstruction of the church of St Cadfan, Tywyn, had four bays (now three) with north and south aisles (Fig 29), whilst St Michael's, Kerry, had a similar arrangement. It is possible that some churches only had one additional aisle, such as the possible north aisles at Llandrinio (Fig 30), and St Mary, Brecon, though in both cases the surviving evidence is fragmentary and it is possible that there may have been south aisles for which no evidence survives.

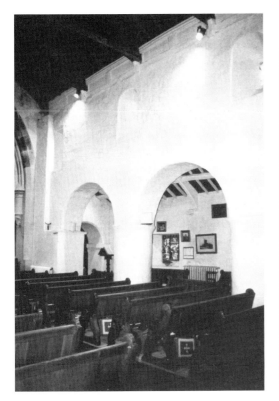

Above left: 29 Interior of St Cadfan, Tywyn, showing Norman south aisle. (Author's photograph)

Above right: 30 Traces of north aisle at Llandrinio (Montgomeryshire). (Author's photograph)

Above left: 31a Traces of south transept, Meifod (Montgomeryshire). (Author's photograph)

Above right: *31b* Remains of north transept, Meifod (Montgomeryshire). (Author's photograph)

A cruciform plan for churches, with north and south transepts and a central tower, is also found across Wales. St Cadfan's, Tywyn, has a surviving north transept. Transepts without aisles are known at Llanbadarn Fawr, Llanddew, Clynnog Fawr, St Dwynwen and Llanfihangel-y-Creuddyn amongst others. At Meifod, transepts appear to have been located at the west end of the church rather than in a central position; Malcolm Thurlby has suggested that this might be interpreted as a *westwerk*, an elaborate western entrance to the church with towers (Fig 247-8) (Thurlby 2006). Interestingly, the evidence from nearby Llandrinio might also be read as indicating a transept at the west end of the building, rather than an aisle.

Early church towers are relatively rare and mainly confined to monastic establishments or were located over the crossings of churches with a cruciform plan, as at Penmon or Llanddew. It is uncommon to find evidence for western towers associated with a simple two-cell church structure. There are a few rare exceptions. At Llaneilian (Anglesey), the stone tower at the west end of the church has an eastern arch with chamfered imposts from the twelfth century (RCHAMW 1937). The west tower at Kerry may date broadly to the twelfth to fourteenth century, as may the low tower at Merthyr Cynnog.

Ralegh Radford attempted to make a simple equation between the status of churches and their plan, arguing that mother churches had cruciform plans, parish churches had two-cell plans, whilst simple non-parochial chapels had only one chamber (Radford 1963). However, this approach has been increasingly criticised; it has been pointed out that some known mother churches did not have cruciform plans (Butler 1996; Thomas 1970); for example, the church at Aberdaron was originally a single-cell structure (Fig 32).

In other cases, some cruciform churches show no evidence that they were ever of superior status, such as Laugharne and Llanfihangel-y-Creuddyn (Thomas 1970, 95-6). It is also clear that church plans were often not all of one period, and that complexity could change over time. The complex growth at Penmon has already been highlighted and at nearby Ynys Seiriol excavations in the late nineteenth century showed that the small barrel-vaulted chancel was rebuilt at some point before the construction of the central tower in the twelfth century; at a later date a southern transept was added, but never a northern counterpart. The remains of the cruciform church of St Dwynwen, Newborough, even suggest that the chancel and transepts date from as late as the early sixteenth century, though it is possible that these were rebuilt on the foundations of earlier fabric (RCAHMW 1937, 119). Conversely, churches could also see the progressive simplification of their layout. Meifod lost its transepts, presumably at some point before the fourteenth century, when the tower was built into the last nave bay (Haslam 1979, 159), and Capel Maelog lost its chancel (Britnell 1990). The probable north aisle at Llandrinio was also removed at some point in the medieval period. The re-ordering of the church at Llantwit Major, probably in the late thirteenth century, also led to the removal of its transepts.

Whilst Ralegh Radford's rigid scheme cannot be supported, it is apparent that, broadly speaking, architectural complexity was a function of the wealth of the church. This might either have arrived through wealth generated by land holdings belonging to a church or through direct patronage by members of the Norman or Welsh elite; Gruffudd ap Cynan is recorded as having given 20 shillings to St Davids, and 10 shillings each to Holyhead,

Penmon, Clynnog, Enlli, Meifod, Llanarmon and Dineirth amongst others (Jones 1910, 155-7). It is noticeable that most of these churches had a significant degree of architectural elaboration in the twelfth century.

In exploring the simple two-celled structures that dominate the archaeological record and that still survive widely as standing structures, the term 'nave' has been used to describe the larger western cell and 'chancel' to describe the smaller eastern unit. This terminology carries certain assumptions concerning the liturgical layout of these churches: the term 'chancel' being used to describe the area of the building where the altar stood, whilst the 'nave' being used to describe the body of the church, where the congregation stood. In practice this may not always have been so.

It is far from certain that the altar was initially located in the chancel. At major early Anglo-Saxon churches such as Reculver and Winchester the altar lay at the east end of the nave, rather than in the chancel (Taylor 1973). A similar pattern is also recognisable in some smaller, later Anglo-Saxon churches, such as Raunds (Parson 1996). The evidence for altar position is limited in Wales. At Capel Maelog there was evidence for the location of the altar in the second phase of the building. The base of a stone altar at the east end of the church was set back from the wall of the apse. This was approximately above the east wall of the Phase 1 church, perhaps indicating that the altar of the earlier church was placed against this wall (Britnell 1990, 49).

At both these sites, the evidence for the location of the altar comes from later phases in the church, with no indication of the earlier site of the altar. It is possible, but not certain, that the altars were relocated at the same time the chancels were built, but there is no firm evidence for this. This appears to reflect the wider elaboration of the eastern end of parish churches in twelfth and thirteenth-century England to provide more room around altars, which were often moved from the nave to a chancel that may have replaced an apse provided for the clergy (Barnwell 2004).

The altar certainly had a central role in Welsh society, not just as the location of the celebration of the Eucharist, but also because in legal proceedings Welsh law codes regularly demanded that oaths should be sworn on the altar (e.g. Jenkins 2000, 70). A women who wished to claim that an individual was the father of her child must come to church where the alleged father's family burial place was and swear with one hand on the altar and another on her child's head (Jenkins, 132-3); the formal denial of fatherhood consisted of a very similar procedure (ibid.). More complex rituals were attached to allegations of theft, which involved oath taking at the church door, at the chancel and at the altar (Jenkins, 159). Clearly, such ceremonies would involve formal or semi-formal processions around the church interior.

At Burry Holmes, the chancel replaced an earlier apse. This may originally have housed the altar; it is intriguing to note that the replacement of an apse by a chancel is known from a number of other sites. The footings of an apse were seen during restoration work at Sully in Glamorgan (Knight 1976-8; RCAHMW 1991), and an apse was excavated at Llanfairpwllgwyn (Anglesey) (Anon 1847). Aerial photographs of cropmarks at Llwydfaen show a single-celled church structure with an apsidal end (Fig 33) (Driver 2006). As seen above, at Capel Maeolog (Radnorshire) the straight end of the church was replaced by an apse, and at Pennant Melangell an apse contained the stone covered grave, interpreted as the burial place of the saint (Britnell 1994).

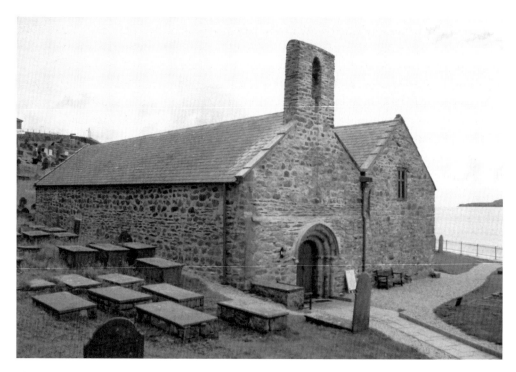

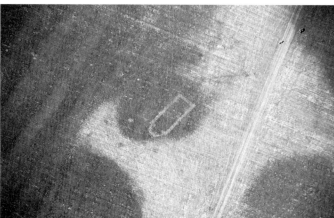

Above: 32 St Hywyn's Church, Aberdaron (Caernarvonshire). (Author's photograph)

Left: 33 Cropmarks of church with apse, Llwydfaen (Caernarvonshire). (Toby Driver © RCAHMW)

In the Welsh borders there is a further cluster of aiseless churches with apsidal ends, including Rye Felton (Shropshire), Craswall, Ford Bridge, Kilpeck, Moccas, Pencombe, Peterchurch, Tarrington, Urishay (all Herefordshire) and Dymock (Gloucestershire). The standing structures at Moccas and Peterchurch are probably from the mid-twelfth century, the latter unusually having four distinct compartments. The replacement of the apse by a square chancel has been identified by excavation at Tarrington and Urishay; in the fifteenth century in the former case and the late twelfth or early thirteenth century in the latter case (RCHME 1932, 182–3; Shoesmith 1987).

It is difficult to assess whether the construction of apsidal ends to churches is a particular feature of Welsh churches in the eleventh or twelfth century. It is noticeable that in most of the examples highlighted the apse was only identified through archaeological work. It is possible that many other Welsh churches had apsidal ends, but have not been recognised. The construction of apses may be influenced by building traditions in neighbouring areas. The presence of eastern apses has already been noted in Herefordshire. However, the known Welsh apses are spread widely across the country, and show no particular proximity to Herefordshire, meaning that it is unlikely that the use of the apse was particularly influenced by these Norman models.

The function of the apses is unclear. Whilst, at Pennant Melangell it appears to have housed a holy burial, the other examples are not associated with churches that have any record of being the site of significant relics. Instead it is likely that they were used by the clergy for seating. The replacement of the apses by chancels again seems to reflect the wider physical separation of the clergy from the congregation over the course of the twelfth century (Barnwell 2004, 53-55).

Internal Fittings

The evidence for internal fittings within early Welsh churches is limited. There is little archaeological evidence; there are a small number of sculptural fragments that might, however, be parts of screens, perhaps serving to divide off the altar from the congregation. Two fragmentary stone slabs from Bangor with carved decoration on them may be parts of such screens (79; Thurlby 2006, 195). Their date is uncertain, they may be tenth century, as suggested by Nash-Williams, or they may be of later date, but deliberately archaicising in style. If the latter, the reconstruction of the cathedral by Gruffudd ap Cynan is a persuasive context for their creation. Another possible fragment of a screen are two carved stone shafts from Llantwit Major, with a straight groove running down one side (G67-8). The groove may have accommodated other stone, or more likely wooden, components. As with the Bangor examples, a tenth or eleventh-century date is most likely. A final curious example is a stone from Llanrhidian variously called a lintel or part of a tomb (G59; Newman 1995). It has clearly been reworked over its life. The end of the right-hand side of the stone has been carved to represent an animal head, suggesting it was one end of a carved stone frieze, with the head originally intended to project outwards. The underside of the left part of the stone appears to form part of an arch (Thurlby 2006, 69). Thurlby also noted the presence of an apparent socket in the top of the stone, suggesting that this may have been for a wooden fitting, and as at Bangor and Llantwit, this was part of a stone and wood screen. Ultimately, the evidence for any of these stone fragments being part of a screen is clearly limited and circumstantial. None of these fragments resemble each other in any way, and the general lack of good examples would suggest that if stone was used to make screens it was relatively rarely. Wood is more likely to have been used for such purposes, though sadly no Romanesque or pre-Romanesque wooden screens survive to suggest the possible form they might have taken.

It is unlikely that Welsh churches of any period up to at least the fourteenth or fifteenth century would have had internal seating for the congregation. However, a number of churches have evidence for simple benches along the walls of the nave, including Rhossili, St Brynach's, Cowbridge, Llanelen and St Barruc's, Barry Island (Williams et al 1985; Parkhouse and Robinson; Schlesinger and Walls 1995; Knight 1981).

The interiors of churches were likely to have varied widely in their appearance. Most probably had plastered walls. It is likely that some may have carried some form of painted decoration, either figurative or decorative. No intact paintings of twelfth-century date or earlier survive, although a little of thirteenth-century date is known. Fragmentary decoration including traces of an inscription and possibly part of a figurative scheme with painted masonry were found at Rhossili (Williams 1985, 254-5). Another thirteenth-century wall painting is recorded from St Cadog's, Cheriton, and a possible image of St John the Baptist from Michaelstone-y-Fedw. However, some churches may not even have had plastered walls; the excavations at Capel Maelog produced no evidence for internal plastering (Britnell 1990). Presumably, some church windows would have been glazed either with plain glass or a decorative scheme, but no early glass survives. There would have had to have been some internal light sources (see Chapter Three).

CHURCH GROUPS

The presence of more than one church on ecclesiastical sites was not uncommon (Blair 1992). However, what might be termed church groups appear to have been particularly widespread in western England, Wales, Scotland and Ireland (Davies 1982a; Edwards and Lane 1992, 9-10; Petts and Turner 2009). There are certainly distinct differences in form and layout between these areas and Anglo-Saxon England. The evidence for church groups is variable; in a small number of cases there is still more than one church or chapel standing on the site, though sometimes what were once originally freestanding structures have been incorporated into the later main church; often these structures have seen substantial rebuilding. In other cases, subsidiary chapels are known only through archaeological excavations. There is also some documentary evidence, including antiquarian observations and limited contemporary records.

At Clynnog Fawr a small chapel stands to the south of the main church. Once separate buildings, they are now linked by a covered walkway (RCAHMW 1960, 36-42) (Fig 34b). Although the fabric of the chapel is predominantly sixteenth century, excavations in the early twentieth century revealed the drystone foundations of an earlier building and a number of cist burials (Stallybrass 1913). Two similar cases are known on nearby Anglesey. At Holyhead the chapel known as Llan y Gwyddel lies a little distance from the main church of St Cybi, within the wall of a Roman fortlet (RCAHMW 1937, 28-32) (Fig 34b). The standing fabric is again of relatively late date (fourteenth century), but excavations have identified the footings of an earlier, possibly twelfth-century phase (Gruffudd 1992). The demolition of the chancel of the chapel in 1832 uncovered at least one burial and long cists have also been found to the south of the church (Lywyd 1832). At Llaneilian, on the north east coast of Anglesey, a chapel known as Myfyr Eilian (grave of Eilian) stands to the south-east of the main parish church, but on a slightly different alignment (RCAHMW 1937, 59-61) (Fig 34c).

The shrine at the west end of the church of St Boda and St Gwynon at Dwygyfylchi, demolished in 1760, is a good example of a chapel known only through early documentary sources (Hughes and North 1984; Gwynn 1906, 18-19). The same is true of the church group at Penmachno, where two churches (St Tudclyd and St Enclydwyn's) stood until the seventeenth century. The current church was built in the mid-nineteenth century on the site of one of the earlier churches (RCAHMW 1956, 168-9). At Abergele at the end of the seventeenth century Edward Lhuyd referred to a 'chappel in ye ch yard'. This may have been a structure to the south of the church, which was accessed by a now-blocked southern doorway. Lhuyd also noted the existence of the Kappel Gwenfrewi at Gwytherin, which probably stood to the south of the current church (Evans 1986, 66-7), and a chapel known as Eglwys Trisant at Clydai (RCHAMW 1925, 75-6). At Llanpumsaint a chapel stood to the north of the main church. In 1710 it was recorded as the 'ruins of a little chapel (whither) on Sundays in wet weather the country people resorted … to dance' (RCAHMW 1917, no.541).

Other antiquarian reports note groups of churches in western English churchyards. For example, Silas Taylor wrote in the seventeenth century that 'in the churchyard at Moccas [Herefordshire] are to be seen the foundations of a very large church to which this standing was but a chapple' (Harl MS 6726). Evidence for possible church groups in south-west Herefordshire can also be found within the Llandaf Charters in a list of churches consecrated by Herwald (1056–1104), the predecessor of Bishop Urban, who probably ordered the compilation of the Book of Llandaf. It states 'In the time of Edward, king of England, and Gruffudd, king of Wales, Bishop Herewald consecrated Henllan Ddyfrig and Llandeilo in one churchyard (*Tempore Etguardi Regis Angliae, et Grifudi Regis Gualiae consecrauit Hergualdis episcopus Henllan Dibric et Lann Teliau in uno cimiterio*) (LL 275). This probably refers to the church of Hentland. It is not clear whether Herewald was consecrating newly-built churches or re-consecrating churches that had been damaged earlier, perhaps following the raids of Gruffudd ap Llywelyn in the area. However, it is noticeable that one church is the Henllan i.e. old or former church, suggesting that it existed before this date. A final possible Herefordshire example comes from Titley, where there are records of a chapel dedicated to the 'Blessed Tylliar' (possibly a corruption of Tysilio) which lay to the north of priory church (Coplestone-Crow 1989).

At Meifod (Montgomeryshire) the *Brut y Twysogion* records that the church of St Mary was consecrated in 1156. It has been suggested that this was simply a rededication of the existing church of Saint Tysilio (Silvester and Frost 1999). However, in 1160, the *Brut* also records that Madog ap Maredudd was buried in the church of St Tysilio, implying that it was still in use after 1156 and that both the churches of Tysilio and St Mary were in contemporary use. A third church is also known to have stood at Meifod, a chapel dedicated to St Gwyddfarch. This stood to the south-east of the main church, in an area no longer in the modern graveyard, but still known as Mynwent Gwyddfarch (Gwyddfarch's cemetery). An earlier reference, though harder to interpret, comes from *Canu Llywarch Hen*. This text refers to the loss of the privileges of the churches (in the plural) of Baschurch following the defeat of Cynddyland and Elfan of Powys by the English (*Canu*

Llywarch Hen stanza 49). This may refer to multiple churches or chapels at Baschurch itself, or instead may mean the churches dependant upon a mother church at Baschurch.

Again, difficult to interpret is the evidence from church dedications. Many sites have more than one dedication. For example, at Llanpumsaint (Church of Five Saints) the parish church is dedicated to SS Ceitho, Celynin, Gwyn, Gwyno and Gwynoro. Although at least one other chapel is recorded from this site, it would seem unlikely that there were originally five churches or chapels within the enclosure. There are also examples of ecclesiastical sites being referred to as possessing several altars. Llewelyn Fardd's *Canu Cadfan* speaks of three altars at Tywyn (to Cadfan?, Mary and Peter):

> Mary's altar from the Lord, trustworthy and sacred relic;
> the altar of Peter in his authority which should be praised;
> and the third altar which was bestowed by heaven:
> the dwelling place is blessed because of its hospitality.
> *Canu Cadfan* lines 25–28 (McKenna 1997)

There is a similar reference in Gwynfardd Brycheiniog's praise poem to St David:

> There is a generous bishop [officiating] over the altars of Dewi
> The five altars of Brefi in honour of saints…
> *Canu Dewi* lines 268–9 (Owen 1991)

It is not clear whether in these cases 'altar' is to be understood as a synecdoche for 'church' or if it indicates the presence of several separate altars within a single building; at least one additional freestanding chapel once stood at St Cadfan's, Tywyn (Davidson 2001, 369).

The purpose of the subsidiary chapels seems to vary, although most appear to have been *capel/eglwys y bedd* (burial chapels/churches) housing the graves or relics of saints. For example, at Llaneilan the chapel is known as *Myfyr Eilian* (the grave of Eilian), and the remains of a later (fifteenth-century) wooden reliquary still survives at the church. The chapel at Clynnog Fawr was known as the *eglwys y bedd* of Beuno. This is typical of the practice of burial *ad sanctos* that might be expected at the burial of a holy individual in the early middle ages (Edwards 2002). Another probable association with relics can be found at Gwytherin where Edward Lhuyd recorded the presence of the Kappel Gwenfrewi; this is likely to have housed the early medieval shrine of Gwenfrewi, a fragment of which still survives (see Chapter Four). At Eglwyswrw (Dyfed), George Owen recorded in the late sixteenth century that a chapel containing the tomb of Saint Errow stood to the south of the main church (Charles 1947, 278; Ludlow 2000).

In some cases there are suggestions that the chapel acted as a focus for burial, but was not specifically associated with a named individual. For example, at Holyhead, the *eglwys y bedd*, known simply as Llan y Gwyddel (Church of the Irishman) is associated with a number of long cist burials (RCHMW 1937, 28–32). At St Bride's (Pembrokeshire) a small chapel formerly stood to the north of the parish church; it was recorded as being surrounded by stone 'coffins', presumably stone-lined graves (RCHMW 1925, 318).

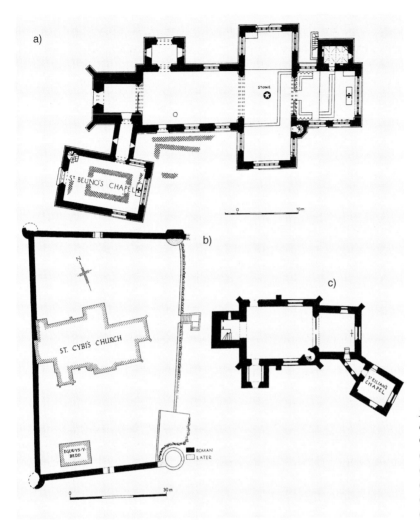

34 Examples of *eglwys y bedd*. (a) Clynnog Fawr (Caernarvonshire) (b) Caer Gybi (Angelsey) (c) Llaneilian (Angelsey)

Spatial Organisation of Church Groups

At Llaneilian and Clynnog Fawr, the chapels lay a short distance to the south of the main church. Chapels are also recorded to the south at Eglwyswrw, Rhoscrowther, Gwytherin, Tywyn, Llanymawddy and St Cybi. The frequent location of chapels to the south of the main church is also reflected in the higher status afforded to the south side of the altar in the Anglo-Saxon church (Deliyannis 1995). A roughly linear, west-east alignment is also known. In some of these cases it is not clear whether the subsidiary chapels were ever truly freestanding, or were originally attached to the main structure. At Patrishow and St Woolos, Newport the *eglwys y bedd* are parts of the main structure, as may have been the now disappeared *capel y bedd* at Llangeler and Llangollen. At Pennant Melangell, the *capel y bedd* of Melangell, as well as being a rare example of an eastern chapel, shows an interesting sequence moving from an apse containing a grave, probably the original focal grave followed by an exceptionally early Romanesque shrine (Britnell

1994) (Fig 35). The pattern of access between such chapels varies. At Patrishow the chapel has external access only and cannot be reached via the main church, it is possible a similar arrangement may have existed at earlier stages at Pennant Melangell. A final possible example of an axial *eglwys y bedd*, is at Llantwit Major, where Jeremy Knight has suggested the original church containing the grave of Illtyd was retained as a burial church when the new east end of the church was built, placing it in a similar position the burial chapel at St Woolos, Newport (Knight and Wood 2006, 166).

Dating Church Groups

The limited archaeological and documentary evidence gives us little indication for the chronology of these groups of churches and chapels. There is, however, little reason to believe these subsidiary structures were in place much before the eighth century. The peak period of the construction of subsidiary chapels and churches in western Britain appears to stretch from the ninth century until the twelfth century. Although most contain later architectural fabric after this last date, it is probable that this represents the continued elaboration of earlier structures rather than the construction of entirely *de novo*.

Parallels to these groups of churches are known from Anglo-Saxon England (Blair 1992; Blair 2005; Jones 1996). The prime example is Canterbury, with a cluster of churches dedicated to St Peter and Paul, St Mary and St Pancras. Other well-known examples include Jarrow, Repton, Glastonbury and Wells. John Blair's extensive review of church groups in England has shown that a linear arrangement is most common, demonstrating strong influence from north-east Gaul (Blair 1992, 250-8). The linear arrangement of some of the Welsh churches has clear parallels with Anglo-Saxon and Frankish church groups, and it is possible that it may indicate influence from these areas on ecclesiastical planning in western Britain. Mausoleums or burial chapels in a linear position are known from major Mercian ecclesiastical centres, such as Repton, Winchcombe and Gloucester, indicating one possible line of influence on this particular arrangement of church and mortuary chapels in Wales (Biddle 1986; Heighway and Bryant 1999; Bassett 1985).

35 *Capel y bedd* at Pennant Melangell (Montgomeryshire) under excavation. (© CPAT)

Groups of churches and the presence of subsidiary burial chapels are also known in Scotland and Ireland. Examples include St Columba's Shrine, St Oran's Chapel, St Ronan's Church, St Mary's Church and the Michael Chapel at Iona (RCAHMS, 1982). A group of churches is also known at St Andrew's Fife (Foster 1998, 45-6) and possibly Whithorn (Hill 1997, 241-51), and several smaller sites. On the Isle of Man, Kirk Maughold appears to have contained at least four keeils in addition to the parish church. Whilst the date of these structures is uncertain, the presence of lintel graves from the site and a number of early Christian carved stones attest to the antiquity of ecclesiastical activity here (Kermode 1968, fig.7). The examples from Scotland and the Isle of Man all appear to occur on sites of some status, either major monastic sites or places with some evidence for royal or other high status links. In this they are closer to the Anglo-Saxon and Frankish examples than the Welsh and Cornish examples.

In Ireland church groups are again widely spread. Eight churches survive at Clonmacnoise (County Offaly), though only three are pre-Romanesque (Manning 1998; Bradley 1994). The phrase *Erdam Chiaráin*, twice described in the annals as standing at Clonmacnoise, may well have been an alternative name for Temple Ciáran. Manning has suggested that *erdam* or *airdam* may mean 'a small subsidiary church close to and associated with a larger one, but not physically attached to it' (Manning 1998, 72). Temple Ciáran has strong parallels with a group of other small chapels or oratories at ecclesiastical sites in Ireland, with associations with the burial places of a founder saint. Examples, include the saint's *leaba* (bed) at Labbamolaga and Inismurray and the *teach* (house) of St Declan at Ardmore, as well as probable cases at Fallmore (Mayo), Glendalough, Kells, Louth and Derry (Herity 1993, 194).

In general, unlike the Scottish, Anglo-Saxon and Frankish examples, the Welsh subsidiary chapels tend to be small in size, and are often linked with churches of relatively low status. Some ecclesiastical sites with known church groups had local or regional importance, such as Meifod or Clynnog Fawr, but many were of relatively little importance by the time their status is first recorded in the late middle ages.

Few ever seem to have been as important as the greatest church groups of neighbouring regions like Canterbury or St Denis, although it is important to note that very little is known about the planning of major ecclesiastical centres in western Britain such as Bangor or St Davids.

Not all church groups in Wales and Cornwall were burial chapels. It is likely that at some sites, such as Hentland and Meifod additional churches were not primarily mortuary chapels. It is possible they may have been consecrated to create additional congregational areas. However, it is also possible that the decision to construct an additional church or chapel may again reflect a regionally distinctive response to the problems of architectural space. Rather than adding to an existing church, the decision may have been taken to build a new structure leading to a multiplication of chapels on one site rather than development of an architecturally complex central church. It is noticeable that additional churches apparently stopped being constructed in western Britain and Wales in the eleventh or twelfth century – precisely the same period that the church architecture of these areas shifts from simple single-cell or nave and chancel plans to more complex floor plans, including transepts and aisles (Butler 1996). The construction of connecting corridors, linking external chapels to the main church structures, such as at Clynnog Fawr and Llaneilian appears to be an attempt to reabsorb these separate structures back into the main body of the church.

CHAPTER FOUR

OBJECTS OF WORSHIP: ARTEFACTS AND RELIGION

In medieval Christianity the celebration of the mass required more than simply a building. The early mass had a bi-partite structure. The first section consisted of readings and prayers, the second section, the Eucharist, comprised the oblation, the consecration of the gifts and, finally, communion. Each section required a different range of equipment to celebrate it appropriately; the first part of the service was particularly reliant on the provision of key holy texts and liturgical material, in the form of gospels, lectionaries and sacramentaries. The celebration of the Eucharist needed a range of vessels for the offering and blessing of the gifts and to assist with the associated rituals. In addition to the primary purpose of these items, they regularly had wider symbolic purposes, acting as items of veneration in their own right, particularly when associated with an individual reputed to possess particular sanctity.

However, these more portable elements of early Welsh Christianity have not survived well. The cumulative impact of Viking raiding, Norman ecclesiastical intervention, zealous promoters of the Reformation and the seventeenth-century Puritan ideal and over enthusiastic Victorian church restorers has meant that relatively few early liturgical items and ritual objects have survived. Nonetheless, a small amount of material has been recovered and it is possible to begin to reconstruct the range and changing patterns of use of religious items in the early Welsh church.

LITURGICAL VESSELS

The celebration of the Eucharist requires a basic suite of liturgical vessels: a chalice for the wine and a paten for the bread. This basic equipment can be supplemented by a wide range of additional vessels and equipment. However, the earliest surviving examples from Wales date from as late as the thirteenth century (Alexander and Binski 1987, 307-8). Any attempt to reconstruct the kind of objects used must thus remain necessarily speculative. In early medieval Ireland, the earliest surviving Eucharistic objects date to the eighth century and include the spectacular Ardagh chalice and the objects from Derrynaflan, including a chalice, a paten and its stand

(Ryan 1980; Ryan 1989, 127-8). The earliest examples from Anglo-Saxon England, including chalices from Hexham (Northumberland) and Trewhiddle (Cornwall), date to the ninth or tenth centuries (Bailey 1974; Wilson and Blunt 1961; Ryan 1990). Thus in neighbouring regions there is a horizon of survival of objects relating to the Eucharist from the eighth and ninth centuries, and the surviving items are mainly of precious metal or metal plate. It seems reasonable to suggest that similar objects may have been used and manufactured in Wales from around the same period.

However, this still does not resolve the problem with identifying liturgical objects of a pre-ninth century date, for which recourse to Anglo-Saxon or Irish parallels is of little help. One possibility is that the objects were made of a material that is less archaeologically visible. Wood was commonly used for making vessels in the early medieval world, using a range of techniques including lathe-turning for smaller objects and the construction of the vessels from staves (cf. Morris 2000). The fragmentary remains of two lathe-turned bowls were found at Dinas Emrys and are probably from the sixth to eighth century, and a stave-built bucket of similar date was recovered from a bog at Ty'r Dewin (Evans 1905; Savory 1960). There is no reason to think that these particular vessels had a liturgical function, but it does highlight the possibility of the use of other materials to make such items.

It has been suggested that some of the earliest liturgical vessels were ceramic (Radford 1957). There is a distinctive range of pottery types being imported into Atlantic Britain between around AD 400 and AD 800 from Mediterranean and western French sources (Campbell 2007). Several types of these imports bear overt Christian imagery. A number of items of Phocaean red slipware carry stamped crosses. Although none have been found in Wales, examples are known from Phillack in Cornwall and Dublin (Campbell 2007). A fragment of D ware (more correctly, *dérivées paléochrétiennes du groupe atlantique*) found at Dinas Emrys, imported from Atlantic France at some point in the sixth century carried a stamped *chi-rho* symbol (Savory 1960, 61, Pl.8b, fig. 7,36; Fig 36).

However, it is clear that the religious symbols were just one element of a range of imagery used on imported pottery of this type (e.g. Hayes 1972; Rigoir, Rigoir and Meffre 1973). Neither do any of the sites at which these objects were recovered have any known ecclesiastical function. It is hard to argue that these ceramics were deliberately imported to be used for liturgical purposes. It is possible that they were subsequently re-used for religious reasons, though it is unlikely that such opportunistic use was common. Although the best evidence for the vitality of the western sea routes between Atlantic Britain and western France and through to the Mediterranean was the spread of imported pottery (Campbell 2007), it is possible that some unequivocal liturgical items were reaching Wales along this route. It is known that Byzantine metalwork was reaching Britain in this period. However, the distribution of most of the items, mainly so-called 'Coptic' copper-alloy vessels, is mainly focused in Anglo-Saxon England, particularly East Anglia and the south-east (Harris 2003, 64-9; Mango et al 1989). The axis of this trade is likely to have been from Byzantium via northern Italy, the Alps and the Rhine bringing items into Britain via Kent and the east coast. However, this spread of material did not extend as far west as Wales. There are hints though of material arriving from Byzantium via the western route. A bronze Byzantine censer of probable seventh-century date was found in Glastonbury during drainage work in the 1980s (Fig 37) (Rahtz 1993, 99-100). The nearest

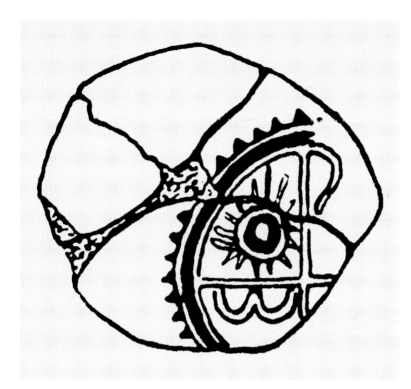

Left: 36 Chi rho symbol from fragment of 'D ware' from Dinas Emrys. (Savory 1960)

Below: 37 Seventh-century censer from Glastonbury (Somerset). (©The Trustees of the British Museum)

parallel to this item is a censer from Spain (Ripoll López 1993, 52-3). Unlike the Byzantine objects found in eastern England and along the Rhine trading route, which mainly consisted of secular vessels (though some bore religious imagery), most Byzantine material from Spain was found in ecclesiastical contexts (Harris 2003, 66-7; Ripoll López 1993). This suggests that the censer arrived at Glastonbury via the same western trade route that brought the Mediterranean imported pottery to western Britain, rather than via the eastern Rhineland route that carried 'Coptic' vessels. There is another hint of Byzantine items arriving in Wales via the western route. A scrap of silver sheet from the early medieval defended site at Longbury Bank is intriguing. The excavators noted that the only large silver sheet objects found in northern Europe at this period were Byzantine dishes (Campbell and Lane 1993, 30). Although based on extremely limited evidence, the Longbury Bank fragment and the Glastonbury censer may attest to the arrival of metalwork from the eastern Mediterranean, some with a liturgical function, arriving in Wales and western Britain between the fifth and seventh centuries.

Ironically, however, the best insight into early Welsh liturgical items may come from metalwork found in Anglo-Saxon areas of England; this is for several reasons. First, the acid soils that predominate in much of Wales generally provide a poor environment for the survival of metalwork, particularly the thin silver and copper alloy sheet that is likely to comprise the majority of such objects. Secondly, the early Anglo-Saxon burial rite that predominated before their conversion to Christianity from the seventh century onwards features the widespread placement of objects within the grave. These grave goods are usually items of personal adornment of Anglo-Saxon manufacture. However, some graves also contained items of metalwork that are likely to have been produced in Wales and western Britain and reached Anglo-Saxon areas through trade or exchange. The most distinctive form of British metalwork found in these graves is a class of metal vessel known as 'hanging bowls' (Brennan 1991; Youngs 1989; Bruce-Mitford 2005). These are shallow, circular or oval bowls constructed from sheets of copper alloy and usually provided with three or four hook mounts (escutcheons) from which they appear to have been suspended. They often featured decoration in the form of bronze strips attached to the vessel body by solder; the escutcheons were also regularly decorated, often with enamel and millefiori. Despite being found mainly in Anglo-Saxon areas scholarly consensus is that they were largely produced in western and northern Britain. A mould of an escutcheon has been found at Craig Phadrig (Invernesshire) (Bruce-Mitford 2005, *no. 113*) and a possible waster of an escutcheon was found in the River Avon between Malmesbury and Chippenham (Bruce-Mitford 2005, *no 96*).

The function of hanging bowls is likely to have varied widely. They are a diverse class of objects, varying considerably in size, decoration and form; it is unlikely that they were all used for a single purpose. Many undoubtedly fulfilled a secular role, as decorative items or possible vessels containing wine or other alcoholic drink; they may equally have contained water and been used for formalised ablution during or after a feast. Whilst the majority of hanging bowls may have had such a secular purpose, it is possible to argue that some may have had a religious function. A number of bowls and escutcheons are decorated with a distinct cross, including examples from Camerton (Somerset), Faversham (Kent) and Whitby (North Yorkshire) (Allen 1898, 48; Horne 1929; Peers and Radford 1943, 47-50; Bruce-Mitford 2005, *6, 132, 101*). A copper alloy skillet found at Shalfleet on the Isle of Wight bears some similarities in design to hanging bowls, including a distinctive rim form (Basford and Geake 2006); a mount in the form of an expanded armed cross is attached to the surface of the handle.

The context of some of the hanging bowls may also imply a liturgical function. The only escutcheon to be found in Wales comes from St Arvans and is one of a number of finds of early medieval metalwork to come from an area to the west of the church, suggesting a focus of religious activity at the site from the seventh century (Redknap 2007, 36-7). A bowl found accompanied by a series of cone-shaped mounts, another silver bowl, a group of silver penannular brooches and a porpoise bone were found buried at the east end of an early medieval church on St Ninian's Isle (Shetland) (Wilson 1973, 55-7; Youngs 1989, 119-110). It is likely that they belonged to a church or monastery. A bowl found during excavation at St Paul-in-the-Bail, Lincoln was found in a cist grave that lay within an apsidally-ended building or possibly a smaller successor structure that lay on the same axis as the later church and in the centre of the Roman forum. This early structure is likely to have been a church, possibly from the sixth or seventh century (Jones 1994). The location of the burial within the church accompanied by the bowl may imply that the grave was of an important ecclesiastical figure, and that it had a religious function (Bruce-Mitford 2006, 53; Jones 1994). It is possible, therefore that a small sub-set of the corpus of hanging bowls may have had some form of liturgical purpose. It is unlikely, though, that they were used as chalices, as the bowls were clearly designed to be suspended, rather than placed on an altar. Instead they may have been used to contain holy water or used for the ritual ablution of hands or liturgical items (Bruce-Mitford 2005, 32).

Whatever the precise form of early liturgical vessels, it probable that by the end of the first millennium AD the Welsh church was using bronze and silver chalices and patens similar to those being used in Ireland, England and mainland Europe. However, as noted above no early examples survive. It is not until the thirteenth century that we have surviving chalices and documentary evidence for them (Redknap 2004a, 24-6). An agreement between the abbot of Enlli (Bardsey Island) and the canons of Aberdaron dating from 1252 records the canons of Enlli gifting a silver chalice to the Aberdaron community (Pryce 2005, 634). The chalice and paten found hidden in rocks near Dolgellau are also likely to date to the middle of the thirteenth century and are probably associated with the nearby Cistercian foundation at Cymer (Alexander and Binski 1987, 307-8; Lord 2003, 100-101). There are few other chalices of this date from Wales; those that are known are primarily from graves where they appear to have accompanied the burial of the clergy. A silver chalice is known from the grave of Richard de Carew, Bishop of St Davids (1256–80) (Clear 1866) (Fig 38). Most such chalices, however, were made of lead rather than bronze or silver and appear never to have been used to celebrate the Eucharist, but were instead always intended to accompany burials. A small pewter chalice was found in a grave at the church of SS. Stephen and Tatheus in Caerwent (Redknap 2004a, 24-5).

In addition to chalices and patens there was also a need for some other liturgical vessels. Holy water and wine was kept in cruets. These could be made from a range of materials. A pewter cruet marked with the letter A (for *Aqua* = water), dating to the thirteenth or fourteenth century was found in the bottom of a well at White Castle in Monmouthshire (Lewis 1969), whilst a glazed earthenware example is known from Eglwys Gymyn (Lewis 1968) (Fig 39).

Left: 38 Silver chalice from the grave of Richard de Carew, Bishop of St Davids (1256–80). (Clear 1866)

Below: 39 Ceramic cruet from Eglwys Gymyn (Carmarthenshire). (Lewis 1969)

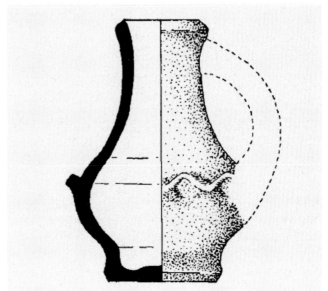

OTHER LITURGICAL EQUIPMENT

As well as the vessels needed for the celebration of the Eucharist, early medieval Christian worship required a range of other equipment for the correct conduct of the ritual aspects of the mass. The evidence for such items is slight and can only give us a glimpse of the range of such items that might have once existed. Although now not used in the western church, the liturgical fan, or *flabellum*, was used in the early church to protect the altar and the Eucharistic gifts from dirt and flies (Richardson 1993). Such fans were known in early medieval Ireland, where the fan (*cuilebad*) of St Columcille was preserved as a relic at Kells until 1034, when the *Annals of Ulster* record it was lost in a shipwreck on the way to Scotland, and there are numerous other documentary references to such an item (ibid). It has also been suggested that there are several artistic representations of *flabella* from Ireland, including on the cross-slabs at Carndonagh and Fahan Mura (both in County Donegal). It is likely that several objects associated with the symbols of the Evangelists in the early ninth-century Book of Kells were intended to be *flabella* (St Mark's Gospel, fol 129v). Although no documentary references to their use are known from Wales, they do appear to be depicted on a number of carved stones. A group of stones from Pembrokeshire (Clydai; St Dogmael's; Jeffreyston) and the surrounding area may represent *flabella*, as may an example from Llangyfelach (ECMW, 244, 308-9, 385-6, 388) (Fig 40).

Left: 40 Possible depiction of a *flabellum* on a cross from Clydai (Pembrokeshire)

Below: 41 Possible holy water sprinkler of West British workmanship from Swallocliffe Down (Wiltshire). (© English Heritage)

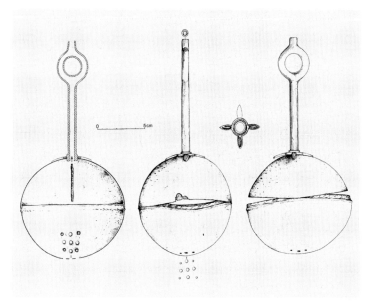

Another aspect of church liturgy was the sprinkling of the congregation with holy water as they entered the church, as well as an act of blessing in other appropriate contexts. No holy water sprinklers are known from Wales, but a sprinkler of probable west British, rather than Anglo-Saxon workmanship is known from a seventh-century grave at Swallowcliffe Down in Wiltshire (Speake 1989, 30-41; Youngs 1989, 56) (Fig 41). The sprinkler is made of two copper-alloy hemispheres soldered together and attached to a hollow handle. Initially, interpreted as a censer, its likeness to a similar item found in an eighth-century Viking grave in Norway made it clear that it was probably used for the ritual aspersion of holy water (Youngs 1989, 122). The object had presumably reached Norway as an item of booty taken by Viking raiders, and may have originated either in Northumbria, western Britain or Wales; parallels can be drawn with its decorative scheme of processing animals and some Anglo-Saxon manuscript art, such as the Chad Gospels which probably have a West Mercian origin (see below).

Incense was not a significant feature of early Christian worship in Britain and Ireland, and it is usually assumed that it was not regularly used in the western church until the tenth century (Dix 1945, 428-9). However, it has been recently argued that several passages in the eighth or ninth-century Stowe Missal – which probably contains liturgical material from the seventh century – refer to the use of incense (Hunwicke 2002, 6). This sacramentary is of Irish origin and this may indicate the early use of incense in the Insular church. The discovery of a seventh-century censer of Byzantine origin at Glastonbury has already been noted

42 Twelfth-century censers from (left) Penmaen (Glamorgan) and (right) Corwen (Merionethshire). (Allen 1891 and Anon 1859)

(Rahtz 1993, Fig. 100). However, there are no other censers known from Wales or elsewhere in western Britain dating between the seventh century and the eleventh century. A thurible found in a ruined chapel at Penmaen on the Gower Peninsula is of architectural form (Allen 1891) (Fig 42). This form of censer has its origins in the tenth or early eleventh century, with parallels known from Anglo-Saxon England from Pershore and Canterbury (Backhouse et al 1984, 89–90). However, the Penmaen example has closer parallels with censers from Bearsden, near Glasgow, Viborg (Denmark) and a recently discovered example from South Shropshire, which are more likely to date to the mid-twelfth century (Scott 1969; Reavill and Geake 2005, 343–5). A different form of censer was found at the church in Corwen (Anon 1859) (Fig.42); rather than being architectural in form it is roughly spherical. There are few similar objects from Britain, but it probably dates to the twelfth century. A similarly shaped censer is depicted on a copper plaque from Winchester dating to 1150 (Zarnecki, Holt and Holland 1984, 261–2), another close parallel is shown on a page of the *Ottobeuren Collectar* dating to *c.*1150–1200.

Liturgical combs were used in the early medieval church as part of the ritual preparation of the priest before celebrating the Eucharist and in ceremonies connected to the anointing of bishops. A number of walrus and elephant ivory examples survive from late Anglo-Saxon and early Norman contexts (Zarnecki et al 1984). One late eleventh-century example from the British Museum has a Welsh provenance (ibid; Beckwith 1972, *47*) (Fig 43). It is double-sided and carries a fragmentary inscription of a probable religious nature. The central panel shows two figures in combat – an armed man vanquishing an unarmed individual. The armed man wears a helmet with a nose guard of distinct Norman design and the motif of men fighting against a background of foliage is broadly reminiscent of combat scenes depicted on some products of the Hereford School of Romanesque sculpture, such as the font from Eardisley.

LIGHTS AND CANDLES

Lighting within early medieval churches had two functions. There was a general need for visibility within structures that had little external light sources. It was also necessary for the altar to be lit with candles to provide an appropriate context for the celebration of the Eucharist. Candles in churches are likely to have been made of wax. The *Cyfnerth Redaction of the Laws of Hywel Dda* notes 'The lineage of bees is from Paradise, and it was because of man's sin that they came from there and that God gave them his grace; and therefore mass cannot be sung without the wax' (Jenkins 2000, 183). Whilst candles were probably used earlier, it was not until the eleventh century that they began to be placed in liturgical contexts on altars (Borg 1985, 86-8). Fragments of an iron pricket candlestick were found at Capel Maelog (Britnell 1990, 72, *80*), whilst the leg of a more elaborate three-footed candlestick of probable mid-twelfth century date comes from excavations at Pennant Melangell (Courtney 1994) (Fig 44).

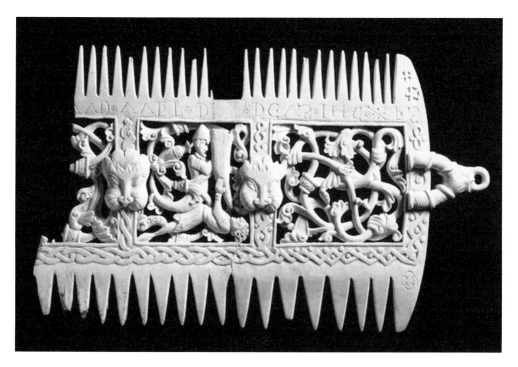

43 Ecclesiastical comb with reputed Welsh provenance. (©The Trustees of the British Museum)

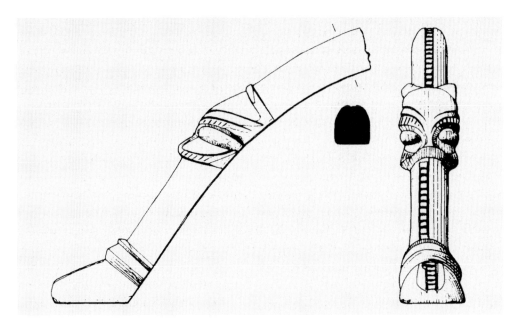

44 Candlestick from Pennant Melangell (Montgomeryshire). (Britnell et al. 1994 © CPAT)

It is likely that oil lamps would also have been used to light church interiors. A number of stone oil lamps or oil lamp holders are known from Wales, all probably from the eleventh century or later. A limestone example from Llangwm Uchaf is decorated with a loose ribbon plait (Knight 1972). A similar lamp is known from Monmouth Priory and simpler ones made of rectangular blocks of limestone are known from Talley Abbey and Burry Holmes (O'Neil 1941). Brecon Cathedral is home to an exceptional cresset stone with space for 30 lights, the largest known in Britain. However, its precise date remains uncertain.

BELLS

Bells had a range of functions in the early church. They clearly acted to mark important events or to summon people to prayer. In Anglo-Saxon England, Bede records that the nuns at the monastery of Hackness were told of the death of Hild by the sound of a bell that was similar to the one that summoned them to prayer (*EH* 4.23). The *Life of St Columba* records the use of bells several times to summon the monks of Iona to prayer (*VC* 7).

However, it is also clear that they could become associated with individuals. Manuscripts and sculptural representations of bells from Ireland often show figures associated with a bell and a crosier, showing that a bell could function, along with the crosier, to symbolise an abbot, bishop or other important ecclesiastical figure (Bourke 1980). The *Additamenta* of the Book of Armagh, dating from the eighth century, notes that a bell, as well as other items including a crosier, was given to Fíacc when he was consecrated as a bishop (Bieler 1979, 176; Edwards 2002, 252).

This association could extend beyond death, and in common with Ireland, Scotland and Brittany, Wales had a tradition of bells associated with key church figures becoming sanctified as relics. The evidence from the eleventh and twelfth-century saints' lives give a clear idea of the extent to which bells had supernatural functions imputed to them; the *Vita Cadoci* claimed that Gildas' bell resurrected two people and spoke with a human voice (*VSC* 27).

It is perhaps due to the preservation of such relics that eight early medieval bells survive from Wales and the Marches. Examples are known from Llanrhyddlad, Llanarmon, Llangwnadl, Llangystenin, Dolwyddelan, Llangenny and Marden (Fig 45) (Fisher 1926). A bell from Bosbury sometimes attributed an ecclesiastical function is of a different form, and unlikely to be early medieval in date. There is considerable variation, however, even among the confirmed medieval bells. All the bells are roughly rectangular in shape with a handle on top of them; they range in size from approximately four inches high (Llanrhyddlad) to 12 inches (Marden). The larger bells are made from folded iron sheet coated in bronze and riveted together, whilst the smaller ones were made from cast bronze. This corresponds to Bourke's Class 1 (folder sheet) and Class 2 (cast) bells (Bourke 1980, 52-3). His analysis of the much larger (73) corpus of bells from Ireland has led him to suggest that Class 2 bells date to *c*.AD 700–900 with Class 1 bells being manufactured from at least AD 600, though with considerable overlap between the two forms.

45 Ecclesiastical bells. Llangystennin (Caernarfon) and Llangwynadl (Caernarfon). (Fisher 1926)

Their size and the shape of their handles suggest that these were primarily handbells, and were clearly intended to be portable. They are largely lacking any additional decoration, although the bell of Llangwnadl does have a simple zoomorphic handle. Some bell relics in Ireland were housed in elaborately decorated cases, such as the twelfth-century St Cuileáin's bell shrine (Ó Floinn 1994); no examples of such cases are known from Wales. In addition to the surviving examples, there are various historic records of other possible or probable early medieval church bells. Gerald of Wales wrote of the bell named Bangu, housed at Glascwm, which was reputed to have belonged to St David (*Journey* 1.1). The antiquarian Edward Lhuyd recorded several other bells, including three quadrangular bells from Cwm in Flintshire, reportedly found on the hillside above the church and named the Yellow, White and Grey Bells, apparently as they were made from different metals (Fisher 1926).

CROSIERS AND STAFFS

Crosiers and staffs were key symbols of authority and status for abbots and bishops. As items often closely related to important religious figures, they easily became adopted as relics for veneration (Edwards 2002, 252-5). There is a distinct Insular form of crosier found in Ireland and Scotland (Johnson 2004; Michelli 1986, 1988); the wooden staff is adorned with decorative metal strips, knops and a metal drop. There are two basic shapes for these metal drops; a loosely curved crook with a vertical drop, such as that found on the Prosperous Crosier (Johnson 2000, 151), whilst the other has a more 'horseshoe' shaped drop, such as that seen on the Kells Crosier (MacDermott 1955). The former probably dates to the ninth or tenth century whilst the latter appears to come into use in the eleventh century. The eleventh century also saw the spread of new crosier forms, showing wider European influence, such as the T-shaped *tau* crosiers (cf. Webster et al 1984, 119-20). The only example from an Insular context is one from County Kilkenny (Henry 1963); one is also shown on the late eleventh-century Doorty Cross, Kilfenora (County Clare) (Edwards 2002; Harbison, 1992, fig 367). The more traditional volute or spiral-shaped crosier head only appears to have come into use in the late eleventh century (ibid 1984). All three forms are shown on the Doorty Cross (Harbison).

There are a number of contemporary and later documentary references to crosiers or staffs associated with important religious figures being venerated as relics in Wales. St Padarn's crosier, known as *Cyrwen* ('holy staff with crooked head') is mentioned in a late eleventh-century poem as being housed at Llanbadarn (Williams 1980, 181-9), whilst Cadfan's crosier was venerated at Tywyn according to the *Canu Cadfan* written in the mid-twelfth century (lines 50-1; Pryce 2001), and a fifteenth-century poem mentions a staff associated with Saint Cybi at Holyhead (Baring-Gould and Fisher 1911). Gerald of Wales recorded seeing the staff of St Curig at the church of St Harmon's in Radnorshire 'covered on all sides with gold and silver, and resembling in its upper part the form of a cross', which he noted was particularly effective in curing glandular swellings (as long as the one penny oblation was paid first) (*Journey* 1).

Although no actual crosiers of pre-twelfth century date survive from Wales, it is possible that there may be some visual images of early examples. It has been suggested that a figure on a

Above left: 46 Possible depictions of ecclesiastical staffs and crosiers: (left) detail from Llanbadarn Fawr cross (centre) cross from Llandyfaelog-Fach (Breconshire) (right) carved slap from Llaniestyn (Anglesey)

Above right: 47 Thirteenth-century gilded copper alloy crosiers from the graves of Bishop Richard de Carew (1256–80) at St Davids. (Clear 1866)

cross from Llanbadarn Fawr may be carrying a crosier (Fig 46). Peter Lord has suggested that a spiral shape on the image may be a volute-headed crosier and draws parallels with the Doorty Cross (Lord 2003, 43). However, the Llanbadarn Fawr cross is probably from the tenth century, earlier than both the Doorty Cross and the introduction of this style of crosier to Britain. It is more likely that the shape simply depicts folds of cloth on the figure's robe. It is important to remember that a staff or sceptre was also a secular symbol of power. The image of Hwyel Dda in the mid-thirteenth century manuscript MS Peniarth 28 shows him enthroned and carrying a sceptre (Huws 1998). In some cases there was doubtless an elision between the secular and ecclesiastical symbolism of a staff. For example, the figure on the cross at Llandyfaelog-fach is usually interpreted as a warrior, and has a sword at its waist and long object at its shoulder (Fig 46) (B16). It has been suggested that this might be another sword or a spear, but it is possible it is a staff of office. Admittedly, the simple inscription on the cross (+BRIAMAIL | FLOU) gives no indication as to whether this monument commemorated a churchman or a secular individual, though it does call to mind Gerald of Wales's description of his surprise at seeing the lay abbot of Llanbadarn Fawr carrying a spear rather than a traditional crosier (*Journey* 2.4).

A final intriguing possibility of a representation of an early staff can be seen on the late fourteenth-century carved stone slab placed over the shrine of St Iestyn at Llaniestyn on Anglesey. It depicts a full-length image of the saint in robe and carrying a staff surmounted with an animal head and a spherical knop (Gresham 1968) (Fig 46). This show no similarity to other known fourteenth-century models, by which time the volute-headed crook was most common, but does show some resemblance to earlier Insular crosiers. It is possible that this carving was based on an actual crosier or staff held in the church at the time. In general by the thirteenth century the volute-headed crook was the most common. These can be seen on ecclesiastical seals, such as the images on the seal of Abbot Adam of Neath Abbey (c.1266) or Cadwgan, Abbot of Bangor (Lord 2003, Figs. 146). They are also depicted on stone sculpture, such as the probable image of Henry of Abergavenny, Bishop of Llandaf (c.1220) over the door at Llandaf Cathedral (ibid, Fig.161). Two thirteenth-century gilded copper alloy crosiers are also known from the graves of bishops Iorwerth (1215–29) and Richard de Carew at St Davids (Lord 2003, Figs 156-7; Clear 1866) (Fig 47). It is also probable that some ecclesiastical staffs of office had simple cross-shaped terminals. A probable example of this was the staff of St Curig at St Harmon's, which was described by Gerald as 'resembling in its upper part the form of a cross' (*Journey* 1.1). A representation of such a staff can also be seen on the Hereford School font at Eardisley being carried by the figure of Christ.

BOOKS AND MANUSCRIPTS

Religious books were of key importance in the early church in Wales and beyond. They were not significant just for the knowledge contained within them, but as artefacts in their own right. This can be seen in the effort spent on the preparation, writing and illustration of texts themselves and the expense and craftsmanship expended on adorning their covers. In a period when literacy was primarily confined to the clergy, the control and display of the written word was an important way of expressing social, political and religious power. The importance of books can be seen in the depiction of a monk carrying a book satchel on the Conbelin Cross from Margam (Glamorgan) (*234*) (Fig 48).

However, there are only a limited number of early manuscripts that can with certainty be attributed a Welsh origin. It is extremely difficult to locate the place of manufacture of such early material without an explicit statement within the text itself. Obviously, the use of Latin as the only liturgical language means that it is not easy to use linguistic factors to identify the origin of religious books, though later vernacular glosses do help to identify volumes that have at least spent some time in Wales. Analysis of artistic styles is also of limited value; although early medieval manuscripts are often vividly illuminated, there is a strong shared repertoire of designs and imagery used in Insular and Anglo-Saxon material. It is not until the eighth century that it becomes possible to identify even material that *might* have been made in Wales, though obviously there must have been earlier, now lost, examples. Even for the period between the eighth and twelfth century it has been estimated that the total number of surviving books or fragments is probably less than 20 (Huws 2002, 3). This poor survival is caused by a range of factors, including the destruction of many monastic libraries during the Dissolution, the damage wreaked on monasteries during the revolt by Owain Glyndŵr and the impact of Norman reformation on native Welsh ecclesiastical establishments, as well as the more general recycling of valuable parchment.

The earliest surviving volume that can be said, with certainty, to have been used in Wales are the Chad Gospels (also known as the Lichfield Gospels or the Llandeilo Gospels) (Brown 1982; Henderson 1987, 122-9). This gospel book, written in an Insular half-uncial hand, was produced in the ninth century. There is considerable debate about the actual origin of this book. It has been held at Lichfield Cathedral since the late tenth or early eleventh century, as it contains a reference to Leofric, Bishop of Lichfield from 1020 to 1026. The book has a number of marginal annotations recording amongst other things (Fig 49):

> Here it is shown that Gelhi, son of Arihtud, bought this Gospel from Cingal, and gave him for it his best horse and gave for the sake of his soul this Gospel to God and St Teilo upon the altar …
> (Lindsay 1912)

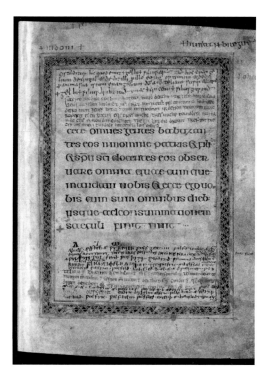

Above left: 48 Book satchel depicted on Conbelin cross, Margam (Glamorgan)

Above right: 49 Text page with Welsh ninth-century marginalia from the Chad Gospels. (By kind permission of the Chapter of Lichfield Cathedral)

Above left: 50 Image of St Luke from the Chad Gospels. (By kind permission of the Chapter of Lichfield Cathedral)

Above right: 51 Illuminated initial page from the Gospel of St John, Hereford Gospel. (By kind permission of the Dean and Chapter of Hereford Cathedral)

Left: 52 Llangyfelach figure

The 'altar of St Teilo' is generally accepted as being the monastery of Llandeilo Fawr in Carmarthenshire. It is unlikely, though, that it was actually made there. It is perhaps more likely that it arrived in Wales following the sacking of Lichfield by Viking raiders in the 870s (though of course this does not explain how it returned to Lichfield). There is considerable debate about its original place of production. It sits comfortably within a group of lavishly illustrated Insular gospel books produced in Northumbria and Ireland, including the Lindisfarne Gospels, the Book of Kells and the Book of Durrow. It contains eight decorated pages, including portraits of two of the evangelists and a carpet page (Fig 50). These all show a range of stylistic influences. The carpet page shows parallels with those in the Lindisfarne Gospels, whilst there are also strong indications of Mercian models for other aspects of the illustrations. Although a Northumbrian origin has frequently been suggested, the strong similarities between the colour scheme on the eighth-century carved stone angel, believed to have been part of the shrine of St Chad and the pigmentation of some of the illustrations within the gospels have led to recent suggestions that it may have been a Mercian product, possibly decorated at Lichfield itself (Brown 2007).

A gospel book from Hereford (Hereford Cathedral P.i.2) is textually related to the Chad Gospels, though it is likely to be a little later in date (Fig 51) (Gameson 2002). It had probably found its home in Hereford in the early eleventh century (Dumville 1992). The manner in which the initials are decorated is strongly reminiscent of those in the Chad Gospels; however, a recent reassessment of the textual history and structure of the Hereford Gospel has argued for a Welsh origin (Gameson 2002). The possibility that the Chad Gospels and Hereford Gospels have different origins despite their similarities is intriguing, suggesting an artistic school or style of illumination that seemingly straddles the Anglo-Welsh border. There is one final surviving ninth-century text of possible Welsh origin, the *Liber Commonei*, contained within St Dunstan's Classbook, which came from Glastonbury Abbey and was written AD817x35 (Hunt 1961, VII-XII; Lapidge 1986, 92-3). It has glosses to the Latin in Old Welsh, and has decorative initials with animal heads (Edwards 1995, 151).

By the ninth century, the presence of scriptoria in Wales seems certain. Despite the poor survival of the texts themselves, their wider importance can be recognised in the influence of manuscripts and manuscript art on stone sculpture. This can be seen in a variety of ways; script, decoration, layout and formulae.

The palaeography of the Group 3 crosses shows a clear manuscript influence, with a move away from the use of mainly capital forms on most Group 1 inscriptions towards the use of half-uncials, such as can be seen beginning on the stone from Llangadwaladr (ECMW, 57). However, recent work suggests that this move might not have been influenced directly by manuscripts, but by writing on wax tablets, which provides food for thought about the precise process of commissioning and carving inscriptions (Charles-Edwards 2005). Nonetheless, the presence of developed geometric capitals on some inscriptions, such as that from Caldey Island does seem to suggest that the carvers were also influenced by direct manuscript models (ECWIS II, P6).

The range of formulae and vocabulary used on some stones also indicated a manuscript model. This is evidenced on a stone from Llanwnnws (CD27). The inscriptions reads 'CHRISTUS Q[U]ICUNQ[UE] EXPLICAU[ER]IT H[OC] NO[MEN] DET

BENEDIXIONEM PRO ANIMA HIROIDIL FILIUS CAROTINN' meaning 'Whoever shall [have] explain[ed] this Name, let him give a blessing for the soul of Carotinn, son of Hiroidil', which directly echoes wording used in the Irish Gospels of MacRegol (*c*.800) (ibid.). As well as showing manuscript influence in the broad wording of this stone, it can also be recognised in the abbreviations and contractions used, such as H with a dot over it (for *hoc*) and N~O~ (for *nomen*); practices which again have clear manuscript origins.

The layout of manuscripts can also be seen to influence the layout and design of some elements of stone sculpture. Again, this is mainly found on the Class 3 stones. For example, one cross from Llangyfelach has a central figure wearing a rectangular tabard-like item of clothing (Redknap and Lewis 2007) (Fig 52). There is no attempt to depict the drapery accurately and the rigid shape of the costume calls to mind the Symbol of St Matthew from the Book of Durrow (Dublin, Trinity College Library, A.4.5 (57), f. 21v). As well as examples such as this referencing the layout of manuscript pages, there are even cases where the setting of the inscription appears to imitate the structure of a book. One of the crosses from Llantwit Major has three pairs of panels carrying the inscription. The layout of these panels side by side is reminiscent of an open book or possibly even a wax tablet of the type known to have been used for a range of purposes in the early medieval world, including learning to read and write, as well as potential use as a notebook (Charles-Edwards 2003) (Fig 53).

Despite this clear evidence for the influence of manuscripts on many aspects of stone sculpture there are no surviving examples of Welsh ecclesiastical manuscripts to fill the gap between the ninth-century material and a small group of late eleventh-century and early twelfth-century documents. This later group consists of a Psalter and Martyology (Trinity College Dublin MS 50) (Fig 54), a copy of St Augustine's *De Trinitate* (Cambridge, Corpus Christi College MS199) (Fig 55), a version of Macrobius's *Commentary* on Cicero's *Dream of Scipio* (London, BL Cotton MS Faustina CI, part II, folios 66-93) and fragments of *De Natura Rerum* by Bede (Aberystwyth, Nat Lib Wals, Peniarth MS540) (Edwards 1995; Peden 1981; Huws 1978). It is likely that these documents all have a common association with Llanbadarn Fawr, and the family of Sulien, a late eleventh-century Bishop of St Davids (Lapidge 1974; Conway 1997). The *De Trinitate* manuscript was created by his son, Ieuan ap Sulien, and he included a poem to his father (*Carmen Iohannis de uita et familia Sulgeni* 'Ieuan's poem on the life and family of Sulien'). The psalter and martyrology was also illustrated by Ieuan ap Sulien (probably around 1079), but written by a scribe; the volume was owned by Rhygyfarch, Ieuan's brother. Rhygyfarch was also responsible for two poems in the Macrobius manuscript (Lapidge 1974). All four volumes have some level of illumination, though it is only extensive in Rhygyfarch's Psalter and Martyrology and the *De Trinitate*. These decorations consist mainly of elaborated initials, though the Psalter also has three decorated pages marking key divisions within the text (Edwards 1995, 148-9). The latter show some parallels with some pages in the Chad Gospels, but a range of other artistic influences are clearly at play (Edwards 1995, 154). Not surprisingly there is evidence for an Irish stylistic contribution; Sulien spent some time in Ireland. However, a range of wider Anglo-Saxon and Scottish influences has also been recognised (ibid.). These books are important as some of the last products of an Insular school of manuscript production; the use of Insular minuscule script was soon to be replaced by Carolingian minuscule, reflecting the increased influence of Norman practice (Huws 2002, 11).

Left: 53 Paired panels on cross from Llantwit Major (Glamorgan) possibly representing an open book or wax tablet

Brlow left: 54 The Rhigyfarch Psalter: first psalm. (By kind permission of Trinity College, Dublin)

Below right: 55 De Trinitate. (By kind permission of the Master and Fellows of Corpus Christi College, Cambridge)

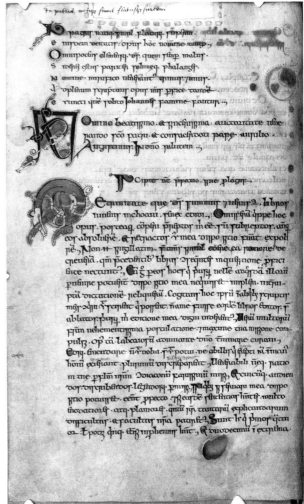

Decoration was not limited to just the pages in early medieval books. Their covers would also have been elaborately adorned, particularly when the books themselves were objects of veneration and treated as relics. However, little evidence for their covers survives, as most early books have been rebound since they were first produced, sometimes several times. It is likely that the 'worm-eaten book covered with silver plate' recorded as being at St Davids in the mid-sixteenth century was an example of such a book (Huws 2002, 5). Another possible example is the Book of St Beuno, also known as 'Tiboeth' from Clynnog Fawr (Phillips 1910–15); the later poet Iolo Goch compared a girl's eyes to the jewel of a clasp 'similar to the Tiboeth stone', presumably describing a decorated book mount or fastening on the volume (Johnston 1993, 100-101). It is also probable that the gospels from St Asaph that were sent on a fund-raising tour in the later thirteenth century were also highly decorated.

However, all these references are relatively late, and may not be referring to the early medieval decoration of the book covers. However, there are a couple of examples of possible early book mounts, though sadly no longer attached to any books. One such mount, of eighth-century design and Anglo-Saxon workmanship, has been found near Penterry and another possible ninth-century book mount of Irish style has been found at Din Lligwy (Redknap 2007, 50, 54). Some caution is needed though, as this kind of simple mount could have been attached to other objects, such as a shrine, and need not necessarily have been used on a book cover. One exceptionally rare example of a surviving decorated book cover, albeit damaged, is the rear cover of the Book of Llandaf. This was a thick oak board, which appears to have originally been covered with silver plate (Huws 2002, 144-6). The cover had a gilt-bronze image of Christ in Majesty attached to it, dating from the third quarter of the thirteenth century (Stratford 2002). However, this is probably not original, and may have been attached during a fifteenth or sixteenth-century rebinding. There is evidence, though, that it may have replaced an earlier, mounted decoration, perhaps another Christ in Majesty, as traces of the incised marks of a mandorla, probably containing a decorated metal mount, can still be recognised (Huws 2002).

FONTS AND BAPTISM

Although baptism was a key element of Christian life in early medieval Wales there is very little evidence for the presence of stone fonts until the eleventh century. This reflects the wider pattern found elsewhere in Britain; in Anglo-Saxon England stone fonts only appear at the same period (Blair 2005, 459-63). Before this date it not clear what form baptism took. It is possible that some other form of vessel was used to contain the holy water; there were a range of suitable containers that could have held the water during the ceremony (discussed above). If parallels with Anglo-Saxon England exist, it is may have been that wooden vessels were used. Aelfric, writing in the later tenth century, used the term *font-faete* (font vat); the term *font-stan* (font stone) only entering the literature in the later eleventh century (Jones 2001). Two possible early wooden fonts are known from Wales, though both are likely to be from the eleventh century or later. The wooden font from Efenechdyd is carved from a single piece of wood (Fig 56); it has been variously dated to between the twelfth century

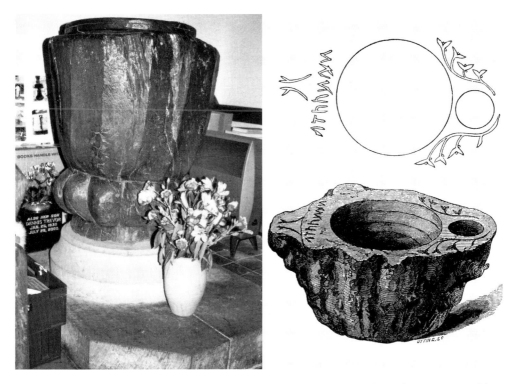

56 Wooden fonts (left) Efenechdyd (Denbighshire). (Author's photograph) (right) Dinas Mawddwy. (Barnwell 1872)

and the fifteenth century (Thurlby 2006 1274; RCAHMW 1914). Another similar, though more crudely carved, font was found in a bog at Dinas Mawddy; unusually it has a second smaller bowl integrated into it, possibly intended to act as a chrismatory (Barnwell 1872) (Fig 56)

Undoubtedly, it was the direct and indirect impact of Anglo-Norman settlers that led to the adoption of stone fonts, though the extent of artistic influence varies widely across Wales. The thriving traditions of Romanesque stone carving that developed in some of the border areas of Wales, such as the Hereford and Dymock schools, saw the production of elaborately carved stone fonts (Gethin Jones 1979; Thurlby 1999). Not surprisingly the font that shows the closest links to the Hereford School is at a site with known patronage by a Norman lord. Brecon Priory was established by Bernard de Neufmarché, Lord of Brecon in the early twelfth century. The chalice-shaped font is adorned with six carved medallions inhabited by animals, and has strong links, both in shape and decoration, to the font from Stottesden in Shropshire (Thurlby 1999 148-50; Thurlby 2006 11-12). In addition to such outliers of existing Norman traditions, it is possible to recognise regional and local patterns in twelfth and thirteenth-century fonts in Wales (Fig 59). These might be on a quite small scale, such as in the Abergavenny area, where a group of bowl-shaped fonts with arcs on the underside and thick rope moulding are all found within an area of no more than 10 miles south and east of Abergavenny (Gardner and Fisher 1917; Newman 2000). A much more extensive regional tradition can be found in Pembrokeshire, and

Above left: 57 Carved stone font with arcading, Llaniestyn (Anglesey). (Author's photograph)

Above right: 58 Font from Penmon Priory, Anglesey

extending into Cardiganshire, comprising over 50 scalloped table-top fonts (Thurlby 2006, 187-9, 260-1). Due to the relatively simple carved design on the fonts it is difficult to develop a more detailed appreciation of the chronology of these fonts, beyond a broad twelfth-century date, and thus understand whether their distribution is linked to patronage, the output of single or multiple workshops or a simple spread of a fashionable style.

A group of fonts bearing distinctive arcading are found on Anglesey (Fig 57). There is some variation in the precise depiction of this motif. The arcading on an unusual rectangular font from Llabeulan and one from the church of St Lwydian, Heneglwys, appears with a lozenge chevron beneath it. The simpler arcades on the fonts from Llandeussant and Llanbadrig contain decoration between the columns – simple depressions in the former case and bosses on the latter. At Llaniestyn the arcading is relegated towards the base of the font, whilst the simplest example, that from Llanfechell, has no additional decoration beyond the two arches on each side.

Other distinctive regional font traditions include simple fonts with three or more carved stone heads, such as the font from Llandyssiliogogo, Silian and St Harmon, with other examples from Breconshire and Carmarthenshire. These have been linked to the influence, direct or otherwise, of Rhys ap Gruffudd ('Lord Rhys') in the later twelfth century, though some must be later (RCAHMW 1913, xx).

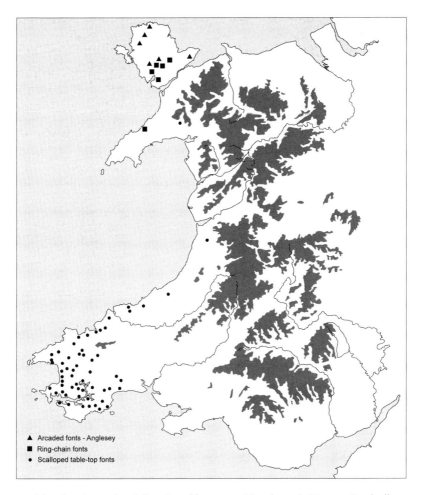

59 Map showing regional diversity of font types. Map drawn by Yvonne Beadnell

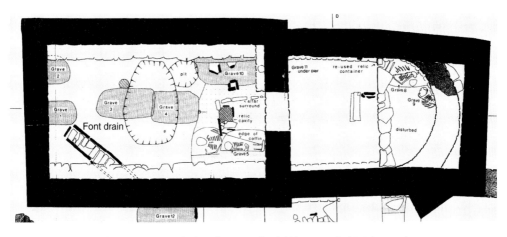

60 Font drain at St Barruc's chapel, Barry Island (Glamorgan). (Knight 1981)

It is not only Norman stylistic influences that can be seen on Welsh fonts. Another group of fonts from Anglesey draws on artistic traditions linked closely to the Irish Sea and Hiberno-Norse world. Interlace is used on the fonts from Llangristiolus, Cerrigceinwen, Newborough, Trefdraeth and Pistyll (just across the Menai Straits on the Llyn Peninsula). The use of ring-chain on the Pistyll and Llangristolus fonts appears to be closely linked to the use of the motif on one of the crosses from Penmon. It is probably safest to interpret the use of interlace in this context as indicating a relatively late use of the native tradition, perhaps even consciously archaicising, rather than evidence for a precocious early use of fonts. A twelfth-century date for these examples seems most likely; it is possible they are linked to the patronage of Gruffudd ap Cynan (d.1137) or his son Owain Gwynedd (d.1170) (Thurlby 2006, 234).

Most fonts are unlikely to be *in situ*; they are almost certain to have moved location within their churches according to the evolving demands of the liturgy. However, it is possible to extract a little evidence about the architectural context of baptism from a study of the archaeology and architecture of the churches. There are no baptisteries to compare with that known from the Anglo-Saxon church at Potterne (Davy 1964). At the church of St Woolos, Newport, Malcolm Thurlby has suggested that the present location of the font, in the chapel at the west end of the church, is its original position (Thurlby 2006, 164). This chapel was probably also an *eglwys y bedd* (burial chapel) containing the remains of St Gwynllyw (Knight and Wood 2006). The juxtaposition of the burial of a saint and font clearly has strong symbolic connotations. Baptisteries are known from the west end of churches in Anglo-Saxon England (e.g. Barton-upon-Humber; Rodwell and Rodwell 1982) and on mainland Europe (e.g. St Riquier, France). However, at Newport it is important to be aware that the font was heavily restored in the nineteenth century, and its current position may not be original.

It was necessary to drain fonts on some occasions, and in some cases carefully constructed drains or soakaways were provided to channel the water away (Parsons 1986). At the west end of St Barruc's Chapel, Barry Island, just such a probable drain was excavated (Knight 1976-8, Fig. 4) (Fig 59). This, again, suggests a western location for the font, hard up against the west wall. There is circumstantial evidence that other fonts may also have stood close to the walls of their churches. A number of fonts from Anglesey have an area with little or no external carving, including those from Llangwyllog, Cerrig Ceinwen, Llanbeulan, Llechynfarwy, Newborough, Trefdraeth and Penmon. This suggests that when they were carved it was not expected that they would be visible from that side, or may even have been carved *in situ*.

RELICS

It has already been seen that items associated with individuals of particular sanctity often became objects of veneration in their own right. They made the transition from functional object to relic. However, whether these artefacts or the remains of the holy dead themselves were the focus of special worship, they were usually placed or encased in some form of decorative cover or container, the reliquary. Whilst the use of reliquaries as vessels for sacred objects would have been widespread in Wales, relatively few examples survive.

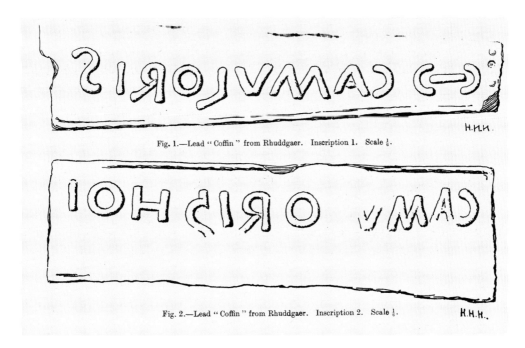

Fig. 1.—Lead " Coffin " from Rhuddgaer. Inscription 1. Scale ⅛.

Fig. 2.—Lead " Coffin " from Rhuddgaer. Inscription 2. Scale ⅛.

61 Inscription on lead sheet, possibly an early reliquary, from Llangeinwen (Anglesey)

Most such items are from the eighth century or later. There is, however, one possible earlier example. Three lead plates were found at Llangeinwen, Anglesey in 1878 (*27*; Wynn Williams 1878) (Fig 61). One plate depicted traces of the symbols *Alpha* and *Omega*, while the other two pieces carry the Latin inscriptions CAMVLORIS H O I and CAMVLORIS. The former inscription has usually been reconstructed as CAMVLORIS HIC OSSA IACENT ('Camulorix, here lie his bones'), and the item is frequently described as fragments of a lead coffin. This is an unusual object; it is the only example of a lead coffin from early medieval Wales, and would be more at home in a late Roman context were it not for the inscription. Indeed it is not certain that the fragments of lead even come from a coffin at all. The two longest pieces appear to be complete, but are only approximately 95cm long, whilst the third fragment is slightly less at 65cm in length, and also seems to have been complete. Although the length may suggest a child's coffin, the shorter piece is far too long to be a foot or head plate, yet too short to be a cover or base (Toller 1977, 5). In the immediate area of the find were tile, pottery, ashes and calcined bone. The presence of tile and pottery suggests Roman or later medieval occupation, but there is nothing to suggest that the ashes and bone were human, as suggested by Wynn Williams (1878, 140). The entire site was clearly much disturbed. There are a number of possibilities. If the bones are accepted as human, this might suggest an earlier date, and the unusual dimensions of the lead object may suggest some form of lead ossuaria, of a Roman date, which, unlike lead coffins, are sometimes inscribed, although the inscription is not like any known (Smith 1880, 172-3). An alternative explanation is that the possible reference to 'bones' rather than a body, may indicate some form of

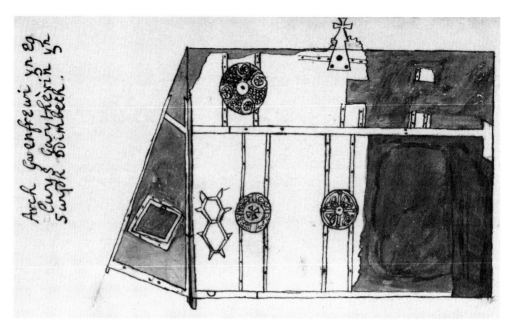

62 Drawing of reliquary of St Gwenfrewi at Gwytherin (Denbighshire) by Edward Lhuyd, *c.*1690. (© Bodleian Library, University of Oxford)

casket for the bones of a saint, rather than a proper coffin. Whether an inscribed Roman coffin or ossuaria or an early medieval reliquary, the Llangeinwen object remains highly unusual.

Most Welsh reliquaries appear to fit into the well-established Insular traditions. This can be seen most clearly in the case of the reliquary casket from Gwytherin. Until recently this was only known from number of seventeenth and eighteenth-century illustrations, derived from an original by Edward Lhuyd captioned '*Arch Gwenfrewi yn eglwys Gwytherin yn swydh Ddimbech*' ('the shrine of St Gwenfrewi [Winefride] in the church of Gwytherin, Denbighshire') (Butler and Graham-Campbell 1990) (Fig 62). This depicted a casket, triangular in cross-section, with short supporting legs. It was seemingly decorated by three attached roundels, metal strips and possible metal sheet and surmounted by a cross-shaped mount. It was not until a fragment of the original was discovered at the Catholic church at Holywell that it was possible to assess the scale of the item, which was probably nearly 40cm long and 30cm high (Edwards and Gray Hulse 1994). It clearly belongs to a well-known group of Insular house-shaped shrines found in Ireland and Scotland, such as the reliquary of St Manchan (Kendrick and Senior 1937; Blindheim 1984; Youngs 1989, 134-40). However, its decorative roundels appear more akin to eighth and early ninth-century Anglo-Saxon metalwork than Irish metalwork, though parallels have been drawn with some of the mounts on the St Manchan's Shrine (Redknap 2007, 55). Opinion remains divided as to whether this is a product of English, Irish or Welsh workmanship (Butler and Graham Campbell 1990, 46; Redknap 2007, 55). Not big enough to have contained the body of St Gwenfrewi, it is more likely to have held either small corporeal relics, such as bone fragments or teeth, or small associated items, such as brandea (small pieces of cloth that have been placed amongst corporeal relics and thus become imbued with sanctity).

Even though the evidence for the Gwytherin reliquary is only partial, it is the best that survives from Wales. Other similar reliquaries are known simply through the survival of metal decorative mounts. The earliest possibility is an Anglo-Saxon style gilt copper alloy mount from St Arvan's, possibly from a casket, book or reliquary, decorated with a *chi-rho* monogram (Rednap 2007, 44, Pl. VIII. 19). This probably dates from the seventh century. Similar in form to the Gwytherin examples is the circular mount from Din Lligwy, mentioned earlier (Redknap 2007, 54). There is also an important group of enamelled shrine mounts from eastern Wales and the Borders. Part of a handle from a portable house-shaped reliquary was found during excavations at Llangors Crannog; this site was probably destroyed by Mercian forces in late ninth century giving a good *terminus ante quem* for the artefact. It is decorated with blue glass studs and red and yellow enamel work, and has a clear range of Irish parallels (Redknap 1995; 2007, 61-2). Two further Irish enamel mounts have been found in Herefordshire – one at Weston under Penyard in the territory of the Welsh kingdom of Ergyng (Fig 63) (La Neice and Stapleton 1993), and another from the other side of the Wye at Weobley. It is clear that such Irish enamelled metalwork could be found equally in Welsh and Mercian contexts, as further examples from Breedon-on-the-Hill (Leicestershire) and a recent discovery at Whitchurch (Shropshire) demonstrate (Dornier 1977, Fig.41.1; Reavill, Leahy and Geake 2008).

A small group of stone reliquary containers is also known. Excavations at the chapel of St Barruc on Barry Island discovered a fragmentary stone box, which is likely to have been used to store a small reliquary containing relics related to Barruc (Knight 1981) (Fig 64).

Above left: 63 Enamelled mount from Weston-under-Penyard. (© Herefordshire Heritage Services, Herefordshire Council)

Above right: 64 Stone reliquary containers: (top) St Barruc's Chapel, Barry Island (Knight 1981) (bottom) Llanidan, (Anglesey). (Way 1870)

Another stone container was found beneath the church at Llanidan (Way 1870). It is conventionally dated to the fourteenth century, but it is stylistically very simple, and it is possible that it dates from an earlier period (Lord 2003, 24). It is also possible that the rectangular font from Llanbeulan may in fact have originally been a reliquary or shrine. Although stylistically linked to a group of other fonts in Anglesey (see above), its shape is unique. The presence of an equal armed cross at one end finds no parallels among fonts of this period. Peter Lord has suggested that it was originally an altar, though this is unlikely (Lord 2003). However, it is possible that it may have originated as a shrine. Whether a shrine, altar or font, it is hard to find comparable specimens for this unusual item.

Relics were often kept in special locations within the church structures, particularly the chancel. In addition to the stone reliquary container, work at St Barruc's Chapel found a relic cavity beneath the altar. It is likely that relics could also be kept in the aumbreys in the chancel. A letter to Philip Augustus, King of France, sent by Llywelyn ap Iorweth in 1212 notes that Llywelyn kept an earlier letter from Philip Augustus in the aumbrey of a church 'as if it were a sacred relic' (*in armariis ecclesiasticis tanquam sacrosanctas relliquias*) (Pryce 2005, 235).

The Chronology and Function of Relics

Relics did not simply work as objects of religious devotion, though this was clearly one of their key purposes. By the eleventh or twelfth century, when the first written documentation appears, it is clear that they took a central role in the functioning of the Welsh legal system. The swearing of oaths and compurgation was crucial in this process. The law codes show that relics were regularly used to validate these oaths and providing an element of holy sanction. For example, when an individual who had stood surety for another wished to deny a claim by a debtor they were required to declare 'By the relic which is here, I am a surety from you for what is said, and falsely have you sworn …' whilst placing his lips to the relic (Jenkins 2000, 64). A man who wished to deny having had sexual intercourse with a woman 'in bush and brake' was required to swear on a 'bell without a clapper' (Pryce 1993, 43). The twelfth-century saints' lives also record a similar use for relics; the *Vita Cadoci* notes the use of Gildas's bell for swearing oaths (*VSC* 27).

Sacred objects were not simply confined to churches. It is clear that from the eleventh century, if not earlier, relics could regularly be taken from churches and used elsewhere for a range of purposes. Evidence from Welsh royal acts suggests that the possession of a relic whilst travelling conveyed an element of sanctuary or immunity to the bearer. Llywelyn ap Gruffudd declared that if Maredudd ap Rhys was accused before him he could travel 'without escort or relics to show his innocence' (Pryce 2005, 347; Pryce 1993, 201-2). The protective nature of relics is also implied by a passage from Welsh legal texts that states that if a person carrying relics does wrong he does not derive any protection from them (Jenkins 2000, 82-3). Relics could also be removed from a church for the swearing of oaths. In homicide cases the laws stated that the relics should be taken by a servant along with the accused murderer to exact the required *galanas* (blood money) from the kindred of the accused (Jenkins 2000, 445). In boundary disputes between two abbots or bishops the Welsh laws also required that they swear oaths on the disputed boundary (Jenkins 2000, 427). The importance of swearing on relics on the spot of the dispute is also seen in the legislation on the death of livestock and the destruction of crops, where it is necessary for relics to be bought to the relevant land (ibid, 205).

It is possible that some relics could be held in the possession of individuals rather than ecclesiastical communities. A letter patent issued by Dafydd ap Llwyelyn in 1241 noted that Dafydd 'has sworn on the holy cross that he has carried around with him' (Pryce 2005, *300*). It may be the treatment of relics by as private property may explain why fragments of a reliquary were found at Llangors (Campbell and Lane 1989); it could have housed relics held personally by Tewdwr ap Elisedd, the King of Brycheiniog at the time of the site's destruction.

The precise type of relic used in legal procedures is not always clear, though in some specific cases the relics used are specified. A quitclaim by Lleison ap Morgan in favour of Margam Abbey made in 1205/1207 records that 'Lleison has sworn on the relics of the monastery, namely on the body of Jesus Christ, the most precious wood of the True Cross and the relics of the holy apostles, martyrs, confessors and virgins (all of which relics are contained in one cross)' (Pryce 2005, *158*). Bishops and abbots had to resolve boundary disputes by swearing on their crosiers and gospels (Jenkins 2000, 127).

Gerald of Wales noted

> The common people … in Wales, have such a reverence for portable bells, staffs crooked at the top and encased in gold, silver or bronze and other similar relics of the saints, that they are more afraid of swearing oaths upon them and then breaking their word than they are upon the Gospels
> *Journey 2*

This preference can be seen clearly in an analysis of the acts of the Welsh kings, where the vast majority of acts validated by swearing on gospels were agreements between Welsh rulers and Norman kings and nobility (e.g. Pryce 2005, *284, 328, 361*), whereas, oaths relating to agreements between Welsh lords used a wider range of relics.

Gospel books did, however, have an important role in mediating power in early medieval Wales. Rather than functioning primarily as relics, they appear to have been used to record land grants and similar transactions. The earliest examples are the marginal annotations in the Chad Gospels, which were records of the settlement of land-disputes between two lay individuals and deposited with the community of St Teilo and placed in the Gospel book (Jenkins and Owen 1983, 51–2; Jenkins and Owen 1984; Jenkins 1994, 74–79). An example of how such a procedure may have taken place is known from Herefordshire in the reign of Cnut when Leofflaed, wife of Thorkel the White, was given the right to some land. The text in the Hereford Gospel concludes 'Then Thorkil rode to St Aethelbert's Minster, with the consent and cognisance of the whole assembly, and had it recorded in the gospel book' (Jenkins 1994, 79; Gameson 2002).

A similar process may be envisaged in a Welsh context. Whilst known elsewhere in the early medieval world, the use of Gospel books as cartularies appears earliest and most widely within a Celtic milieu, and Dafydd Jenkins has suggested that the practice had its origin in western Britain or Ireland (ibid, 85–6; Davies 1998, 108-9). The gospel books were, however, not just used as repositories for charters, but also as records of those for whom the churches prayed, so-called *liber vitae*, and it is suggested that the group of marginalia from the Lichfield gospels known as Chad 8 represents just such a list (Jenkins and Owen 1983, 55-6). There are also charters contained in the Book of Llancarfan in which the donor made the grant for his soul so that his name might be written in Cadog's book at Llancarfan — the phrase used is '*pro anima N*', which also makes an appearance on Group 3 stones of the eighth to tenth centuries (Davies 1982a; e.g. ECMW, 220-3).

CHAPTER FIVE

DEATH AND BURIAL

By the tenth century the burial of the dead in enclosed cemeteries surrounding churches, with the bodies placed in west-east aligned graves accompanied by few, if any, grave goods characterised the mortuary ritual across western Christendom (Bullough 1983; Hadley 2002; Zadoro-Rio 2003). However, this represented the final result of a long process of the development and evolution of burial practices. This process was influenced by both developing Christian doctrinal views on death and burial, and the social and political demands of early medieval societies. There was also considerable geographical variation in the early Christian burial rites at international, national and regional scales in the first millennium AD. Conversion to Christianity in this period did not result in a complete rupture in existing burial traditions; rather new theological and institutional demands were brought to bear on the pre-Christian rites. Any exploration of burial in Christian Wales must thus have a clear understanding of the treatment of the dead in the preceding Roman period.

THE ROMAN BACKGROUND

By the third century AD inhumation was the dominant burial rite in Britain, largely replacing cremation, which had been the main tradition in the first and second centuries AD. In much of Britain it is possible to distinguish two key variants in the late Roman burial rite (Petts 2004; Quensel-von Kalbern 1999). One rite consisted of inhumations placed west-east with few, if any, grave-goods. Burials of this type were often found in cemeteries showing a high level of spatial organisation with the graves arranged in rows. This contrasts with a burial tradition which comprised graves accompanied by a range of grave goods, including pottery vessels and dress items; these burials tended to be aligned north-south. Bodies in both traditions were usually placed in an extended position, though in the latter rite there was a significant minority of individuals placed in the grave prone, in a crouched position or even decapitated (seemingly after death). Burials of both types can be found in Wales. For example, inhumations accompanied by pot and glass vessels are known from the forts at Caerleon and Chester amongst others (Boon 1972, 106-13; Mason 1987, 154-5; Pollock 2006, 23-54). Importantly, some cemeteries that are known to have continued in use into the early medieval period may have a late Roman origin (Pollock 2006, 74). The radiocarbon dates from the cemetery at Atlantic Trading Estate, Barry Island, range from cal. AD 241–409 to cal. AD 664–946 (Price 1985, 1986, 1987); it is possible that this site may have originated as part of a larger cemetery of Roman origin, as cremations with glass vessels and burials with decorated lead coffins were recorded in the 1940s nearby (Sell 1996). Cemeteries utilising extended inhumations with no grave goods are not just linked to major centres of Roman activity, such as forts and towns, they are also known from rural sites. A good example is the group of nine extended inhumations from Kemeys Inferior (Tuck 2003).

One of the real challenges in trying to characterise the nature of changing burial rites in late Roman and early medieval Wales is the difficulty in dating cemeteries in this period. Obviously, graves containing no grave goods can only be dated by radiocarbon analysis of skeletal material (a rarity in the acid soils of Wales) or other organic material. It is extremely hard to be certain whether a particular burial of this type was placed before or after the early fifth century, though the presence or absence of grave-goods has been used to provide a rough guide to the date of a cemetery. The general assumption has been that the tradition of accompanying the dead with grave-goods ceased in western Britain at the end of the Roman period, whilst the practice of placing the dead in the grave unaccompanied continued to become the dominant early medieval burial rite. However, it is increasing becoming clear that the situation is a little more complex than this (Petts 2009). The practice of placing grave-goods continued into the fifth century and beyond. For example, at Biglis the burial of an old woman inserted into a corn-drying oven provided a radicarbon date of cal. AD 419–648; the woman was buried wearing two gilded bronze bracelets (Parkhouse 1988, 15-16). Excavation on the cemetery associated with the early medieval ecclesiastical site at Llandough found a number of burials accompanied by grave-goods, including the remains of hobnailed shoes or boots. These have often been seen as almost diagnostically Roman, and in early reports of the excavation it was assumed that these indicated a Roman origin to the cemetery (Thomas and Holbrook 1995). Radiocarbon dating of some of these burials now suggests a secure early medieval date (Holbrook and Thomas 2005, 20). It is possible that the hobnails are not deliberately placed grave-goods, but residual material which was accidentally redeposited in the grave fills (the site is close to a Roman villa). However, in a number of cases the hobnails were recovered from around the feet of the skeleton suggesting they were worn by the dead individual. A range of other grave-goods, such as knives and dress accessories, are known, if only in small quantities, from other early medieval cemeteries in western England, such as Cannington in Somerset (Rahtz et al. 2000) and Bromfield in Shropshire (Stanford 1995).

It is not even certain whether the use of inhumation rather than cremation can be a hard and fast indicator of early medieval date. A pit cut into the edge of a Bronze Age burial cairn at Pentre Farm, Pontardulais, contained skeletal material and charcoal which provided a radiocarbon date of cal. AD 420–665 (Ward 1975, 3-15). It is highly unlikely that this is an isolated example of early medieval cremation in Wales. Cremated human bone with a similar date (cal. AD 395–460) has been found at Tintagel (Cornwall) (Barrowman et al. 2007, 312). It is highly probable that outside areas of extensive Roman influence, such as towns, forts and rural areas in the south-east of the country, the late Iron Age tradition of cremation burial may have continued to be used into the early medieval period. This means that it may be possible that some of the cremation burials from Wales usually ascribed an Iron Age or Roman date may be early medieval. It is also important to note the continuation of cremation as a minority rite in Ireland in the fifth century and beyond, particularly in the east of the country, areas where contact with Wales and Cornwall is attested (O'Brien 1992).

Whilst it is clear that there may have been some use of cremation into the fifth century and beyond, it is equally apparent that the dominant burial rite in the early medieval period was extended inhumation, occasionally with grave goods. This burial practice not only shows direct continuity from late Roman burial, but is also part of a tradition that was common across much of the Late Antique world, particularly in Gaul, Spain and North Africa (Petts 2004). In these regions, oriented extended inhumation was widespread.

EARLY MEDIEVAL BURIAL: THE USE OF COFFINS

The evidence for use of coffins is partial, due to the problems of survival. Whilst stone and lead coffins survive well in the archaeological record, wooden coffins rarely do, and can usually only be recognised by the presence of iron nails or coffin fittings. Thus coffins constructed from wood, but without using metal fastenings, are only recognisable in exceptional circumstances. In Roman Wales, coffins were commonly used (Pollock 2006, 90–91). Wooden, nailed coffins were the most common, but stone and lead coffins were far from rare. The stone coffins were usually carved out of local stone, but there is no tradition of elaborate decorative carving, as was common elsewhere in the Empire (e.g. James 1977, 29–61). Equally the decoration on lead coffins was rarely complex, and it seems that many so-called 'lead coffins', were actually only coffin liners for wooden or stone coffins (Toller 1977). The only possible use of a lead coffin in early medieval Wales is suggested by the lead plates found in 1878 at Llangeinwen on Anglesey (Nash-Williams 1950, 27; Pollock 2006; Williams 1878) and even this is far from certain (see Chapter Four).

There are few cases of wooden coffins of early medieval date with metal coffin fittings. The extensively excavated cemetery at Llandough produced relatively little direct evidence for coffins, though a number of iron objects recovered from graves may have been coffin nails (Holbrook and Thomas 2005, 27). However, there is some evidence for wooden coffins without such metal fittings or fastenings, presumably secured by wooden nails. The only evidence for such coffins is often dark organic stains in the soil. Many such examples are known from Llandough, although they were clearly only a minority of the total number of burials (Holbrook and Thomas 2005, 27). A similar pattern was found at Capel Maelog, where less than 10 per cent of the identified graves contained evidence or possible evidence for a coffin (Britnell 1990, 53). Intriguingly, the evidence from this site seems to suggest that coffin use was more common in the earlier phases of the cemetery. Similar coffin stains are also known from many of the graves found at Tandderwen (Denb.) and nine graves from Plas Gogerddan (Murphy 1992; Brassil et al. 1991). One of the coffins from Plas Gogerddan produced a radiocarbon date of AD 344–605, whilst at Tandderwen dates of AD 36–682 and AD 730–1149 have been obtained. At both sites the preservation was too poor to allow the coffin shape to be identified, though in one case at Tandderwen, it was possible to identify the wood used as oak. Over the Welsh border, wooden coffins were recognised at the British cemetery at Bromfield in Shropshire dated by artefactual evidence to the sixth century (Stanford 1995).

Both the Bromfield coffins and those from Wales seem to be of simple plank construction, and in Grave 50 at Tandderwen separate elements of the side and base of the coffin could be recognised. At Capel Maelog the evidence from Grave 8 suggests that rather than having a wooden coffin, the body was covered with two planks meeting with a central ridge. The body rested on another wooden plank, but there was no evidence for side planks. Similar cases of possible wooden linings or panels being placed over the body are known from Llandough, such as Grave B110, where despite the presence of staining indicative of a wooden plank in the grave, a limestone slab was placed at its feet (Holbrook and Thomas 2005, 27). Probable wooden linings have also been identified in five graves at Llandegai, where it appears that stone slabs were used to hold wooden planks in place (Longley 2004, 109).

STONE CISTS AND LININGS

The use of stone cists or stone slabs to line graves has a long tradition in Wales extending back into prehistory. Some Iron Age graves, such as those from Llangeinwen and Merthyr Mawr were placed in cists (Hughes 1909, 56-7; Savory 1954/6, 53-4). The practice continued into the Roman period (Pollock 2006, 189). Their use ranged from simple stone linings, often utilising bedrock displaced during the excavation of the grave, as at Rogiet, to complex stone cists, such as those from Abernant Farm, Kemeys Inferior (Hudd 1908; Tuck 2003). This use of stone in graves again parallels practices elsewhere in late Roman Britain, where cists and stone-linings are common (Philpott 1991). The evidence suggests that the use of stone in graves emerges earliest in rural contexts, both in Roman Wales and Roman Britain as a whole (Pollock 2006, 89; Petts 2001).

There is considerable regional variation in the use of stone in graves in early Christian Wales, with most cases limited to the north-west and south-west (particularly Pembrokeshire). In Gwynedd cist burials are known from the *capell y bedd* at St Beuno's Chapel in Clynnog Fawr (Stallybrass 1914), though at this site only two cists are known, but nearly a dozen dug-graves. At the University Tennis Courts, Bangor, three out of the 14 burials were placed in partial cists, which covered the upper body only (Hughes 1924, 1925). Again, the number of cists is small compared with the dug-graves, and at the nearby site of Berllan Bach, out of 78 graves, none are placed in cists (Longley 1996).

A near or total absence of stone-lined graves can also be seen at Llandegai (Longley 2001) and at Ty Newydd, Bardsey Island (Arnold 1998). It is only in Anglesey that cist burial really seems to become the dominant rite. At Capel Eithin two of the three phases of burial appear to be dominated by cist graves, including stone-lined graves and lintel-graves (Smith et al. 1999). Elsewhere, at Arfryn, Bodedern (White 1969–70, 1971–2), another multi-phase burial site, at least half of the graves had some form of stone lining. Like Capel Eithin the earliest phase of

65 Cist burials at Ty Mawr, (Anglesey). (© Gwynedd Archaeological Trust)

burials comprised dug-graves, suggesting that the use of cist graves was an innovation in the early medieval period. At Llansantfraid, Tywyn y Capel, a large sand mound contained a large number of lintel-graves in up to four tiers (Stanley 1846; Boyle 1991). In contrast to other sites on Anglesey, the phase of stone-lined graves appeared to precede the phase of dug graves. Other cist burials are known from Anglesey. Isolated cemeteries are known from Llanbedr-goch (Hughes 1904), Llanddyfnan (Johns 1956), Llanfaethlu (Lloyd Griffiths 1895) and Llanrhuddlad (Lloyd Griffiths 1895), and some more recently excavated examples, such as Ty Mawr (Fig. 5a). All these sites are small cemeteries situated away from church sites, with no dug-graves, though cist graves are also known from church-sites, such as Lechynfarwy (Neil Baines 1935).

A similar pattern can be seen in Pembrokeshire. At Caer, Bayvil, a mixed cemetery of stone-line, cist and simple earth graves was situated within the ramparts of an Iron Age enclosure (James 1987, 73), though less than half of the 61 graves contained stones. Stone cists or lined graves are recorded from many other sites in the county, often close to extant or former church or chapel sites (e.g. Bridell, RCHMW 1925, 31; Caldey Island, Evans 1918; Dinas, James 1987, 72; Eglwyswrw, Ludlow 2003b; Llanwnda, RCHMW 1925; Llanbydder, James 1987). Many of these sites are recorded only as antiquarian observations, meaning it is quite possible that more ephemeral simple dug-graves have gone unrecorded; where modern excavation has taken place, for instance at Eglwyswrw, such graves were also recorded.

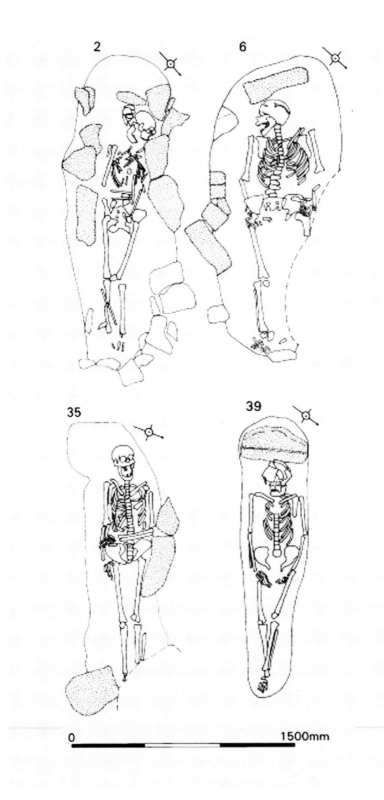

66 Graves with
stone linings,
Llandough,
(Glamorgan)
(© Cotswold
Archaeological
Trust)

Away from the north-west and south-east of Wales the use of stone linings is far less common. Although several groups of early medieval burials have been excavated at Caerwent, only the Vicarage Garden cemetery revealed any cist burials. Out of 76 excavated graves only 13 had any kind of cist: four were stone-paved, eight were stone-lined and one was a lintel-grave (Campbell and Macdonald 1993). At Llandough at least 16 burials were lined or partially lined by stone packing having been dug through the bedrock; this is a very small proportion of the overall number of burials (Fig 66). A higher proportion of cist graves were found at the Atlantic Trading Estate cemetery, but there may be a functional explanation, as the graves were cut into wind-blown sand and the stone linings may have been used to prevent the collapse of the cut before burial (Price 1987).

It is not easy to develop a precise chronology for the use of stone-lined graves; there is little evidence that variation in constructional details can be linked to date. There are two cases of stone cists being covered with Class 1 inscribed stones, Arfryn and Pentrefoelas (Anon 1912, 142; *183*; White 1969–70, 1971–2), although it is not clear whether these stones were re-used or placed in primary contexts. Whilst bone preservation is often poor, a number of cemeteries from Pembrokeshire have produced radiocarbon dates (St Bride's, cal. AD 893–1206; Llanychllwydog cal. AD 782–1152; Caer, Bayvil, cal. AD 649–878) making it clear that stone-lined graves were being used throughout the early medieval period and into the medieval period. The presence of Dyfed gravel-tempered ware within stone cists at Eglwyswrw suggest that such graves were being created well into the post-Conquest period (Ludlow 2003b, 41). Other indicators of the use of stone cists during this period include a stone cist from Cilgerran churchyard, which contained thirteenth-century coins (Anon 1859).

There are some indicators that the use of stone-lined graves became increasingly common over the course of the first millennium AD. The excavations at the church site of Llanelen (Glamorgan) revealed a series of graves. The earliest phase, consisting of eight dug graves, was succeeded by a second phase dating from possibly the seventh century to the thirteenth century. In this second phase most graves were stone-lined (Schlesinger and Walls 1997). A similar pattern appears to have occurred at Arfryn and Capel Eithin on Anglesey (Smith et al 1999; White 1971-2), though notably the situation was reversed at Tywyn y Capel, Llansantfraid (Anglesey), whilst at Caer (Pembrokeshire), there was no discernible chronological preference for dug or stone-lined graves (James 1987, 59).

The evidence above shows that burial in cist or stone-lined graves was common in early medieval Wales. However, it is too simplistic to see this as a single phenomenon across the entire region. Their use is more common in the north-west and south-west, but occurs occasionally elsewhere, particularly in the south, where it is likely that this demonstrates continuity from the Roman period. Nationally there does appear to be an increase in their use through the early medieval period. This phenomenon is not just limited to Wales. In south-east Scotland, in the areas of Lothian and Clackmannanshire, there is also a remarkable efflorescence of long-cist cemeteries, seemingly growing out of a local tradition of short-cist burial (Alcock 1991). In these regions the change from short-cists to long-cists is intimately related to the move from crouched inhumation to extended inhumation in the immediate post-Roman period. It is apparent, though, that there was a similar process happening through much of western Europe in the fourth and fifth centuries (Petts 2004). In Brittany the practice of surrounding graves with re-used Roman *tegulae* is seen as diagnostic of the late fourth and fifth centuries (Galliou 1989). Stone-lined graves were often used in late Roman Spain (TED'A 1987), a practice continuing into the Visigothic period (Ripoll 1991).

GRAVE STONES AND EPIGRAPHY

Despite clear evidence of continuity in burial practices from the late Roman period into the early medieval era in Wales, there are also some notable changes. Most clearly visible in the archaeological record is the use of stone burial memorials carrying inscriptions in both Latin and Irish (see Chapter Two). Although carved gravestones are well known from Roman Britain, the practice had largely fallen out of use by the fourth century. Recently, a strong case has been made for the continuation of the Roman epigraphic tradition into the fourth century in northern England, where a small number of rough stones of this date have been identified, particularly associated with Hadrian's Wall and associated military installations (Dark and Dark 1996; Todd 1999). There are, though, no such late examples currently known from Wales until the reintroduction of epigraphy in the fifth century. Mark Handley has noted that the chronological distribution of epigraphy in Roman and early medieval Wales largely parallels that known from elsewhere in the Empire (the so-called 'Mrozek curve'; Handley 2001). This is true, but does not help much in explaining the reintroduction of the practice in Wales or understanding how it was revived. The Welsh stones bear only a general similarity to the late Roman ones from northern England, meaning it is more likely that the practice was reintroduced from mainland Europe, rather than elsewhere in Britain. The parallels between some of the epigraphic formula used in Wales and Cornwall and those from the Continent are well attested. Handley has rightly highlighted the fact that there is nothing inherent in the choice of formula used to suggest that the exempla were specifically from western Gaul as has often been suggested, although the evidence from documentary sources and the likely origin of D and E ware known to have been traded into Britain, still make this the most likely origin (Thomas 1990; Campbell 2007). The use of Irish ogham on these stones is also obviously not a Roman influence (although it is likely that Roman grammar may have had some indirect influence on the development of ogham as a script), attesting the complex range of influences that were at play in the revival of funerary epigraphy in fifth and sixth-century Wales.

It is notable how little explicit acknowledgement of Christianity is apparent on these Group I stones. There are a few cases which make explicit recognition of the faith of the individual being commemorated; references are made to bishops (*sacerdos*) (Bodafon, Caerns; Llantrisant, Anglesey, Nash-Williams 1950) and priests (*presbyter*) (Aberdaron, Caerns. *77, 78*). However, in general, the key aspect of social identity that is recorded is kinship, particularly (though not exclusively) via the male line. It is also notable that there is a distinct gender bias in the provision of these memorials, with the vast majority recording men; even when women are recorded they are often mentioned in a secondary position to a man (Petts 1998). A significant number of these stones are, however, decorated with crosses, which might be seen as a clear indicator of Christian identity (e.g. Trallwng; Silian; Egremont; Clydai; B45; CD29, CM18, P15). A closer examination of these cross carvings makes it clear that in many cases the cross was carved later than the primary inscription and in some cases partially obscures it (Longden 2003). This practice is not limited to Wales and examples are known in Ireland (MacAlister 1945) and the south-west of England (Okasha 1993). Whilst it is not possible to be precise about when the crosses were added, it was probably in the seventh or eighth century AD, or even later, as part of a retrospective campaign of 'Christianising' memorials. Not all grave markers need have been inscribed stones. It is quite possible that wooden markers and uninscribed stones were used in this way. For example, an unmarked stone at Llanychlwydog was probably associated with burials (Murphy 1987, 88).

CEMETERY ORGANISATION

The notion of the 'enclosed cemetery' has been a powerful one in early Christian archaeology. It has been suggested that burial grounds surrounded by a formal boundary were a diagnostic feature of the archaeology of early Christianity in the Insular world. This theory was developed most extensively by Charles Thomas

> But alongside these sprawling open cemeteries there are others which are enclosed, by a rude stone wall, by a low bank with an external quarry-ditch, even (as with monasteries) by some pre-existing earthwork; and these enclosed burial grounds are invariably oval or circular in plan.
>
> There is growing evidence that these cemeteries, *in particular the enclosed ones* [my emphasis], antedate any other form of Christian structure in the countryside of post-Roman Britain, and can thus be viewed as the primary field monument of insular Christianity.
>
> (Thomas 1971, 50)

He subsequently modified this view acknowledging that the enclosures themselves were 'secondary' within a 'primary' phase' (Thomas 1994) and suggesting they dated to the sixth or seventh century. However, archaeological excavation in Wales and south-west England had failed to identify any cemeteries of this early date with evidence for formal enclosures. For example, the cemeteries at Tandderwen, Llandegai, Plas Gogerddan, Arfryn and Capel Eithin have no evidence for any formal boundary features. Whilst the cemetery at Atlantic Trading Estate, Barry Island does have a boundary feature to its south, this appears to act as a revetment against the sand dunes to the south, and does not seem to extend round the other sides of the cemetery (Newman 1985, 1986) (Fig 67). A rare exception to this pattern is the re-use of an Iron Age enclosure as an early medieval cemetery at Caer, Bayvil (Fig 68). This site is located in north Pembrokeshire in an area of known Irish influence in the early medieval period. The re-use of prehistoric enclosures for cemeteries in this period is well-attested in Ireland. For example at Lough Gur a late Neolithic circular enclosure contained over 50 early medieval inhumations, whilst 15 inhumations were placed within a Neolithic earth-banked enclosure at Carbury Hill (Grogan and Eogan 1987; Wilmot 1938). This suggests that the similar pattern of re-use at Caer is indicative of Irish influence on local burial practices, rather than any indicator of Christianity (Petts 2002). Monastic *valli* (ditches defining the boundaries of monasteries) may well have existed in the fifth to eighth centuries. However, there is little evidence that they were sub-divided at this early period to mark out formally defined burial areas. Admittedly, there has been very little adequate excavation on early medieval ecclesiastical centres in Wales, but what little evidence there is from sites such as Llandough, Bangor and Carmarthen, suggests that the internal space within these sites was not divided up by ditches or similar boundaries until the eighth century or even later (Petts 2002, 30-32).

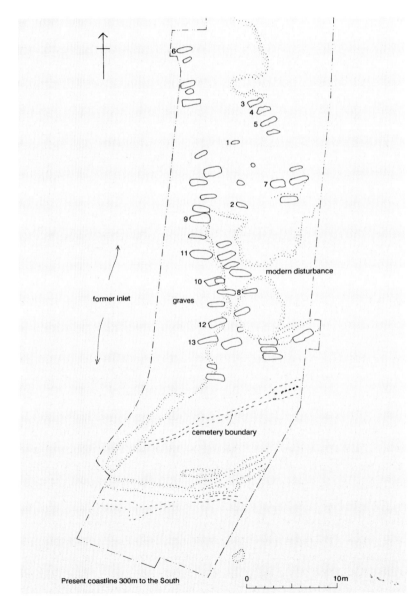

67 Early medieval cemetery, Atlantic Trading Estate, Barry Island, (Glamorgan). (© Glamorgan Gwent Archaeological Trust)

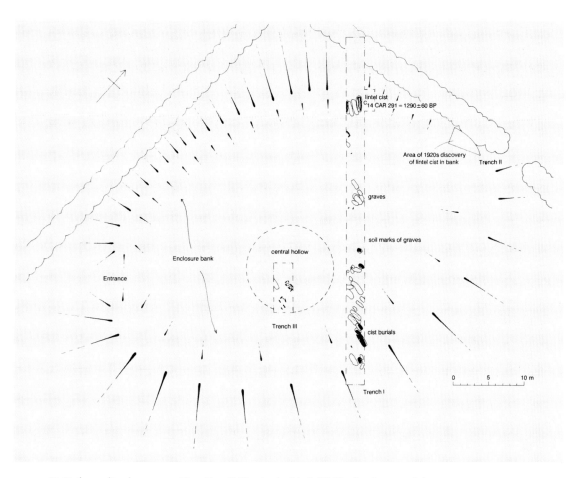

68 Early medieval cemetery, Caer, Bayvil (Pembrokeshire). (© Heather James 1987)

Whilst, it is no longer possible to accept that cemetery enclosures are indicative of the earliest stages of Christianity in Insular Britain, there are certain features of layout that appear diagnostic, if not of early Christianity, at least of early medieval cemeteries in Wales and the south-west. It is becoming increasingly clear that small rectangular structures or enclosed areas were commonly placed around certain graves. Such features are now known from excavated cemeteries at Tandderwen, Llandegai, Plas Gogerddan, Capel Eithin and Trefollwyn in Wales and in south-west England at Kenn in Devon and Stoneage Barton in Somerset (Weddell 2000; Webster and Brunning 2004) (Fig 69). Similar rectangular enclosures probably associated with early medieval cemeteries are also recorded as cropmarks at Bryn y Garn, nr Margam, Croes Faen, Bryn Crug, Corwen, Penrhyn Park, Tyddyn Pandy, Fynnon and Llangoedmor.

There is some variation in these enclosures; the nine at Tandderwen were between 5m and 10m across, whilst the best-preserved example from Plas Gogerddan was only 4.5m across. The excavators of Tandderwen suggested that the ditches of many of these features surrounded low earth mounds. Eastern entrances are also known from Plas Gogerddan and

Kenn and Stoneage Barton in south-west England. It is possible that these enclosures were in some cases the foundation trenches for small rectangular structures. Evidence from Plas Gogerddan suggests that they were foundation trenches for wooden plank walls. The enclosure at Capel Eithin appears to have been defined by a trench holding wooden beams in place; the central grave was sealed by a clay surface, implying the structure was roofed.

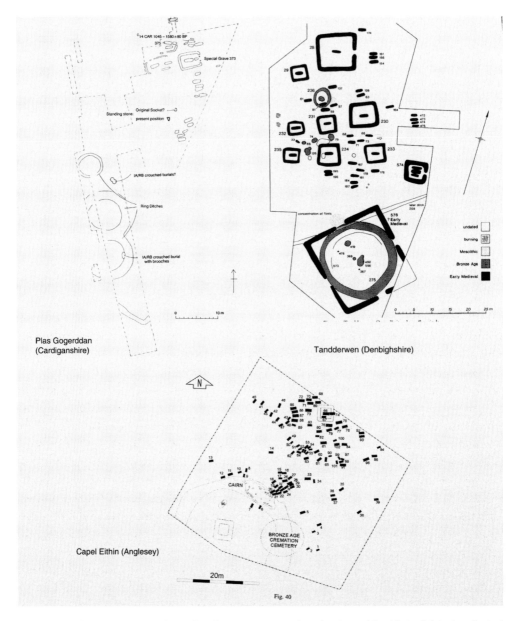

69 Rectangular structures in early medieval cemeteries in Wales: Plas Gogerddan (© Dyfed Archaeological Trust); Tandderwen (© Clwyd Powys Archaeological Trust); Capel Eithin (© Gwynedd Archaeological Trust)

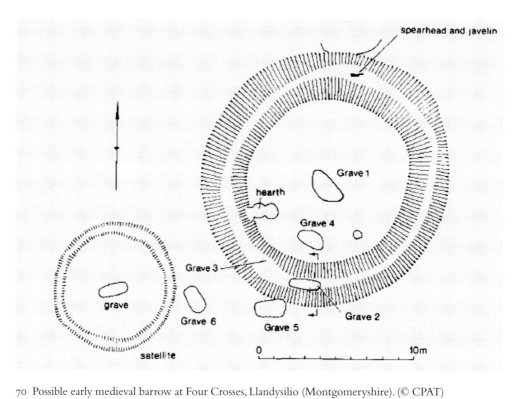

70 Possible early medieval barrow at Four Crosses, Llandysilio (Montgomeryshire). (© CPAT)

It is not entirely clear how far these features can be lumped together as a single phenomena; it is possible to distinguish between the rectangular enclosures or buildings with
wooden walls, such as at Plas Gogerddan and the features which are more likely to be small
square barrows, such as Tandderwen. The suggestion that the Capel Eithin monument was
an enclosed structure places it in a separate category. However, the nearest parallels to both
type of monument appear to be of Roman origin. Rectangular mausolea and enclosures are
found in a number of late Roman cemeteries in Britain. At Poundbury (Dorset), there were
a number of small stone mausolea decorated inside with painted wall plaster. Whilst more
sophisticated than the early medieval Welsh examples, they have broad structural similarities; simpler, ditched enclosures with no visible entrances are also known from the same site.
(Farwell and Molleson 1993). The cemetery at Lankhills, Winchester, contained a number
of enclosures with east entrances. A very similar sub-Roman feature has been found at
Queenford Farm, Dorchester-on-Thames, where a woman was buried in a small rectangular
enclosure outside the main cemetery boundary (Chambers 1987).

The strong similarities between these late Roman burial enclosures and the early medieval
Welsh examples make it likely that the latter drew on Roman models for their inspiration. It
is also likely that they drew on Roman exempla for square barrows. Within Wales a series of
square barrows are associated with the auxiliary marching camp at Tomen-y-Mur (Bowen
and Gresham 1967, 230-5). Most of these are of Roman date, although at least one appears

to partially overlie the Roman road suggesting a post-Roman date. A Group 1 inscribed stone from Tomen-y-Mur reading *D(is) M(anibus)*BARRECTI(?) CARANTEI(?) has been recorded (Edwards 2002, 27; *285*). The phrase *Dis Manibus* is a phrase found commonly on Roman gravestones, but this is a unique example of its use in the early medieval period. Square monuments are known from outside some Roman forts on the Northern frontier, such as at Low Boroughbridge (Cumbria), where a group of square ditched enclosures containing cremations have been excavated (Lambert 1996, 122-3); other square barrows include those close to the fort at High Rochester (Northumberland) (Wilson 2004).

In addition to the use of rectangular enclosures and barrows, more traditional round barrows and cairns appear also to have been used as burial monuments in early medieval Wales, both newly constructed and re-used prehistoric examples. It is not always easy to date such cases, though the use of extended inhumation is a likely indicator of an early medieval date. For example, such a burial was inserted into a Bronze Age barrow at Kilpaison Burrows, Rhoscrowther (Fox 1926). The placement of Group 1 stones on barrows is also known, and is probably indicative of the re-use of such mounds for burial (Edwards 2001, 18-23; Knight 1991, 140-1; Petts 2002). The stone from Penbryn was found lying against a cairn containing a Roman burial (CD28). In Glamorgan the so-called 'Bodvoc' stone was sited in the centre of a Bronze Age ring-cairn on Mynydd Margam, and the stone from Clwydi Banwen (G7, G77) was also recorded as being related to a barrow. The stone on Cefn Gelli-Gaer (Glamorgan) is situated in a small enclosure, which was probably a dug-out Bronze Age barrow (G27).

In addition to re-used prehistoric burial mounds, it is probable that some barrows were newly constructed in the early medieval period. At Four Crosses, Llandysilio, on a gravel terrace in the Upper Severn Valley eight ring-ditches forming part of a scattered barrow cemetery were excavated in the mid-1980s. Most of these barrows were prehistoric (Middle Neolithic to Middle Bronze Age) in date (Warrilow et al 1986) (Fig.5f).

Adjacent to one of these prehistoric barrows was a smaller satellite barrow containing a single burial. This was aligned west-east and presumably placed in an extended position (though there was no bone preserved), a position quite compatible with an early medieval date. The rare deposition of an early medieval iron javelin and spearhead in the neighbouring larger barrow may have been related to funerary rites linked to the construction and use of the satellite barrow (Barford et al 1986).

The phrase *in hoc congeries lapidum* known from the stone at Penmachno (ECMW, 101) is usually translated as 'in this heap of stones' and is probably indicative of barrow use. Whilst Nash-Williams suggests that it is merely a variant on the *in hoc tumulo* formula, there is no reason not to assume a more literal interpretation.

THE RISE OF THE CHRISTIAN CEMETERY

The period from the seventh to ninth century was one of major transition in the burial rite in Wales. Whilst there is clear continuity in the use of extended inhumation, often in stone-lined graves, major changes can be seen in the ways in which these graves were marked and the spatial organisation of the cemeteries. Group 1 stones appear to fall out of use by the seventh century, though some may have been carved into the eighth century. Replacing them as grave markers were the simple cross-marked Group 2 stones. Although none have been found in context over a grave in Wales, similar stones have been found in direct mortuary contexts elsewhere in Insular Britain (Edwards 2001, 30; Thomas 1971, 125-6; Fisher 2001). Their use shows a definite move towards anonymity in the marking of burials. Only a small proportion of these stones (around 10 per cent) have personal names carved on them, and these rarely have additional information relating to kinship or filiation. Unlike Group 1 stones on which personal and family identity were emphasised but religious affiliation rarely expressed, we see a reversal of this situation on Group 2 stones, which indicate faith rather than familial ties.

The move away from kinship identity appears to be reflected in cemetery organisation. It is in this period that the move towards what will ultimately develop into enclosed cemeteries begins. Cemetery sites with rectangular enclosures or barrows, such as Plas Gogerddan and Tandderwen, fell out of use by the ninth century. It is also noticeable that whereas Group 1 stones are widely recorded from locations away from later church sites, Group 2 stones are much more likely to be found at known ecclesiastical foci (Edwards 2001, 31; Lewis 1976, 185). This is most likely because these church sites, or more precisely, the simple cemeteries that preceded them on the site, were established once Group 1 stones had stopped being produced. This can be seen on a localised scale in the Gwaun valley, which runs eastwards from Fishguard in North Pembrokeshire. The only Group 1 stone in this area is from Llanychaer (P48); however, Group 2 stones are known from the churches at Llanllawer, Llanychlwydog, and Pontfaen (Edwards 2007) and nearby Llanwnda and Morvil (P32-5, P32-46, P51-4, P64, P86).

There thus appears to be a horizon of new cemeteries from the seventh or eighth centuries, which show evidence for an increasingly overt Christian identity, and less focus on secular expressions of kinship. However, there is still relatively little evidence for the formal enclosure of these cemeteries by a boundary feature, such as a ditch or fence. Admittedly, there is very little solid excavated evidence for the date of the first, distinct cemetery boundaries. In fact, about the only example, is that at Capel Maelog (Radn.) (Britnell et al 1990) (Fig. 5g). This site commenced in the ninth century as a cemetery; it was not provided with a church and an enclosing ditch until the late eleventh or twelfth century. This seems to suggest strongly that the enclosure of cemeteries was relatively late in the evolution of the Christian burial rite in Wales, rather than, as Charles Thomas suggested, a very early feature. However, this does place much weight on the archaeological evidence from a single site; are there any other sources of evidence that might help refine this chronology?

Evidence from place-names also suggests that from the eighth century at earliest, there was a change in the organisation of cemeteries in Wales, with a move towards formally enclosed cemeteries. The word *Llan* is commonly found in Welsh place-names. It derived from the Brittonic place-name element *lann*, which came to be used to refer to a church in early medieval Wales, Cornwall and Brittany (Petts 2002, 311). The meaning of the word appears to have developed from 'rough meadow' to 'small enclosed meadow' to 'enclosure' to 'churchyard, church, monastery' (Thomas 1994). This clearly demonstrates the central role of the enclosure as a metonym for an ecclesiastical site. Its final semantic range was wide – it could describe a monastic enclosure and by extension the monastery itself, but it could also be used to describe an enclosed cemetery, not necessarily one with an associated church structure. It also came to refer, in some cases, to the wider estate attached to a religious institution, including detached portions of it (Davies 1982, 145).

However, whilst language scholars have a clear understanding of the evolution of the meaning of the term, the chronology of this process is less secure. An early date for the transition from a secular to an ecclesiastical meaning has been put forward by Charles Thomas. He notes that Rhigyfarch's Life of St David, mentions a monastic school run by Paulinus, called in the text '*in insula Wincdilantquendi*' (James 1967; Thomas 1994, 100-1). Thomas argues that this can best be understood as a description of an ecclesiastical site known as '*lantquenti*' which lay in an isolated place or an island ('*in insula*'); the whole supplemented by an untranslated phrase '*Wincdi*'. Crucially for his argument he suggests that Rhigyfarch's source for this passage was pre-AD 600 in date, noting that the author stated that he used 'the oldest manuscripts in the land … written in the archaic fashions of the elders' (James 1967). In the words of Thomas, the name 'traps the word [lan] like a butterfly in the flight from British (Gaulish, Romano-Celtic) landa ('Vindolanda') through the fifth- entury (?) apocope as land into sixth century –lant- (written), /land/ (spoken), and then lann through assimilation of –nd to –nn, probably by the end of the sixth century at the latest' (Thomas 1994, 111 n.36). The implication is that as the name Wincdilantquendi includes the element *lant* (with a terminal 't') the name must belong to the end of the sixth century at the latest. However, there is clear written evidence from ninth-century charters from Brittany and the eleventh-century *Cornish Life of St Petroc* that in some cases place-names could retain the unassimilated nd/nt until much later than Thomas's sixth-century date (de la Borderie 1901, 220-1; Jackson 1953, 508; Grosjean 1956; Petts 2002, 69-41). Even if Thomas' arguments are accepted, it is far from clear that in the context of the Life of St David the term *lan* was being used to describe an ecclesiastical site, rather than simply an area of land, particularly given the unusual structure of the place-name.

Place-names incorporating the element ⋆*lann* also appear in the Llandaf charters. Despite the uncertainty about the chronology of the charters and the high level of corruption within them, it is noticeable that ecclesiastical sites, which in the later charters had ⋆*lann* names were often called *podum* in earlier charters, with no examples of the reverse occurring (Davies 1978). This suggests that the term was not used to form place-name elements in the earlier charters within the collection. Whilst again, it is hard to be precise about the chronology of the charters, it seems likely that ⋆*lann* names are only being used from the ninth century onwards at earliest. More thorough explorations of the evolution of ⋆*lann* place-names has taken place using Cornish material, where evidence suggests that names using ⋆*lann* were not being formed after the eleventh century, though the earliest documentary evidence for such names is from the ninth century, implying a fairly narrow chronological band for their creation (Padel 1976). In Brittany similar place-names are known, with documentary records of their use from the early ninth century (*Langon* = landegon) and the late ninth century Wrmonoc's *Vita Pauli Aureliani* (Lanna Pauli) (Cuissard 1881–2; Guigon 1997).

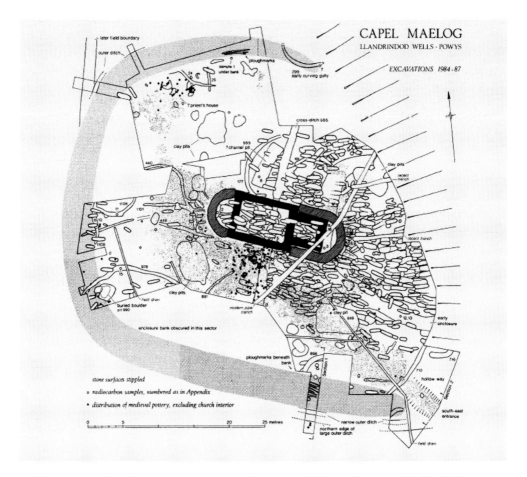

71 The remains of the church, cemetery and boundary at Capel Maelog (Radnorshire). (© CPAT)

The spread of *lann place-names is limited to Wales, Cornwall and Brittany, with a few outliers, such as Landican (Cheshire), *Lantokai* (now Street, Somerset) and *Lanprobus* (now Sherbourne, Dorset) (Gelling 1992; Padel 1976, 25; Barker 1984). However, it does not appear in other areas of Britain which certainly saw pre-Augustinian Christianity, such as Southern Scotland and the West Midlands. It is unlikely that in these areas earlier Christian names were supplanted by Anglo-Saxon toponyms, as other early Christian place-names, such as *eccles* and in southern Scotland *both/bod*, are known in these areas (Cameron 1968; Taylor 1996). Instead, the distribution of *lann names appears to complement the pattern of Anglo-Saxon occupation in the eighth century, whereas *eccles* and *both/bod* names are found in areas occupied by both the British and the Anglo-Saxons (Petts 2002, 42).

This all appears to confirm the model derived from the archaeology and the distribution of the sculptural evidence. From the fifth to eighth centuries, apart from a small number of people who were buried at ecclesiastical sites, the majority of the population were interred in cemeteries, which probably belonged to specific lineage or kinship groups. These expressed little in the way of overt affiliation to the Christian church, and instead the focus was on expressions of kinship. In the eighth century, there appears to have been a distinct change in burial in Wales. Whilst the basic tradition of extended inhumation continued, there appears to have been a distinct break in the location of cemeteries. Many old family cemeteries seem to have fallen out of use, and instead there is a new generation of burial sites coming into use. This dislocation in the use of cemeteries probably equates to a break in the role of family groups structuring burial rites, and an increased emphasis on the role of the church in overseeing funerary behaviour. The emphasis on the expression of kinship identity found in the use of Group I stones is replaced by a greater focus on badges of affiliation to the church, particularly through the use of cross-incised stones. The evidence for later crosses being carved onto Group I stones suggests that there may have been a deliberate attempt to 'Christianise' earlier cemetery sites that were deemed too 'secular', even if not overtly pagan.

At first these cemeteries were not formerly marked out or bounded in any way. However, it is probable that between the eighth and eleventh centuries these Christian burial sites were increasingly marked as separate and distinct places in the landscape through the use of ditches, fences, walls and banks. It is probable that this formal marking went hand in hand with the rise of the distinct rite of consecration, the overt sanctioning of their function as cemeteries by the Church. It is doubtless because of this link between enclosure and consecration that the place-name element *lann became such a key marker of burial sites in this period. By the thirteenth century executed thieves, traitors and mad men were forbidden from being buried in consecrated (and by definition enclosed) ground (Pryce 1993; Jenkins 2000). The notion that a good Christian could be buried outside a consecrated cemetery had become unthinkable.

SPECIAL BURIAL

Whilst the move towards enclosed cemeteries and the change in the nature of funerary epigraphy can be read as a withdrawal of the role of kinship identity from the sphere of mortuary rites, it might be better to see this as a transformation rather than a complete abolition. For both secular and ecclesiastic elites, kinship continued to be an important structuring element in death and burial, though the way in which it was expressed changed.

Within ecclesiastical communities, kinship became structured around the key holy men or saints, who were believed to have acted as the founding fathers of particular communities. Holy men who became the *de facto* ancestor figures of monastic establishments ousted the quasi-mythological figures that headed many secular genealogies. The members of these communities, if not sharing biological kinship, at least shared an ancestry of faith and worship (Charles-Edwards 2002). With strong evidence for a hereditary dimension to ecclesiastical office, this symbolic kinship may not have been merely fictive. In practice, the rising importance of saints as 'father figures' appears to have been signalled materially by the increased importance of the tombs of holy men (Edwards 2002). Evidence for the development of these special tombs is difficult to date. Although it has been suggested that the structure at Capel Eithin may have been an early example, there is no reason to believe that there is anything specifically ecclesiastical about it. The earliest direct evidence we have for a focal tomb associated with a holy man comes from the *Historia Brittonum* (early ninth century), which contains the story of how St Illtud built a church around the body of a holy man which had been brought to the saint. The construction of a church above a grave is paralleled at Capel Maelog, where a stone-lined grave surmounted with white quartz pebbles became a focus for other burials. When a church was constructed on the site in the later twelfth century the chancel arch was positioned directly above this grave, which may well have been visible still (Britnell et al. 1990, 36). There is no direct date for this grave, but a nearby burial produced a date of cal. AD 778–1116. Whilst there is no certainty that this burial was of someone of religious significance rather than a secular notable, the manner in which the church was subsequently situated above it implies it was a long-term focus of veneration, which is perhaps unlikely for the grave of a lay dignitary.

By the eleventh century the evidence from the saints' lives indicate that it was believed that holy figures would be buried in graves within their monasteries. In some cases, they were seemingly actually buried in the church structure; Brynach was placed beneath the eastern wall of his church and Gwynllyw and Tatheus beneath the floors of their churches (*Vita S. Bernachi; Vita S. 16 Gundleii* 10; *Vita S Tathei* 17). Important clerics were also clearly erecting major stone memorials by the tenth century. Abbot Samson erected a cross at Llantwit Major for himself and King Juthahel (Redknap and Lewis 2007). This is probably the same monument that the twelfth-century *Life of St Illtud* recorded as being erected by the earlier, sixth-century Samson of Dol (VSI 15). The presence of a biblical personal name may mean that Idnert son of Iacobus, who appears on an inscribed stone of ninth-century date, may also be a member of an ecclesiastical family (CD9).

The changing ways in which high status burials were commemorated also found expression in changes in the repertoire of carved stone monuments used. Following on from the introduction of the simple cross-incised stones, a new range of sculptured crosses and cross-slabs began to be used from the ninth century onwards. These crosses had a range of functions, but it is clear from the epigraphic formula that they were used to commemorate the dead (see Chapter Two), although not necessarily marking the grave itself. The epigraphy refers instead to the soul, rather than the body, of the departed (Petts 2003, 201-4). In some cases the crosses may even have been erected before the death of some of those recorded on them; this can be seen on the Ebisar cross from Llantwit Major, which reads 'Samson set this up for his own soul and for the soul of Iltut, of Samson the king, of Samuel and of Ebisar' (G66). The dead and the living became juxtaposed on funerary monuments in the way that did not occur on Group 1 or 2 stones. This can also be seen in the increased references to the individual who set up the cross, such as the stone from Llanhamlach, the inscription on which read 'Matthew, Mark, Luke and John; Moridic set up this stone' (B32). These stones also sometimes record the craftsman responsible for its execution: 'Conbelan placed this cross for his own soul and for the souls of Saint Glwys, of Nerttan and of his brother and his father. Prepared by me, Sciloc' (Merthy Mawr, G98). The importance of the craftsman reflects the wider increased investment on funerary sculpture found on these, often very elaborate, crosses, compared with the far simpler Group 1 and Group 2 stones.

THE HOLY DEAD

The corporeal remains of churchmen could undergo a further transformation, as they became the focus for veneration. This development was one that occurred across Christendom, and the growth of the cult of relics and the rise of pilgrimage to significant holy sites is one of the characteristics of medieval Christianity.

Valuable evidence for the cults centred around the veneration of the graves of holy men comes from the study of place-names, particularly the element *merthyr* which comes from the Latin word *martyrium* meaning the 'grave of a martyr or shrine' (Roberts 1992, 42; Thomas 1971, 89). It is probable that when used in Wales it indicates that the site once housed the physical remains of a specific saint. Surviving examples include Merthyr Mawr, Merthyr Dyfan, Merthyr Tydfil, Merthyr Cynog and Merthyr Fâch. In many cases, *merthyr* names were subsequently replaced by place-names using alternative elements, such as *Llan*, for example Merthyr Meirion (now Llanfeirian), Merthyr Caffo (now Llangaffo).

In Wales, the small purpose-built chapels were known variously as *capel y bedd* (chapel of the grave), *eglwys y bedd* (church of the grave) or *cel y bedd* (cell of the grave). These structures usually lay within the main enclosure at an ecclesiastical site, but were subsidiary to the main church (Petts and Turner 2009).

Traditionally, when an individual was deemed worthy of veneration, their physical remains or relics would be translated – moved from their original grave and placed in a new, often raised, tomb or shrine, or fragmented and placed in a reliquary. Nancy Edwards has suggested that in Wales this process did not occur until the advance of Norman religious and political influence in the twelfth century (Edwards 2002). Indeed, much of the surviving evidence for the act of translation belongs to this period and in the context of expanding Norman power. For example, the relics of Dyfrig were translated from Bardsey to Llandaf, an incident recorded in the Book of Llandaf (Davies 2003). The relics of Gwenfrewi were excavated from their original burial location at Holywell and translated to Shrewsbury in 1137 (Edwards 2002). It is possible that the relics of Gwynllyw may have been translated from their original burial place in the floor of the church at St Woolos at the same time that the church itself underwent major reconstruction in the Romanesque style in the early twelfth century (Knight and Wood 2006).

The clearest evidence for a twelfth century phase of translation comes from Powys, where there is evidence for a series of elaborate stone shrines in a Romanesque style. The best surviving example is the shrine of Melangell at Pennant Melangell (Britnell et al. 1994). Although the current shrine is reconstructed from fragments discovered during archaeological work at the site, it gives a good idea of the way such as a shrine might appear. Standing behind the main altar the house-shaped body of the shrine has gables decorated with substantial foliated crockets; the ensemble stands on columns with capitals again decorated with foliage scrolls (Britnell 1994; Thurlby 2006) (Fig 72). The relics of Melangell were presumably moved from their original context in the grave housed in the eastern apse and placed within the new raised stone shrine. Stylistically, this shrine probably dates to the mid-twelfth century. It may have been erected by Rhirid Flaidd, a local nobleman described as 'Proprietor

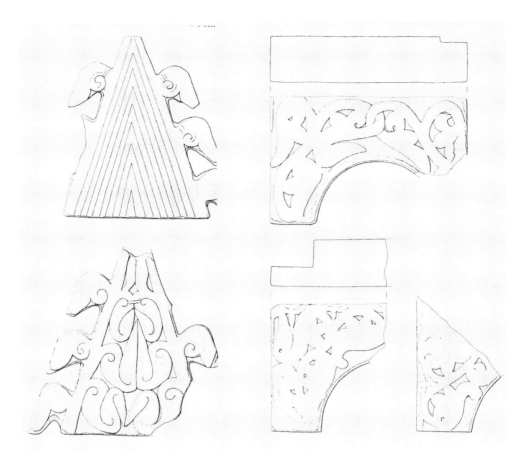

72 Fragments of the shrine at Pennant Melangell (Montgomeryshire). (© CPAT)

of Pennant' in a poem by Cynddelw. Although this is the best-preserved example of such a shrine in central Wales, there are fragments of other stylistically similar shrines known from a number of other sites in Powys. A fragment of a crocketed gable is known from Llanrhaeadr-ym-Mochnant, whilst other elements are known from Llangollen, Llantysilio-yn-Iâl and Clocaenog. This distinctive cluster of shrines appears to represent a regionally-specific response to Norman ecclesiastical influences in this part of Wales, close to the English border.

THE NOBLE DEAD

It was not just the holy dead who became the focus for special commemoration. Despite the general trend towards increased anonymity and the reduced emphasis on kinship found in the general burial rite in the later first millennium, aristocrats and royalty appear to have bucked this trend. From as early as the eighth century it also appears that aristocratic and royal families were starting to adopt particular ecclesiastical centres as dynastic burial grounds. The kings of Gwynedd appear to have used Llangadwaladr as their burial site very early in this process, as is shown by the stone commemorating the burial of Cadfan (d.645), which records him as *'wisest (and) most renowned of all kings'* (ECMW, 13). This stone may not have been erected on Cadfan's death; the church was probably founded by his grandson Cadwaladr (d.664), and it is possible this may have been contemporary with the commissioning of this stone.

It is likely that such use of churches as burial sites at this relatively early period saw the elites and the Church coming to a mutually satisfactory arrangement, with those wishing to be buried giving land or other resources. For example, in the Llandaf charters, King Awst and his sons Eiludd and Rhiwallon give the church at Llangors and their bodies for burial. The gifting of their bodies is clearly seen as a favour; either because it would involve the payment of burial fees or because it implied a more general on-going favourable relationship between the family and the monastery.

A similar example of the gifting of a body occurs in one of the charters appended to the *Life of St Cadog*, in which Conbelin gave 'land called Lisdin Borrion for the traffic of the heavenly kingdom together with his own body' (VSC 66) to the monastery at Llancarfan. By the tenth century it is clear that a church burial was expected for members of the elite and that the location of the burials of important figures was a subject worth commemorating (Petts 2007). For example, the *De Situ Brecheniauc* and *Cognacio Brychan* (probably eleventh century), which contain stories about King Brychan and his progeny, record the burial sites of Brychan and some of his relatives. Although, these figures would have been active in the fifth or sixth centuries, before church burial was widely established, the documents record later traditions that they were interred at churches: 'Anllach lies before the door of the church at Llanyspydyt. Reyn, son of Brychan, lies at Llanvayloc. The grave of Kynauc, in Merthyr Kynauc in Brecheiniawc.' (CB 16)

The increased use of major monastic establishments as centres of burial for royalty and powerful aristocratic families can also be recognised through the distribution of funerary sculpture. For example, crosses were erected at Llantwit Major for the souls of Hywel ap Rhys (King of Glywysing), King Samson and King Juthahel (G63, G65, G66). Similar clusters of crosses in Glamorgan are known in Margam and Merthy Mawr. The probable Viking-style hogback from Llanddewi Aber-arth (Cardiganshire) is likely to indicate the burial of a local lord (CD7), whilst 'Budic, the wife of Guindda' recorded on a stone slab from the tenth or eleventh century from Clodock is probably the wife of a local magnate (H1). It is also possible that the man named Guorgoret on a cross at Margam may be the individual of the same name who appears as a witness in a charter in the *Life of St Cadog* (ibid G78; VSC 55). However, in general, without explicit references in the epigraphy it is difficult to be sure whether many of these memorials were erected by churchmen or secular lords. The patterns of patronage that led to the clusters of crosses at Margam or Llan-gan remain unclear.

The focus on establishing possible dynastic burial sites continued into the twelfth and thirteenth century. There was a notable shift towards using the new Cistercian foundations patronised by the leading families in Wales. The family of the Princes of Deheubarth were frequently buried at Strata Florida (though Lord Rhys himself was buried at St Davids), with many being placed in the chapterhouse (*BYT* 1231, 1235, 1255), whilst Aberconwy became a major burial site for the lineage of Llywelyn ab Iorwerth (*BYT* 1236, 1269). The family of Madog ap Gruffudd Maelor, king of Powys Fadog were buried at Valle Crucis. It is possible that these sites had previously been dynastic burial sites before the foundation of the Cistercian monasteries at them. There is good reason to think that many of the Welsh Cistercian foundations were placed on the site of pre-existing ecclesiastical establishments, pre-Conquest sculpture is known from Strata Florida, Llanllŷr and Margam Abbey, whilst place-name evidence is indicative of a native foundation preceding Valle Crucis. Some native foundations also continued to be used as royal burial grounds into the twelfth century, such as Meifod, which was probably the burial site of the Kings of Powys (*BYT* 1259-60).

CHAPTER SIX

BELIEF AND LANDSCAPE

Whilst the church and churchyard formed the symbolic focus for Christian worship in early medieval Wales, they were not the sole sites of devotional practices. The landscape itself became imbued with symbolic and religious meanings. The expression of religious belief could be found at a range of differing scales and locations, from marking boundaries, engaging with monuments of the prehistoric and Roman past and moving through the landscape on local, regional, national and international pilgrim routes. However, as with other aspects of early Christianity, the relationship between landscape and belief altered and developed over the period AD 400–1200.

AD 400–800

The landscape into which Christianity was introduced in the fourth or fifth century in Wales was not a blank one. Despite the presence of large areas of uplands and mountains, many areas of Wales, particularly in the lowlands and coastal plains, were relatively densely occupied. Romano-British settlements were common across much of the country and frequently associated with field systems, highlighting the fact that agricultural landscapes were widespread, and by extension the issue of land rights, inheritance and boundaries must have been a key aspect of social life. Late Roman settlement is also known in upland areas, though often more difficult to date. It is likely that transhumance was practiced in these areas, with herds of sheep and cows being moved into upland pastures during the summer and down to lower areas in the winter months. This practice continued into the medieval and even post-medieval periods as is attested by the well-known *hendre/hafod* system found across the country. Thus on the dawn of the introduction of Christianity into Wales, the landscape was one of both boundaries and divisions and movement and fluidity.

However, it is important not to see the late Roman landscape of Wales as simply a zone of agricultural production; it was also a landscape of belief. Relatively little work has been done on expressions of religion and ritual in Roman Wales (though see Pollock 2006 for a thorough exploration of the burial evidence). It is clear though that whilst formal temples were constructed in either the Classical or Romano-British/Gaulish style in and around the towns in the region, the majority of the population expressed their religious beliefs through engaging either with natural features, such as lakes, rivers and wet places, or ritual activity on the site of prehistoric monuments (Bradley 1990; Aitchison 1989; Petts 2002b; Williams 1998). The practice of placing votive items at natural features shows strong continuity through the Iron Age and Roman period in Wales. For example, the hoarded items from Llyn Cerrig Bach date from between the second century BC and the late first century AD, indicating long-term depositional practices at the site (MacDonald 2007); they had been deposited in a small lake, which had subsequently become a peat bed. The elaborate Iron Age Capel Garmon firedog was found in a similar context (Fox 1939). Votive hoards continued to be placed well into the late Roman period; a hoard containing three small bronze dogs, a statuette of Mercury, three votive plaques (two decorated with dogs), a twisted wire bracelet and nearly 550 coins dating from the first century to late fourth century AD, was found in a spring at Llys Awel, near the hillfort of Pen-y-Corddyn (Manley 1982).

The evidence for Roman burial at prehistoric monuments is small but significant, considering the small number of Roman burials known from Wales (Pollock 2006). The clearest example is the Roman burial from Penbryn where a Roman urned cremation contained in a small Black-Burnished ware jar (c.AD 120–150) was accompanied by an aureus of Titus (c.AD 74). These were found in a small cairn south-west of the church. Significantly, this cairn was then apparently re-used for burial in the early medieval period, and was the site of the Group I *Corbalengi* stone (CD28). Another probable cremation comes from Gwenffrwd, Llantwit-iuxta-Neath, where amongst a cairn-field of at least 36 cairns, excavation revealed that one contained small pieces of burnt sandstone, and sherds of Romano-British buff-coloured pottery. This was interpreted by the excavators as the remains of a Roman cremation.

Probable Roman ritual activity at prehistoric sites was not limited to mortuary rituals. Roman pottery and coins have been found at Neolithic long barrows and Bronze Age round barrows from across Wales. For example, Roman pottery was found at the long-barrow at Din Dryfol (Smith and Lynch 1987, 115-17) and six late Roman coins come from the long barrow at Carn Goch (RCHMW 1997, 54-5). Roman pottery or coins have been recorded associated with round barrows at Bishopston Burch, Ynys Gwrtheyrn, Llaneddwyn and Four Crosses amongst others (RCHMW 1976, 233; RCHMW 1921, 305; Warrilow et al. 1986).

Christianity was clearly appearing in a countryside that was already imbued with sanctity and holy places. Seen in this context it is perhaps not surprising that in the early years of the church in Wales, the evidence for explicitly Christian activity in the landscape is relatively slight and difficult to interpret. It has often been suggested that many of the early Group I carved stones re-used prehistoric standing stones. Although the inscription types used are clearly of external origin (see Chapter Two), the form of these stones is not. Gaulish grave-stones are usually rectangular grave slabs set into the ground, whereas the Welsh stones are predominantly upstanding (Knight 1992). It has also been suggested that some stones, such as Maen Madoc, Ystradfellte (B50), Maen Lhwyd, Llandeilo Fawr (CM21, CM29) and Llangyndeyrn were actually re-used prehistoric monoliths. This has obvious implications when considering the wider re-use of prehistoric monuments.

Left: 73 Possible prehistoric cup marks on a carved stone cross from Llanveynoe (Herefordshire). (Author's photograph)

Below: 74 Comparative height and width of prehistoric standing stones and early medieval inscribed stones in Wales. (Petts 2002)

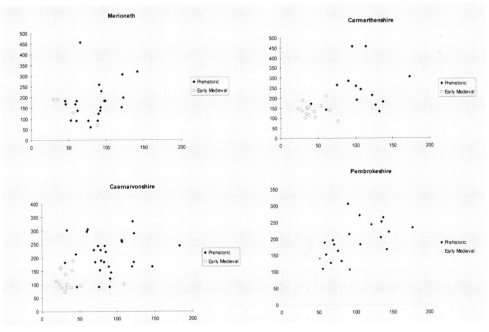

One of the key problems is dating something as simple as an unshaped stone. Very few prehistoric standing stones had any carving on them: the most common prehistoric motif is the simple incised cup and ring mark. Although there are some Early Christian inscribed stones with apparent cup-marks it is not clear that they are prehistoric: the indentations on the inscribed stones from Llantrisant appear to be gate-hanger holes (33), as do those on inscribed stones from Llannor (ibid). A simple cup-mark may also be found on the inscribed stone from Llanfaelog, but even this is uncertain (Wilson 1983). Only one stone has a ring-marking that resembles prehistoric marks, the incised Crucifixion from Llanveynoe, Herefordshire (Fig 73) (H5); however, this stone probably dates from the ninth/tenth century, and it is equivocal whether the ring marks cut the figure or *vice versa*. They also resemble the roundels on the ninth-century cross-slab from Nash, Glamorgan. These are symmetrically placed on the stone, possibly they were part of the medieval decorative scheme (G34). Thus the evidence for the re-use of cup-marked prehistoric stones would seem to be extremely slight, and certainly far from common. This lack of cup-marked standing stones should, however, be seen in the context of a paucity of rock-art in Wales in general, and of cup-and-ring marks in particular (Morris 1989).

A different approach is to compare the sizes and shapes of stones. Comparing the height and width of prehistoric standing stones with those of Group 1 stones is extremely instructive. (Fig 74). There is little overlap in size: Group 1 stones are shorter and wider than uninscribed standing stones. There is no compelling evidence to suggest that there is significant re-use of prehistoric standing stones. Any possible re-use is highly selective, only choosing smaller standing stones, and ignoring the larger, more spectacular examples. Whilst there are clearly a small number of cases where prehistoric stones were re-used for early medieval epigraphic purposes, they are few and far between, and we should perhaps be cautious in attributing this to ideological or symbolic motives, rather than practical ones.

Routeways

It is likely that many other Group 1 inscribed stones were deliberately placed along key routeways and areas of movement (Fox 1939). There are several good examples of stones being situated along Roman roads (Edwards 2001a). Maen Madoc stands above the Roman road known as Sarn Helen (Fox 1940), and the Carausius stone, now in Penmachno church, was originally from a pass where a Roman road crossed between Cwm Penmachno and Cwm Teigl; two inscribed stones are recorded from a site further along the same road know as Beddau Gwyr Ardudwy ('the grave of the men of Ardudwy') (Edwards 2001a). It is hard to be certain whether these and other stones located close to Roman roads were placed with the intention to deliberately engage with specifically Roman remains, or just routeways in general. The upland and mountainous nature of much of the Welsh interior means that options for major routeways are limited and constrained by the landscape and the presence of accessible passes. The construction of roads along these routes in Roman times may simply be a particularly visible reflection of the long-term use of many of these communication corridors. Equally, in many cases, such as Llanfor, Gelligaer Mountain and Banwen Pyrddin, near the fort at Coelbren, the Roman roads and forts are just one element of a clearly complex and chronologically deep palimpsest of Roman and prehistoric monuments, and it is important to be cautious in picking out just the Roman elements of these landscapes as symbolically important.

It is not only the early Group 1 stones that often appear to have marked important routeways. A simple cross incised on a stone boulder lies next to a prehistoric trackway and later Roman road near Caerhun (Edwards 2001a). In Pembrokeshire, a number of carved stones lie on attested pilgrim routes to St Davids (P36, P59).

Burial and the Roman Past

An alternative influence on the form of the Group 1 stones may be Romano-British milestones (Radford 1971). Their simple, rough-hewn inscriptions do bear certain similarities to the inscriptions found on Group 1 stones. However, the potential zone of influence is limited. Although milestones are relatively common in Britain they are not widely spread in the west, where the Group 1 stones are most prevalent. In Wales, five are found in Glamorgan, two in Breconshire, one in Carmarthenshire and five in Caernarvonshire. Five milestones are also currently known from Cornwall. However, Western Dyfed, the area from which the earliest inscribed stones are found, is devoid of such examples. There are two examples of early Christian monuments re-using Roman stones, both from Glamorgan. At Port Talbot a squared sandstone milestone was used for a Latin *Hic Iacit* inscription, but whereas the milestone inscription was horizontally laid out, the early medieval inscription was vertical (G92). The fact that the Roman inscription had been inverted when the stone was re-used suggests that it was of no interest to the early medieval epigrapher. A similar disregard for Roman inscriptions is found at the Roman fort of Loughor, where a Roman altar was re-used for an ogham inscription (G76); in this case the early medieval inscriptions were not even in the Latin script. Again re-use appears to have been the exception rather than the rule and probably governed by pragmatic concerns.

However, it appears that Roman forts did become the focus of some re-use in the early medieval period. The Roman fort at Pen Llystyn lies at the head of the Llŷn peninsula. A Latin/ogham stone reading ICORI FILIVS / POTENTiiNI ('Icorix, the son of Potentinus') is recorded from a site just to the north of the fort at Llystyn Gwyn Farm. The two superimposed Roman forts at Tomen-y-Mur lie on an exposed spur of Mynydd Maentwrog. They had a strong strategic position commanding the Vale of Ffestiniog and the valley of Trawsfynydd (Gresham 1938). On the basis of the ceramic evidence from the limited excavation at Tomen-y-Mur it is unlikely that occupation continued here much beyond the middle of the second century AD (Webster 2005). However, there is clear indication of later re-use of the fort. A Group 1 inscribed stone stood close to the site, and is the only example of this class of stone to use the pagan Roman formula *Dis Manibus* (EMCW 285). Slightly further away to the south along the road between Tomen y Mur came a further Group 1 stone (Hemp and Gresham 1961), whilst another two miles south from this, yet another early stone was recorded (*289*). Also, on the roads leading from the fort to the north and south-east are a total of eight square mounds surrounded by banks or ditches. It is most likely that they are Roman, as similar features are known from Roman forts elsewhere in Britain, such as the square mausolea outside Binchester and Petty Knowes, High Rochester (Wilson 2004). However, square barrows are known from early medieval contexts, such as at Tandderwen (Brassil et al 1991). The barrows at Tomen-y-Mur vary widely in size, and it is possible that they also vary in date; however, the jury must remain out on their precise chronology.

Early inscribed stones are also linked with the Roman forts at Llanfor and Caer Gai, Llanuwchllyn (both Merioneth), which stand at either end of Llyn Tegid (Bala Lake). The auxiliary fort at Caer Gai stands on a spur above the south-west end of the lake (Jarrett 1969). The main phase of occupation was the first to mid-second centuries AD, although there is a possible late- or post-Roman re-defence of the Roman enceinte and a potential outer circuit of undated, though presumably post-Roman, earthworks (White 1985; White 1986). An inscribed stone commemorating an individual named Salvianus Burgocavi was recorded here in the mid-seventeenth century (*283*). It is possible that it was associated with the field known as Cae Cappel (Chapel Field) (Edwards 2001a).

At the other side of the lake, at Llanfor, a series of Roman military remains are known through aerial reconnaissance, including an early fort and two temporary camps (Wilson 1990). These overlay a complex prehistoric ritual landscape containing a Bronze Age barrow, a pit alignment and a stone circle (ibid; Crew and Crew 1997; Bowen and Gresham 1967; Davies 2006). Unlike the Roman forts on Hadrian's Wall, where there is increasing evidence that they were occupied into the fifth century, the case for such continuity at Welsh forts is far less convincing. Roman activity at the forts in question seems to have ceased by the fourth century. Beyond the gravestones, there is no firm evidence for any early medieval reoccupation, except an undated palisaded enclosure at Pen Llystyn, and the possible re-defence of Caer Gai (Edwards and Lane 1988, 102; White 1986).

However, there are some mythological links with a number of these sites. Llanfor was adjacent to a stone circle called *Pabell Llywarch Hen* (Llywarch's Tent) (Bowen and Gresham 1967, 283). Caer Gai (the castle of Cai) was linked to the Arthurian figure Cai (White 1985) and Tomen y Mur appeared as Mur y Castell in the Mabinogion, the palace of the rulers of Ardudwy (Davies 2007, 59, 63). However, although a motte was placed here at some point in the eleventh or early twelfth century, it is unlikely that it ever acted as a significant central place, and it is possible that the siting of the motte reflects the mythological importance of the site, rather than its military significance. Notably, none of these mythological links refer to the Roman past, but instead allude to Arthurian and saga stories.

This is not to say that the early medieval Welsh had no sense of a distinct Roman past. The general Magnus Maximus (*c.*335–388) was elevated to the purple by his troops whilst in Britain in AD 383. Moving into Gaul, he defeated and killed the Emperor Gratian. After a brief reign he was captured and executed in AD 388. Despite his limited career in Britain, he does figure significantly in early medieval Welsh historical tradition. He is mentioned by Gildas (*DEB* II:13-14, the *Historia Brittonum, HB* 27;29, the Triads (Bromwich 2006, 441-444) and the *Historia regum Britanniae* (v.5-6), and appears as the key figure in one of the branches of the Mabinogion (*The Dream of Macsen Wledig*). He is also included in the extended inscription found on the early ninth-century Pillar of Eliseg (*182*). In these traditions he is regularly linked with the final withdrawal of Roman troops from Britain (which in fact took place 20 years or more after his death), and the initial British phase of settlement in Brittany. However, despite the key role he took in the early Welsh written (and presumably oral) traditions, it is not clear how far there was a sense of the distinct *physical* presence of the Roman past. The few cases of re-use of Roman spolia appears incidental.

Whilst Roman forts were sometimes associated with early burial, there is no suggestion that they are seen as distinctly 'Roman', but were just one element of a suite of early monumental sites (including Roman and prehistoric features) that could be re-used; the association of burials with Roman roads is more likely to indicate the wider importance of key routeways through Wales. The gifting of Roman sites to Welsh saints may occur twice in the collections of saints' lives. Tatheus was given the city of Caerwent by Caradog, King of Gwent, as the site for his monastery (CVT6) and in the *Life of St Cybi* (VCY8), Ethelic gives Llangybi to Cybi. It is possible that this is not the church of Llangybi in Caernarvonshire, but the church at Caer Gybi, a small Roman fortlet at Holyhead (Anglesey), which now contains a church dedicated to Cybi. There are also traditions that it was granted to the saint by King Maelgwn of Gwynedd. In neither case does the hagiographical material make any explicit reference or mention of the Roman origin of these saints.

INAUGURATION SITES

The early medieval landscape of Wales demonstrated the re-use of prehistoric monuments for burial. However, compared with Scotland and Ireland, the large-scale re-use of complexes of monuments for a range of activities, including occupation and ritual activities, is notably lacking. Wales has no equivalent to Dunadd, Kilmartin, Forteviot, or Armagh (Aitchison 1994; Driscoll 2004; Fitzpatrick 2004; RCAHMS 1999). These complex sites are often notably associated with royal inauguration rituals (see Warner 1988, 85-7), and we know from historical evidence that Irish kingship and high-kingship and by extension Dal Ríatan kingship in Scotland, had an important sacral element to it (Ó Cróinin 1995, 63-84, esp. 778-8). This contrasts with the Welsh model for kingship, which has no concept of the specialness of kings or of high-kings. There was no legal difference between kings (*brenin*) and other freemen (*bonheddig*), and the presence of a partitive inheritance system meant that it was rare for one family to build up permanent power for any length of time (Charles-Edwards 1993; Davies 1990). Although there was clearly a belief that kings should be related to those who had previously held royal power, this could be either on the mother's or father's side. Wendy Davies has noted the lack of any indications of a Welsh investiture or inauguration rite, declaring 'It is seriously to be wondered if there were such rituals' (Davies 1996, 112), though it is worth noting that Patrick Sims-Williams has interpreted the name *Devorix* which appears on an early grave stone from Capel Eithin as meaning 'Divine King' (Sims-Williams 1999). There are certainly no historic or textual references to legendary sites associated with royalty. The only reference relating kingship to specific sites is the relatively late note in Gerald of Wales, who refers to ancient royal seats in Wales:

> In ancient times there were three Royal castles in Wales: Dinevor in South Wales, Abberffraw in North Wales, on the island of Anglesey and Pengwern in Powys …
>
> (*Journey* 1)

These seem to relate to the three traditional caputs of the kingdoms of Deheubarth, Gwynedd and Powys respectively. This passage dates to the late twelfth century and cannot be projected back into the early medieval period. The presence of only three important kingships points to a period later than that being currently considered in this book, when there were numerous other polities in existence (Davies 1996, 101); the omission of Morgannwg is most notable. Most importantly although the location of two of these sites (Abberffraw, Anglesey; Dynefwr, Carmarthenshire) are known, neither shows any evidence of being positioned in relationship to any prehistoric landscape, though Dynefwr may potentially be sited on an Iron Age hillfort. Gerald places Pengwern at Shrewsbury, though there is no early support for this identification (ibid. 100). The fissile nature of Welsh kingship and the lack of a clear ideology of sacral kingship may well explain the lack of traditional inauguration sites in Wales comparable with those from Ireland and Scotland.

Stones and Boundaries

Mark Handley has suggested that many of the Group 1 stones were not intended primarily as burial monuments, but as boundary markers. He argues that the paucity of direct indications that the stones were funerary monuments, e.g. *hic iacit* inscriptions (81 out of a total of 242), means that most were primarily boundary markers, and that stones with names in the genitive should be read not as '(The memorial) of X son of Y', but '(The land) of X son of Y' (Handley 1998, 348). He develops this argument noting that it may be possible to recognise a chronological change in the relationship between the burials and boundaries (Handley 1998, 353–4).

He notes that only two out of the 10 inscriptions datable to the fifth century do not have explicit memorial formulae, whereas in the later fifth and sixth centuries stones with simple inscriptions in the genitive outnumber those with explicit memorial formulae. However, the problems linked to dating these stones accurately and the relatively small sample sizes means that any such chronological patterns must be treated with great caution. It is also debateable whether it is possible to draw a clear distinction between boundary markers and burial monuments. In many early societies, burial grounds appear to have been deliberately placed with a view to staking claims to land (Bradley 1987; 1993; Williams 1997). Thomas Charles-Edwards has also suggested that the importance of burial on boundaries was reflected in later literary traditions that record the burials of kings on boundaries or facing enemies, and has argued that the burial on boundaries was 'designed to defend inherited land from the claims of outsiders …' (Charles-Edwards 1993, 262-63). It is highly likely that early medieval burial grounds in Wales were initially placed with such intentions (Edwards 2001). It is not possible, though, to make simple assumptions about the precise location of such graves within the wider landscape; were they placed at boundaries or did they assume a central position within a plot of land? In some cases, such as when burials are found on mountain passes, such as the stone from close to the pass at Bwlch-Carreg-y-Fran (*101*), or other natural boundary features, it is reasonable to suggest that they are also located on human boundaries. In other cases, such as the re-use of prehistoric monuments, similar claims to land rights may be being made, but not necessarily by placing burials on a boundary location.

SAINTS IN THE LANDSCAPE: AD 800–1100

The same pattern of inscribing the landscape with mythological stories can be seen with references to the Welsh saints. Many landscape features from wells to prehistoric monuments are linked to saints even today. However, it is crucial to be cautious when trying to understand how they relate to the earliest phases of Christianity in Wales. Place-names in particular can be notoriously fluid, and it is clear that sites may develop attributions or links with saints well into the post-medieval period. For example, the hill known as Gallt yr Ancr (Hill of the Anchorite) stands above the important church at Meifod (Montgomeryshire). On this hill lies an earthern mound known as Gwely Gwyddfarch (the bed of Gwyddfarch). Gwyddfarch was a saint with attested links with Meifod. However, whilst it is tempting to interpret Gwely Gwyddfarch as a feature linked to this important pilgrimage centre, it is salutary to note that the mound is in fact a post-medieval rabbit warren; it must have received its name in the seventeenth century or later and thus has little to tell us about early medieval landscapes (Silvester pers.comm).

This does not mean, however, that it is never possible to link landscape features to stories related to saints within an early medieval context. For example, the eleventh and twelfth-century saints' lives regularly make reference to specific locations within the landscape. This can perhaps be seen most explicitly in Rhigyfarch's *Life of St David*. This work makes a clear attempt to localise key events in the saint's life in the landscape around St Davids. It notes that the place where he is conceived by his mother, Nonita, is marked by two large stones (*VD* 4); the hand prints she left in stones during her labour 'identified that stone for those who have gazed upon it. On that spot a church has been built, in the foundations of which this stone lies concealed.' (*VD* 6)

The *Life of St Brynach* is a good example of how important stages in the saint's life were linked to particular places in and around Nevern, his main cult centre. The well where he washed off blood from a wound was known as Fons Rubeus (Red Well) and was clearly still known at the time the Life was written (*VB* 4). He is recorded as driving out evil spirits at Pontfaen (*VB* 5), now the location of a church dedicated to Brynach and the site of two ninth to eleventh-century carved-stone crosses (P86-7). The story of how he came upon the site for the construction of the church at Nevern is told (*VB* 7), whilst his visions of angels are linked to the name of the nearby mountain known as Carn Ingli (Mountain of the Angels) (*VB* 8) and an oak tree is called Bread Oak on account of a miracle performed by the saint (*VB* 14). The author of the saint's life uses the presence in the landscape in and around Nevern of places linked with the Brynach to support his written narrative, whilst the Life perpetuates and consolidates existing oral stories. Places in the landscape and the written text are linked together creating a mutually supporting narrative. In essence, we see the landscapes and saints' lives acting as *de facto* charters tying together the ecclesiastical community of the saint with their landscapes and landholdings. We do not need to believe that these episodes of hagiography have a significant historic basis in fact; for us today, their historicity is in many ways unimportant. The key to understanding the appearance of these natural and manmade features in the *Vitae* is the perceived historicity from a twelfth-century perspective. The presence of these standing stones, wells and place-names in this period was a vital testimony in perpetuating long-standing claims to land, and indirectly, power.

However, in many cases the links between the saints and specific places within the landscape are not clearly embedded in the biography of the holy man or woman, and in some situations appear to be *post hoc* explanations of how a particular monument gained its name. The *Life of St Illtud* describes how two robbers were turned into stone: 'Till now too are seen the immovable stones called by the name "Two Robbers". Believe thou the robbers were changed into hard stones, deservedly remaining so, a witness to their iniquity' (*VSI* 23). This is a good example of how the links between the stories of saints and later locations within the landscape also undoubtedly had a wider moral didactic purpose, usually made explicit in the text. Again, in the *Life of St Illtud*, referring to a marsh which swallowed up an evil steward we hear that 'That same marsh is till now apparent to human sight as a sign of the villainy of an ill doer for his ill deed' (*VSI* 20). In some cases, the appearance of a site in the saint's lives does not appear to even have anything beyond a very tenuous homiletic purpose; the description of the miraculous footprint of a cow in a rock near Caerwent appears to merely an attempt to impose a moral function on a pre-existing natural feature: 'This stone soft to the tread in the midst of it and hollow within, Footprints by the foot of a cow are imprinted in to the view' (*VST* II) There are also a range of features within the landscape which have been linked to the activities of saints despite the lack of written records. At Llanllyfni marks on a rock are believed to be the hoof-print and thumb-print of Saint Gredfyw (Baring Gould and Fisher 1907, 148). The Neolithic long-barrow known as Tŷ Illtud has a series of small crosses, some partly enclosed with diamonds and some with crosslets, carved on its interior. The name of the barrow means 'House of Illtud' and it is likely it had become a site of local devotional practice, and linked in oral traditions to events connected with the saint's life (Briggs 1997; Grinsell 1982).

This topographic tradition of linking specific places in the landscape with particular narratives can also be found in the secular tradition; for example, a number of incidents in the *Fourth Branch of the Mabinogi* are explicitly situated in known places within the Ardudwy, Arfon and the Upper Dee Valley, with particular landscape features, such as the holed rock known as Llech Gronw, acting as a validation of the veracity of the story (Davies 2007; Siewers 2005; Sims-Williams 2001).

Holy Wells

As seen above, a range of landscape features are linked to the lives of saints in the written sources including trees, mountains and prehistoric monuments. However, it is perhaps wells and springs that are most commonly linked to saints in their written Lives and today are still linked with the activity of early saints (Jones 1992; Edwards 1994). In the *Life of St David* a well springs forth at the place where he was baptised, at the site where a wicked woman kills her step-daughter (*VSD* 7), and David himself creates springs where water is lacking on several occasions (*VSD* 18). Cadog gave the hermit Tylywai his *bachall* (stick), which allowed him to make springs for drinking water (*VSD* 33, 44). The importance of using a stick to create springs, an action with clear parallels with Moses, is seen again in the *Vita Sancti Cadoci*, when Cadog creates a well whilst travelling in Cornwall (*VSC* 31). In the description of this act Cadog says 'For if any sick person drink from that fount, trusting firmly in the Lord, he shall receive soundness of belly and bowels, and he will throw up in his vomit all slimy worms out of himself'. This highlights another common

75 St Winefrid's Well, Holywell. Print by Francis Place, 1699. (© Trustees of the British Museum)

aspect of the holy wells, a reputation for performing miraculous cures. For example, Brynach's *Fons Rubeus* was known as a place 'where also in honour of the saint the merciful God bestows many benefits of health on the infirm, the healing of wounds through mediation of the Lord being received without delay' *VSB* 4). This therapeutic aspect can be see at its most extreme in the *Life of St Winefride*, which describes in detail how the spring at Holywell arose following the beheading and miraculous cure of Winefride [Gwenfrewi] and lists the miraculous healings associated with this site (Fig 75. *VSW* 12-14). Whilst some wells were reputed to heal specific ailments, Holywell appears to have been able to tackle a gratifyingly wide range of complaints: 'No less does she remove sciatica, eradicate cancer, cure shorten of breath, extirpate piles. Also she removes a hard cough, repels gripings of the stomach and fluxions, clears repressed menses causing barrenness, stops superfluous and excessive blood.' However, if there is ample textual attestation to the presence of holy wells in the eleventh and twelfth centuries, the archaeological evidence for their use in this period, or indeed earlier, is largely lacking.

Ritual activity at wells could undoubtedly take a range of forms, although it is difficult to tease apart possible early medieval practices from activity of later date. For example, simple cross-marks can be seen incised on the rock close to the holy well just below the church at Patrisow (545); these, although similar to the kind of simple devotional cross known to have been carved on early medieval monuments, are inherently undatable. Excavation on sites, such as Ffynon Degla (Denbighshire), St Seiriol's Well (Penmon, Anglesey) and Ffynnon Beuno, Aberffraw have produced no medieval finds, let alone those of earlier dates (Rees 1935; Edwards 1982; Kelly 1991). Many of the post-medieval rites carried out at wells, such as deposition of pins, rags, thorns and flowers in or near the well are unlikely to have left a significant mark on the archaeological record. Not surprisingly, the holy water derived from wells is likely to have been used for a wide range of therapeutic and apotropaic purposes.

The physical location of wells could vary widely. Some were incorporated into the enclosures of churches, such as at Rhoscrowther; the well of St Decuman is probably situated within a larger enclosure surrounding the present church yard which is preserved in the surviving field boundaries. At Llanfair Caerinion St Mary's well, which has now been incorporated into the churchyard, originally lay just outside the enclosure. The well at Llangybi lies a short distance from the church. When located close to churches it is possible that some wells may have had a baptismal purpose, either as the site of baptisms themselves or as a source for holy water.

Hermitages

In medieval Christianity, the notion of the hermit who seeks isolation to become closer to God is a strong one. The traditions of eremitism and communal monasticism developed hand-in-hand in the deserts of Egypt; both forms of devotional life were known in early medieval Wales. The focus on the physical and spiritual isolation of the hermit meant that hermitages were usually located in remote or difficult to access areas. Most of the best-known examples from Wales are in coastal or island locations, reflecting a wider tradition across the Atlantic world and Anglo-Saxon England (Cramp 1981; Wooding 2007). However, it is not always easy to date these hermitage sites archaeologically. The practice was clearly widespread by the twelfth century, and references to coastal hermitages appear in the hagiographical material. The *Life of St Cadog* records that he would spend time on Barry Island and Flatholm during Lent (VC 18), and Samson spent time on Caldey Island (VSI 20) (Wooding 2007b). An ecclesiastical presence on Caldey is attested by the presence of a relatively late Group 1 inscription from the eighth or ninth century re-using an earlier ogham-inscribed stone (P6). The presence of a fragment of carved stone sundial and inscription from Ramsey Island, opposite St Davids (Pembrokeshire) may indicate an offshore hermitage linked to the main monastery (Edwards 2007).

The best-known offshore religious site in Wales is undoubtedly Bardsey Island (Ynys Enlli). Gerald of Wales wrote of its sanctity in the mid-twelfth century, noting that it was reputed that many holy men were buried there (*Journey* 2.6). He was echoing stories promoted in the *Life of St Elgar* from the Book of Llandaf (LL 1-5). The role of Bardsey as a cemetery for saints was widely promoted in later Welsh medieval literature and oral traditions (Wooding 2007b 223-227). However, it is unclear how early the island became a site of ecclesiastical importance. Burials are known from Tŷ Newydd; these are likely to date to the tenth century (on the basis of an Anglo-Saxon coin of *c*.973) in a grave cut (Arnold 1998). This would place the burials as broadly contemporary with a cross-slab of roughly tenth-century date from the island (RCHMW 1964, 19). According to Gerald the island was the site of a community of *Céli Dé* (*Journey* 2.6), who were also associated with offshore ecclesiastical sites at Ynys Seiriol (just off Penmon) and Ynys Tudwal (off Abersoch (Hague 1960). Interestingly in all three cases, the *Céli Dé* communities were transformed into Augustinian houses.

However, it is important to exercise a little caution in assuming all offshore ecclesiastical activity was eremitical. For example, there was clearly much more activity occurring on Ramsey Island than a simple hermitage (James 1993, 107; Wooding 2007b, 218), whilst a ringed pin from Gateholm Island and imported E ware on Caldey Island may suggest high-status activity of secular or ecclesiastical nature at these sites.

Not all hermitages were associated with coastal or offshore sites. According to the saint's *Vita*, Illtud was believed to have spent time in a cave at Llwynarth (near Oystermouth, Glamorgan) (*VSI* 22) and Samson also sought a cave hermitage (vs1.41). Although actual archaeological evidence for such cave sites is known in Scotland, it is lacking in Wales (Ahronson, Gillies and Hunter 2006). Cadog also searched along the river Neath for a suitable site for hermits and Illtud and his wife made hermitages in the Hodnant valley (*VSC* 20), although again no archaeological evidence for such small, isolated hermitages survive (vsi 5–6). In addition, it is important to remember that these saints' lives were written much later than the events described, and probably borrowed a range of *topoi* from other hagiographical material, so any description of early hermitages derived from them must be treated very carefully.

CASE STUDY: DEWISLAND (FIG 76)

The scale of ecclesiastical landscapes linked to saints could vary widely. The most developed example was probably the network of sites associated with the area around St Davids that came to be known as Dewisland (James 1993; Edwards 2001b), which had a sophisticated sacralised topography consisting of a range of chapels, holy wells, cemeteries and carved stones.

Whatever the precise origins of St Davids as a religious site, it is clear that by the ninth century it was becoming increasingly important on a national scale within Wales as a centre for the cult of David (Wooding 2007a; Isaac 2007). He was known in Ireland, Brittany and Wessex, as well as his native Wales (Edwards 2001b, 55; Evans 2003). Attempts to support claims of metropolitan status saw enhanced promotion of the cult in the eleventh and twelfth century, to which can be linked the production of the *Vita Sancti David* in the late eleventh century. The parish of St Davids comprised the entire cantref of Pebidiog, which later became known as Dewisland. Across this landscape was substantial evidence for the culting of David and the creation of a ritualised space. As noted above, a crucial aspect of this literary work was that it explicitly linked moments in the saint's biography with specific locations within the immediate landscape of St Davids, such as the link between his birth and a particular chapel, probably St Non's chapel about 1km south of the town.

Whilst these traditions first appear to have crystallised in the twelfth century, the presence of a cross-incised stone of seventh or eighth-century date implies it developed as a religious site earlier than this (p100). Other traditions linked the well and chapel called Capel-y-Pistill at Porth Clais to David's baptism. There were also a series of sites connected with Irish saints, including St Patrick's Chapel at Whitesands Bay and Fynnon Faiddog (Fountain of Aidan) nearby. St Davids undoubtedly attracted Irish pilgrims to its shrines. The role of pilgrimage can be seen at Porth Stinan, to the west of the town, where a chapel dedicated to St Justinian was probably a site for pilgrims making the short crossing to the chapels of St Dyfanog and St David on Ramsey Island (Ynys Dewi). Later hagiographical material linked Justinian to St David, claiming he was his confessor (James 1993, 13–14).

It is clear that in addition to the chapels and wells, there were a series of burial sites scattered across the hinterland of St Davids. Intriguingly, the sculptural evidence from one of these sites predates that from St Davids itself, which is all ninth century or later. Early inscribed stones have been found at Carnredhyn Farm (Edwards 2007); the inscription includes the relatively unusual term NOMENA, which appears in this context to have implied relics or physical remains (Edwards 2001b). Most of the cemeteries are recorded as collections of cist graves which cannot be precisely dated beyond a broad medieval date (James 1993). However, a collection of cross-carved stones from the ninth to eleventh century from Pen-Arthur Farm do suggest some kind of early medieval ecclesiastical focus (Edwards 2001b; Edwards 2007). The precise status of this site is unclear, though it appears to have stood on the routeway between the harbour site and chapel at Whitesands Bay and St Davids itself. The quality of the carving suggests that they were clearly significant monuments, and presumably this site had a direct connection with the monastery at St Davids; it may have been another hermitage, complimenting the putative off-shore hermitage on Ramsey Island, or it could have been linked to one of the pilgrimage routes leading to the main shrine.

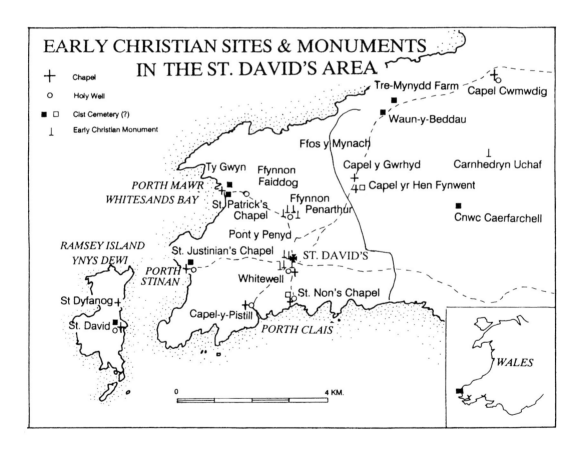

76 Map of Dewisland showing sites linked to St David (from James 1993)

CASE STUDY: PENNANT MELANGELL AND HIRNANT (FIG.77)

Not all religious landscapes were as complex or developed as those around St Davids. In practice, many parts of Wales would have seen the development of small-scale ritualised landscapes, overlapping and existing within the interstices of the existing secular and productive landscapes. Often connected to saints with local rather than regional or national cults, these landscapes would consist of fewer elements, often surviving today only through place-names and traditions, rather than solid archaeological evidence for early cult activity. Obviously place-names and folklore are difficult classes of evidence to deal with, particularly as far as imposing any element of solid chronology. Many of these holy landscapes may only have developed in the later medieval period. However, it is possible to tentatively explore how such ephemeral evidence might be used to create some understanding of these more exiguous and, quite literally, parochial landscapes.

Pennant Melangell and Hirnant are upland parishes located in the upper reaches of the Tanat Valley in Montgomeryshire. Pennant Melangell is best known for its church, important twelfth-century stone shrine and archaeological evidence for a *capel y bedd*. Hirnant, which lies to the south of Pennant Melangell, is less well known. The church, dedicated to Saint Illog contains a little medieval fabric, but was largely rebuilt in the later nineteenth century. However, at both sites the evidence for symbolic importance in the wider landscape is present.

Pennant Melangell was clearly the centre of the cult of St Melangell. The shrine may have been built through the patronage of the nobleman Rhirid Flaidd, who was linked by the poet Cynddelw to the hill known as Moel Dimoel to the south of the church (Jones 1958). Also to the south of the church, is a rock-cut ledge known as Gwely Melangell (Bed of Melangell) (Fig 78). It is tempting to see this feature as a site sanctified by tradition and linked to the story of Melangell. However, it has been suggested that the *gwely* element of the names is in fact a case of folk etymology in action. The word has a semantic range that includes a type of land holding held by a kin group (CPAT nd; Charles-Edwards 1993, 226) and an adjacent field was known as Cae Gwelu. Nonetheless, a crag above this site is called Craig Melangell, perhaps suggesting some kind of longer-standing link between the saint and this location. There are also hints at other ecclesiastical loyalties, with the presence of Craig Llwyn Armon (the crag of Garmon's grove) elsewhere in the parish; Garmon (Germanus) was a saint who had clear links with the kingdom of Powys. On the hillside to the north of the church in Cwm Nantewyn lies a holy well, which was reputed to have cured rheumatism, scrofula and skin diseases (Jones 1992, 202).

Two holy wells are also known in the parish of Hirnant. Ffynnon Isel in the south of the parish on the slopes of Buchel y Foel Ortho was believed to help childhood diseases, whilst Ffynnon Illog on the hill above the church was also a healing well and in the post-medieval period pins were left there as offerings (Jones 1992, 198, 202). Illog was not only remembered in the name of the well and the dedication of the church. According to the eighteenth-century church terrier, the boundaries of the parish to the west of the parish ran 'From Bwlchdu and down to and through Glascwm land and so to Carnedd Illog' (Evans 1880, 46). Carnedd Illog, a stone carin, now destroyed, stood close to a stone called *Carreg y tair Eglwys* (Stone of the Three Churches), where the bells of the churches at Llanwddyn, Llanfihangel and

Hirnant could be heard. After this, the boundary ran from Bwlchgroeslwyd (Pass of the Grey Cross) to Carnedd Bwlchgroeslwyd. Whilst it is not possible to be certain about the precise location of these sites, they are probably in the area of the farm of Ty Croes (Cross House), which lies a few kilometres to the west of the church. The place-names suggest the presence of a stone cross in the general area. At the eastern edge of the parish, the boundary ran 'up the mountain by Fawnog Fawr to Llyn-gloeyw, and so on to Gwely Illog [the bed of Illog]' (ibid.). This clearly echoes the presence of Gwely Melangell in the neighbouring parish.

The extent to which specific places within this remote upland landscape were sanctified is much more limited than that of Dewisland, but in that respect it is probably more typical. Most parishes in Wales are likely to have had a holy well, a stone cross, a cairn or a stone linked in oral tradition to a local saint. The antiquity of such poorly recorded sites is always going to be difficult to ascertain and must remain open. Nevertheless there is no reason to assume that some of these isolated sites may date back to the turn of the first millennium if not earlier.

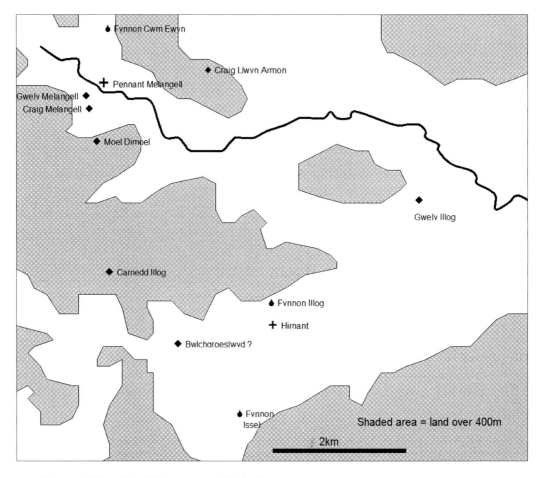

77 Pennant Melangell and Hirnant: a symbolic landscape

78 Rock-cut ledge known as Gwely Melangell (Bed of Melangell), Pennant Melangell (Montgomeryshire). (*Archaeologia Cambrensis* 1894)

STONES AND BOUNDARIES

The landscape of early medieval Wales was increasingly defined by boundaries. The growth of the church as an institution during the second half of the first millennia AD led to changes in the way in which land was held, transferred and defined. In secular society, land was held primarily through kinship groups, rather than by individuals (Charles-Edwards 1993). As in all agricultural societies, control of land was frequently contested at a range of levels, from questioning the ownership of entire blocks of land to haggling over the precise course of boundaries. As seen above, kin groups may well have used burial sites between the fifth and eighth centuries as markers of possession and control.

This practice of land possession by a corporate group meant that the alienation of land was difficult and rare. With the development of monasteries as major participants in politics and society, kings and powerful families wanted to be able to grant them land, incomes and legal rights. As ecclesiastical communities existed outside the existing kinship structures, new mechanisms for controlling the movement and establishment of such grants needed to be put in place. The development of kingship also saw the pressure on monarchs to grant land to individuals rather than family groups to help build up their political power base. The growth of kingship and the increasing importance of monasteries went hand-in-hand; monasteries provided important ideological support to the royal families, who in turn provided protection and economic support. One of the key ways in which these legal and economic relationships were articulated was through the use of written charters. Charters were primarily used to mark temporary or permanent transfers of land, but kings could also grant other privileges, particularly freedom from the tributary obligations required of secular groups and individuals, and the permission to grant the right of sanctuary to those who fled justice. A key element of land charter was that not only did they confirm ownership, but they frequently described the physical limits of a parcel of land in boundary clauses appended to them. These would circumscribe, often in great detail, the precise limits of the area in question; a late twelfth or early thirteenth-century charter defined the land granted as 'all the land and woods from Pulla Hameli [(?) as] the stream there leads west to the highway leads towards Holy Trinity Church near Caerleon and by that highway as the nearer stream falls into the river Usk…' (Pryce 2004, *473*)

Like others in early medieval Welsh society, the church had a range of legal rights, privileges (*braint*) and entitlements (*dylyed*). These included the right to exercise its own legal powers; bishops could exile people and demand penance (Davies 1978, 133; Davies 2003, 68-701). One particular aspect of these privileges was the establishment of zones of sanctuary (*noddfa*) around churches within which individuals were meant to be free from legal or physical threats. This practice of ecclesiastical sanctuary (*nawdd*) was found widely throughout the medieval church; obviously the fact that people could flee the secular legal process by claiming sanctuary meant that the whole process was one that closely involved both lay and ecclesiastical authorities. Whilst there were some elements of this process that applied across Western Christendom, there were also specific expressions of sanctuary rights that were only found in Wales, and there is much emphasis in canon law and local Welsh law on defining the physical and legal limits of sanctuary (Pryce 1993, 163-204).

Thus, as Wales entered the eighth century the clear definition of boundaries and borders in the landscape was becoming increasingly important. As land was becoming alienated from kinship groups and began to be held by churches and individuals, the presence of a family burial ground on a piece of land, whether on a boundary or not, was no longer an effective way of staking a claim to territory. New forms of boundaries, such as those defining *noddfa* and areas where *braint* was applied, began to require definition. Whilst the increased use of charters was a key way in which such boundaries could be defined in law, there was also an enhanced requirement for these boundaries to be marked on the ground. Often the process involved elements of both; for example the *Vita Sancti Cadoci* records the exchange of a piece of land between the community at Nantcarfan and two men called Spois and Rodric for a township called Conguoret (*VSC* 55). It notes that Rodri held a *carta* or *graphium* [a charter] for this grant 'But afterwards Rodri and Spois and his sons came together, Conigc also, and his clergy bought the cross of Saint Cadog and his earth, and going round the aforesaid land of Conguoret, claimed it, and scattered the earth of the aforesaid saint upon it in the presence of suitable witnesses in token of permanent possession'. A similar situation can be found in the Book of Llandaf where a ceremonial perambulation of the property of Llandaf is recorded: 'After these things, the King arose, going around the whole territory, and carrying the gospel-book on his back, with clergy bearing crosses in their hands, together with relics; and sprinkling holy water and the dust from the floor of the church on all the bounds of the territory they perambulated the whole…' (*LL* 71; Davies 2003, 101-111).

It is no surprise then that we find boundaries being marked with stones with a greater frequency than in earlier periods, though as much of the evidence comes from documentary evidence this may be an artefact of the 'textual horizon'. Boundary stones are mentioned in

27 of the Llandaf Charters. Mark Handley has pointed out that although some bear names with no relation to the owner as recorded in the charter, others appear to have been named after the recipient of the grant (Handley 1998, 341). He has suggested that this is a further indication of the continued close relationship between burial sites and boundaries, though the explicit linkage of a stone with a burial site in the charters is very limited. It is possible, indeed probable, that the Maen Brith (Stone of Brith) mentioned in the boundary clause of Charter 190b is the same as the 'grave of Gurai' beginning the boundary clause of its doublet. This could suggest that the 'grave of Gurai' may have been used to mark a boundary, but given the doubt about the date of these boundary clauses, it is also possible that they belong to the ninth or tenth century when burial sites and prehistoric monuments were being mythologised, and the '*sepulcrum*' mentioned is that of a mythological rather than a real historical individual. This can be seen more clearly in a much later charter, granted in 1217 by Hywel ap Iorwerth, which has bounds partly defined by 'the aforesaid road near the dyke below the tombs to the land of the church' (Pryce 2005, *473*).

Stones regularly appear as boundary markers in other Welsh charters and related material. The earliest examples that can be securely dated are the early ninth-century marginalia in the Chad Gospels (Jenkins and Owen 1983). Chad 4 and Chad 6 mention the 'long stone of Gwyddog' (*hirnain guidauc*) and the 'short stone' (*bir main*) respectively in their boundary clause. The former, a monolith of probable prehistoric date still stands (Jones 1972, 313-15). The use of stones as boundary markers is also supported in the Welsh laws, including mentions of boundary stones in the Book of Iorwerth (Jenkins 2000). Crosses, presumably of stone, regularly appear in the charters issued by the Welsh kings in the twelfth century and later. For example, a cross appears in the simple boundary descriptions of the land associated with the church at Trefeglwys by Hywel ab Ieuaf : 'all the land called Bryn Bedwyn from the ditch of the cemetery to the Gleiniant and to the Trannon, and in addition from his own patrimony the land of Tregymer from the cross to the Gleiniant and whatever is contained from the cross in the opposite direction to *Redwastaroth* and again from the same cross to the Trannon and whatever is contained below the aforesaid cross and *Redwastaroth* and waters of the Trannon and the Gleiniant' (Pryce 2005, *3*). In the early thirteenth century a cross is used to define a grant of land to Margam Abbey: '[all the] land of Hafodhalog between the river Kenfig and river Baedan and towards the mountains to the cross near the high road' (Pryce 2005, *473*). This grant incidentally reminds us that crosses could often be placed on key communication routes; a reference to a 'cross, which is on the road known to many' appears in the *Vita Sancti Cadoc.* (VSC 63).

It is noticeable that the earlier charters simply refer to boundary stones, whereas we instead see crosses being referred to in the later charters. Several of the Group 2 cross-incised stones may also have acted as such boundary markers. Although there is nothing inherent in the design or lay-out of such stones that can diagnostically distinguish between the crosses used as burial markers and crosses used as boundaries, it is tentatively possible to identify such crosses on the basis of their position in the landscape, particularly where they are not located within a known churchyard, like the majority of this class of monument. For example, the cross-carved stone at Capel Colman (Pembrokeshire) stands approximately 180m south of the parish church close to a cropmark boundary marking a larger enclosure surrounding the church (P8; Ludlow 2003). One of the stones from Margam may have also marked the boundary of the ecclesiastical enclosure (G79).

The physical extent of *nawdd* or *noddfa* was recorded in a range of documents, and could vary widely in size. These boundaries could clearly be quite extensive: Gerald of Wales notes that some of the major churches offered sanctuary 'as far as the cattle go to feed in the morning and can return in evening' (*Description* 1.18). The *Canu Dewi* describes the *noddfa* of Llanddewibrefi as running 'From Caron with its fair rule, with its purple hue/ From Llyndu, broader was the roused tumult/ As far as Twrch, where the land is bounded by a stone'. It is possible that this stone was the 'longstone of Gwyddog' recorded in Chad 4.

However, the boundaries of most areas of *noddfa* were probably more modest. Canon law prescribed that the area of immunity should be 30 paces from small churches and chapels and 40 paces from larger churches (Pryce 1993, 163). However, the Iorwerth Redaction of the Welsh laws noted that 'Whoever takes sanctuary is entitled to go about in the cemetery and the enclosure (*corflan*) without relics on him ... The dimensions of an enclosure (*corflan*): a legal acre in length, with its end at the cemetery, and that in a circle around the cemetery' (Jenkins 2000, 82.22). The term *corflan* appears to derive from the term *corf* with its meanings of 'defence' or 'boundary' (ibid; Pryce 1993). The *corflan* could also seemingly define the boundary of a form of landholding divided into small strips or quillets, which was again presumably defined with reference to its fixed distance from the cemetery. It is possible that some of the curved enclosure which may be plotted around ecclesiastical centres may in fact be such a *corflan*, rather than the boundaries of the *llan* (cf. Kissock 1997, 132-35). It may have been the boundary of a *corflan* that was implied when one of the Llandaf charters notes the construction of an *ager a refugium* (a sanctuary ditch LL 211).

As noted in an earlier chapter, the carrying of relics could also provide an individual with the protection derived from the right of sanctuary. This can be seen in the *Vita Sanci Wenefredi* when it describes a deacon collecting tithes having 'sacred signs suspended from his neck for protection' (VSW 25) He then reaches the bounds of the estate where thieves 'paying no respect to the martyr or her sacred things' attacked him. Inevitably, the leader of the thieves received his just deserts for this double breach of Gwenfrewi's *nawdd*.

PILGRIMAGE

As in many religions, pilgrimage played an important role in the early Welsh church (Coleman and Elsner 1995; Gray 2001; John and Rees 2002). Motives for going on pilgrimage could be varied, ranging from carrying out the journey for penitential reasons, in fulfilment of a vow, a desire for healing, personal devotional reasons or simply as chance for an individual to travel. Pilgrimages could be short journeys to shrines of only local importance or international voyages to the most significant shrines of Christendom, such as Rome and the Holy Land. Whilst the actual act of travel can be difficult, if not impossible, to capture archaeologically, pilgrimages created their own landscapes and infrastructure providing for the spiritual and practical needs of the pilgrims.

Pilgrims from Wales were certainly heading to international pilgrimage sites in the early middle ages. The *Brut y Tywysogion* records that the kings Cadwaladr ap Cadwallon, Cyngen and Hywel and Bishop Joseph all died in Rome, where they had presumably travelled on pilgrimage. Rome seemed to be the favoured pilgrimage destination and Gerald of Wales noted that 'of all pilgrimages they prefer going to Rome' (*Desc* 1.18) The hagiographical material also records that David, Padarn and Teilo travelled to Rome. Jerusalem appears to have been less frequented, though the *Life of St Cadog* tells a story that the saint went on a journey to Jerusalem, where he took water from the Jordan, which he added to a spring he miraculously brought forth in Cornwall (*VSC* 32). The *Vita Sancti David* also records a visit by David, Teilo and Padarn to Jerusalem, where David was given many relics by the Patriarch of Jerusalem.

Whilst these Lives were not contemporary records of the saint's life, there is nothing inherently implausible about a sixth-century Welsh holy man travelling to Rome or the Holy Land. Two ceramic flasks from the shrine of St Menas in Egypt have been found close to Wales, one from the major coastal site at Meols on the Wirral and another from Preston on the Hill (Cheshire) (Fig 79) (Campbell 2007), indicating links of some form with the eastern Mediterranean. Whilst it has been suggested that these articles were traded indirectly into the area via Anglo-Saxon England, the wider evidence for trade links between Atlantic Britain and the Mediterranean suggest, at the very least, that communication routes to pilgrimage sites in Italy and further east were open and available for use by travellers from Wales. Morgan ap Cadwgan went to Jerusalem in penitence for the murder of his brother in 1129 (*BYT*); a group of Welsh pilgrims also died on their way to Jerusalem in 1144 (*BYT*). In both cases, the dates suggest they were on a traditional pilgrimage, rather than on a crusade.

In addition to pilgrims from Wales heading overseas, pilgrims also travelled into England. Some of the most important medieval pilgrimage sites in England developed relatively late: Walsingham and the shrine of Thomas Becket in Canterbury did not really develop until the twelfth century. The Holy Rood at Chester, which became a major source of devotion for Welsh pilgrims, was probably not in place until the early mid-thirteenth century (Lewis 2005). However, there were other pilgrimage centres in England before this date. Writing in the sixth century, Gildas bemoans the fact that burgeoning Anglo-Saxon power was preventing access to the 'graves and places where they suffered' of early martyrs, particularly naming St Alban, whose shrine was at St Alban's (*De Excidio* 10.2). It is likely that shrines linked to Cuthbert (first Lindisfarne, then Chester le Street and finally Durham), St Chad (Lastingham), St Aethelthryth (Ely) and St Swithun (Winchester) also attracted Welsh pilgrims.

Within Wales there was a well-developed network of national pilgrimage centres. The most important was St Davids which contained the corporeal relics of a number of significant holy men, including David himself and, from 1124, Caradog, as well as other, non-corporeal relics, such as the gospel reputedly written by David and completed by miraculous intervention. Despite its frequent ravaging by Vikings and others, the church of St Davids became the focus of a developed pilgrimage landscape, with a series of subsidiary churches, shrines and ecclesiastical sites in the surrounding area. Its importance was confirmed by the visit of William I on pilgrimage there in 1081. According to William of Malmesbury, who had tried to steal one of St Caradog's fingers whilst on pilgrimage at St Davids, Pope Calixtus II granted an indulgence that made two journeys to St Davids the equivalent of a single journey to Rome (*Gesta* 5.45).

Bardsey was also a key pilgrimage site from the twelfth century onwards. However, it is unclear how much earlier it developed significance as a pilgrimage destination. It was clearly a site of religious activity from at least the tenth century (see above) and presumably earlier. Nonetheless, although Gerald of Wales noted the presence of a community of *Celi Dé* on the island, he did not mention that it was a place of pilgrimage. In the twelfth century the Bishop Urban translated some relics from Bardsey: the teeth of St Elgar and the relics of St Caradog (Davies 2003; LL 5).

Most of the textual evidence for this function for Bardsey is of later medieval date, as have been most of the archaeological finds from the island (John and Rees 2002, 18-19). On the mainland, Aberdaron developed as the key point of departure for pilgrims heading to Bardsey, although again the standing evidence is late. Y Gegin Fawr (The Great Kitchen) traditionally a gathering site for pilgrims is in its current condition of entirely post-medieval date. The additional aisle on the church of St Hywyn, reputedly added to house pilgrims, is of fifteenth-century date.

Holywell, the holy well and chapel associated with Saint Gwenfrewi, also became first a regional and then national pilgrimage centre. Once again though, the evidence for the antiquity of the cult is unclear. The corporeal relics of the saint were kept at Gwytherin until they were translated to Shrewsbury Abbey in 1138 (Edwards and Gray Hulse 1994). The shrine and well at Holywell only emerges into the historical record in the late eleventh century, with the writing of the saint's Life and the granting of the well and chapel to the monastery of St Werburgh in Chester by Countess Adeliza in 1093. Her son, Earl Richard, was attacked by the Welsh when going there on pilgrimage in 1119. However, Gerald of Wales made no mention of the shrine when staying at Basingwerk abbey, in the immediate locality, in the mid-twelfth century, suggesting that the pilgrimage tradition was still very under-developed at this stage.

In general, it appears that the major high medieval pilgrimage sites of Wales, apart from St Davids, developed relatively late. The major Marian pilgrimage site at Penrhys appears to have only become established in the fifteenth century, reflecting the growth of the cult of

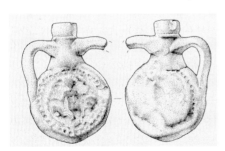

Above left: 79 Flask of St Maenas, Egypt. Found at Meols (Cheshire). Drawn by Mark Faulkner. (Used by permission of the Meols Project)

Above right: 80 Inscribed crosslets on the chambered tomb of Tŷ Illtud. (from Grinsell 1981)

81 Crosslets carved on stone built into Meifod church, possibly connected to pilgrimage activity. (Author's photograph)

Mary in this period (Gray 1996; Williams 1962, 491). However, if these large national pilgrimage sites only developed in the eleventh century or even later, it is far more certain that there was pilgrimage at a more regional level. For example, Meifod, one of the major monasteries of Powys would have attracted pilgrims to its two major relics, including a crosier decorated with gold rivets (*Canu Tysilio* ll.65). There is some physical evidence for this pilgrimage. A stone carved with a series of small crosslets is built into a window on the south wall of the south aisle (Fig 81). Early pilgrims may well have created such informally carved or scratched crosses. Similar examples are found carved into the chambered tomb at Tŷ Iltud, which may have been a focus for small-scale devotional activity connected to the saint (Fig 80). They are also found on the stone known as Maen Dewi (David's Stone) near Fishguard, where they may be connected with one of the pilgrimage routes to St Davids (P16). A number of small crosses are also found on a cross slab at Llawhaden, where the church is dedicated to the Irish saint, Aidan of Ferns, recorded in the *Vita S. David* as one of the Saint's key disciples (P55-6). Although now built into the church structure, it is possible that this was the cross referred to in a *Life of St Aidan*, which records that Aidan marked the spot where he had seen David standing (Baring-Gould and Fisher 1907, 118-9; James 2007, 58).

It is certain that there were also many pilgrim sites of lesser importance. The intimate relationship between the veneration of relics and pilgrimage would have meant that almost any church which contained relics would have acted as a pilgrimage site, even if only at a very local scale. The whole notion of pilgrimage would have elided into veneration and celebrations at a parochial scale. The celebrations attached to the feast of the local saints' days, known later as *gwylmabsantau* ('the patron saints' festival'), would have attracted people from the locality and perhaps further afield, both for the secular celebrations and the religious dimension of the festivities (for later activities at these events see Suggett 1996). It is one of these festivities that Gerald of Wales was probably describing when he wrote of great crowds assembling at the church of St Eluned on her feast day (*Journey* 1.2).

CHAPTER SEVEN

THE EARLY MEDIEVAL CHURCH IN WALES: AN OVERVIEW

In the previous chapters of this book a range of evidence for the early church in Wales has been explored, highlighting what is known, but also marking the limits of our knowledge. This concluding chapter will take these individual threads and weave them together to present a more holistic overview of the development and growth of Welsh Christianity. Inevitably, this discussion will introduce more speculation and inference than has been found in previous chapters, but by building on the data presented earlier, it will attempt to develop a chronological framework for the understanding of the Welsh church and place it in its spatial and temporal context.

'CHRIST MADE A PRESENT OF HIS RAYS': THE CHURCH IN ROMAN WALES

In Anglo-Saxon England the basic process of conversion is reasonably well understood, primarily through the narrative presented in Bede's *Ecclesiastical History*. Whilst Bede is undoubtedly an incomplete narrator, his work does at least offer a broad chronological overview of the spread of Christianity amongst the English. There is, however, no complimentary broadly contemporary history outlining the spread of the church in Wales.

The assumption is usually that the process of conversion was rapid and widespread and took place swiftly in the first half of the fifth century. Certainly by the time that Gildas was writing in the early sixth century, he saw no need to assert the presence of paganism in his jeremiad against the rulers of Britain. They may have been bad Christians, but he never suggests that they were pagan. As a churchman and a highly critical observer, it seems unlikely that Gildas would have missed the opportunity to highlight the continuity of paganism if it had been present.

It is also noticeable that in his historical introduction to the *De Excidio* he places the moment 'Christ made a present of his rays' to Britain was in the last years of the rule of the Emperor Tiberius (AD 14–37 *DE* 9). He suggests mistakenly that Tiberius himself was Christian, and was in opposition to a pagan senate. He follows this with a record of the persecutions under Diocletian and records Britain's martyrs. Once these purges had ceased,

Gildas stated that the church went through a golden period, when 'all her sons exulted, as though warmed in the bosom of the mother church' (DE 12.2).

There is also a general lack of conversion narratives in the hagiographic material. Whilst the majority of the existing material is of a much later date, it does not appear to record any earlier traditions, and the saints appear to have operated in a mainly Christian milieu. One of the few exceptions to this can be found in the earliest surviving saint's life, the *Vita Samsonis*, which records the saint travelling in Cornwall, where he comes across a group of men performing a play before a stone idol and after performing a miracle baptises them (*VS* 1.48–50). However, even if one accepts that there is a kernel of truth here, the case is in fact one of re-conversion following apostasy rather than conversion *de novo*.

This limited documentary evidence all points towards a similar conclusion – the conversion of Wales to Christianity has its roots firmly in the initial spread of Christianity in Roman Britain, not through later periods of missionary activity. This is not to suggest that the whole area was converted at the same time or in the same way. Conversion is a complex process, the conversion of kings and rulers, whether for purely religious motives or as an exercise in *realpolitik,* is unlikely to have equated in a simple way to the direct conversion of their subjects (see Mayr-Harting 1991; Higham 1997; Pluskowski and Patrick 2003). Even when records of mass baptisms are made, it is highly debateable whether such religious spectacles would have led to any fundamental ideological or ritual re-alignment of the participants.

A truly detailed understanding of the process of the spread of Christianity in Wales in the Roman and early post-Roman period is beyond the level of historical and archaeological evidence available. However, it is possible to make some broad inferences about the process. The Emperors Constantine and Licinius issued the Edict of Milan in AD 313, which allowed religious toleration within the Empire, ending the persecution of Christianity. Alongside the conversion of Constantine himself, this led to an expansion of the Church across the Empire. Almost all of the archaeological evidence for Christianity in Roman Britain dates to the fourth century (Petts 2003). The Church was undoubtedly present in Britain before this point, and the persecution of Christians took place prior to the fourth century. The best-known example is the martyrdom of Alban at St Albans, which is most likely to have taken place in the third century AD. Of more relevance to our subject is the martyrdom of Julius and Aaron at Caerleon, which was recorded by Gildas (*De Excidio* 2.10). This indicates the presence of a small Christian community in the town in the Roman period (Knight 2001a; Sharpe 2002; Stephens 1985). Whilst the cult of the two martyrs is attested in Caerleon in the early medieval period, it is not clear how far there was direct continuity between the community in which Julius and Aaron practiced their faith and later Christian cult activity at the site.

Administratively, the diocese (the term diocese at this period having no religious connotations) of Britannia was divided into four provinces; Wales was within the province of Britannia Prima, which probably had its capital in Cirencester. The pattern of Roman control over this province was not even. Most of the central and eastern portions of the territory were administered through a network of *civitates*, subdivisions notionally based on the territories of the pre-Roman tribes. These *civitates* were centred on Roman towns. Whilst the precise boundaries are unclear, the key urban foci in Wales were Carmarthen (Moridunum), the capital of the Demetae, and Caerwent (Venta Silurum), the capital of the Silures (Arnold and Davies 2000, 45-57; James 1993; Brewer 1993). In addition to the tribal capitals, the other major town was Caerleon (Isca Silurum), the legionary headquarters of the Second Legion Augusta. There were also small towns and roadside settlements at Abergavenny, Usk, Monmouth, Cowbridge and possibly Cardiff (Arnold and Davies 2000, 62-3; Burnham and Wacher 1990, 296-300). This network of *civitas* capitals and other urban centres ran from Gwent, along the southern coastal strip of Glamorgan, to eastern Dyfed.

The eastern border of modern Wales was also marked by a series of Roman towns running from Gloucester (Glevum), through Weston-under-Penyard (Ariconium), Kenchester (Magnis), Leintwardine (Bravonium), Wall (Letocetum), Wroxeter (Viriconium) and Chester (Deva). However, beyond the Marches and the southern coastal zone, most of Wales was administered directly through the army, rather than devolved down to the *civitates*. In practice this meant that the main official Roman presence was a network of the roads and forts. By the fourth century, many of these forts, particularly within the heartland of Wales had fallen out of use, although there were new fortifications constructed at Caernarfon (*Segontium*) and Holyhead. This building reflected the new threat of raiding from Ireland. Within this military area, there were no Roman towns and few substantial civilian settlements. This contrast between the areas of Wales governed through *civitates* and their towns, and those controlled by the military is a key one in understanding the way in which Christianity spread in Wales in the fourth and early fifth centuries.

In the Roman world, Christianity was initially a firmly urban religion, indeed the word 'pagan' is derived from the Latin *pagani*, meaning simply 'country dweller'. Consequently, the church was administered through a network of bishops based in urban centres, who would have had authority over the Christians within the town itself and the surrounding district. We have historical evidence for bishops in Roman Britain from the proceedings of the council of Arles (the *Acta Concilii Arelatensis*), which took place in AD 314. The reading of this list is slightly corrupt, but probably reads:

Eborius episcopus de civitate Eboracensi provincia Brittania

Restitutus episcopus de civitate Londiniensi provincia suprascripta

Adelphius episcopus de civitate Colonia Londiniensium

Exinde Sacerduss presbyter Arminius diaconus

Eborius was Bishop of York (*Eboracum*) and Restitus was Bishop of London. The other identifications are less clear. *Colonia Londiensium* may have been either Colchester or Lincoln, with opinion favouring the latter. York, London and Lincoln were probably the provincial capitals of the diocese of Britain; London was the capital of Maxima Caesariensis, York was probably the capital of Flavia Caesariensis and Lincoln the capital of Britannia Secunda. On this basis, the final group, Sacerdus, a priest, and Arminius, a deacon, may well have represented Britannia Prima, which is otherwise without representation. It is possible that the province was temporarily without a bishop at this time. Any bishop would presumably have been based in Cirencester, the provincial capital.

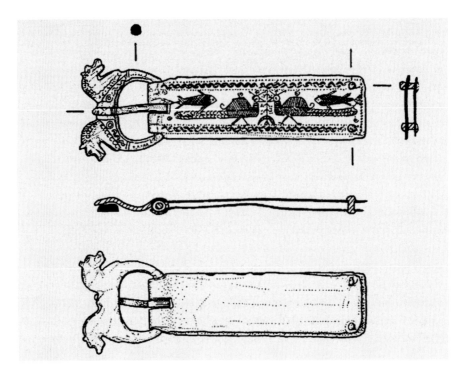

82 Late Roman belt-buckle from Pen-y-Corddyn, Abergele. (© Tim Morgan)

It is not clear whether these were the only bishops in Roman Britain. It is possible to take a minimalist view and see the British contingent at Arles as including the entire episcopal body in Britain. However, it is equally possible that they were in fact representing the other bishops within their provinces, and that they had some form of metropolitan status. It is also important to remember that this list dates to only one year after the Edict of Milan. The state approval of Christianity is likely to have led to the expansion of the Christian community in Britain and the establishment of more episcopal seats during the fourth century. Whilst it is not possible to be certain of the precise location of these putative additional episcopal seats, it is certain that they too would have been centred on Roman towns. Circumstantial evidence from a series of sites along the Welsh borders and in the West Midlands suggests that there were a series of early medieval dioceses that preceded the arrival of the Anglo-Saxon church in this area, and which provided the framework on which later Anglo-Saxon ecclesiastical administrative structures were built. By mapping the earliest known parish and minster boundaries associated with churches in this area, it has been suggested that Gloucester, Worcester, Wall, Leominster and Wroxeter were all the foci of pre-Anglo-Saxon dioceses (Bassett 1991; Bassett 1992a, 1992b; Hillaby 2001). It is almost certainly Wall which was referred to in the seventh-century *Marwnad Cynddylan*, which recorded a raid on Caer Lwytgoed (*Letocetum* = Wall) and the destruction of the 'chief bishop wretched in his four-cornered house' and the 'book-keeping monks' (Williams 1935, 50-52; Rowland 1990, 181).

All these towns had Roman origins and it is likely that the associated diocesan structures also had a fourth-century origin.

The historical arguments for a network of late Roman dioceses along the eastern border of Wales can be supplemented by the limited archaeological evidence for Roman Christianity in Wales. Not surprisingly, there is no structural evidence for any churches of Roman date, but there are a number of artefacts indicating the practice of Christianity. A Roman silver spoon traced only to Monmouthshire bears a small, inscribed *chi-rho* symbol and an alpha and omega, as well as traces of a personal name. It is clearly Christian and similar to a number of other spoons of Christian identity from late Roman Britain (Mawer 1995, 45-56; Sherlock 1976, 235-7; Petts 2003). In 1906 a pewter dish was found in a pit cut through the floor of a room in House VIIN in Caerwent. The pit also contained seven late Roman pottery vessels and a knife. On the base of the pewter dish a graffiti *chi-rho* symbol had been crudely scratched (Mawer 1995). A bronze buckle carrying two confronting peacocks, with fish above each of their tails was found in disturbed ground on the hillfort at Pen-y-Corddyn, near Abergele (Clwyd) (Burnham 1993). (Fig 82). A similar strap-end, also decorated with a peacock, was found at Kenchester (Magnis) (Mawer 1995). The use of the peacock on such items is diagnostically Christian, and indicates a broad Christian affiliation of their wearers (Petts 2003). This limited artefactual evidence is confined to the civilian zone within Wales and corresponds to the broad zone of Roman urbanism in the south and east of the country.

'WONDERFUL THINGS ARE FOLLOWED BY THINGS MORE WONDERFUL': THE CHURCH IN WALES AD 400-700

Thus, as the Roman Empire ceded control of Britain to its own inhabitants in the early fifth century, Christianity was already in place in Wales, although limited to areas that had been governed through the system of *civitates* based on the Roman urban network. In most of central, northern and far western Wales the church had yet to make any real impression; however, we know from the testimony of Gildas that within 150 years the rest of the country had been converted. How did this process take place and what hard archaeological evidence is there for it?

It is clear that a diocesan structure was rapidly established (Fig 84). Two stones from north-west Wales make reference to individuals with the title *sacerdos*. A stone from Bodafon (Caernarvonshire) is inscribed simply 'SANCTINVS SACER[DOS] IN P[ACE]' (Sanctinus *sacerdos* in Peace) (Fig 83) (*83*), whilst a more extravagant epitaph from Capel Bronwen, Llantrisant, Anglesey is translated as '-)iva (PN), a most holy woman, lies here, who was the very loving wife of Bivatig(irnus) (PN), servant of God, *sacerdos*, and disciple of Paulinus, by race a (-)docian, and an example to all his fellow citizens and relatives both in character (and) in rule of life, (as also) of wisdom (which is better) than gold and gems (or gold from gems)' (*33*). The term *sacerdos* is a specifically Christian term, though there can be some debate as to its precise meaning. We have already seen it in the excerpt from the Council of Arles, where it has a meaning distinct from *episcopus* (bishop). However, in the early medieval period, the semantic range of the term could be extended to include 'bishop' (Davies 1978). This appears to indicate the presence of bishops in this part of Wales by the mid-sixth century. It is likely that as it was the site of his burial, Bodafon was also the location of Sanctinus' seat, whereas the Llantrisant stone records the burial of the Bivatigirnus's wife, and the site may not have had a direct link to the bishop. Another bishop from the north-west is known from histori-cal sources; the *Annales Cambriae* records the obit of s.a. 584, of 'Daniel of the Bangors', who is recorded in the Irish Martyrology of Tallaght as 'Deiniol, bishop of Bangor' (Lawlor and Best 1931). Potentially, this indicates at least three different episcopal sees in Gwynedd in the fifth and sixth centuries AD. There may be a number of explanations for this. One possibility is that these dioceses existed at different times with relatively little chronological overlap. The presence of a see based at a particularly site need not be a long-term arrangement. They distribution of sees is likely to have reacted to the ebb and flow of dynastic power struggles, with completing dynasties struggling to exert control over sources of ecclesiastical as well as secular power. However, evidence from the south-west may suggest an alternate explanation for these multiple bishoprics.

A section within the twelfth-century lawbooks *Llyfr Blegywryd* and *Llyfr Cyfnerth* discusses the 'seven bishop houses of Dyfed' (Charles-Edwards 1971). This records a series of churches: Mynyw (Pebidiog), Llan Ismael (St Ishmael's), Llan Degeman (Rhoscrowther), Llan Teulydawc (Old Carmarthen), Llan Teilaw (Llandeilo Llwydarth), Llan Geneu (in Clydai) and Llan Ussyllt (St Issell's?). This broadly equates to one 'bishop-house' for each cantref. Thomas Charles-Edwards has argued that this material records the state of affairs in Dyfed at some point before the ninth century. There are a number of possible ways of interpreting this arrangement. One

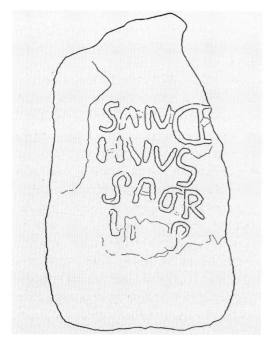

83 Inscribed stone at Bodafon (Caern.) recording possible bishop (*sacerdos*)

possibility is that the bishop houses are key estates centres controlled by a single bishop. In Wales, kings would have had a manor (*maenor*) in each cantref, which acted as a demesne farm, providing resources for the royal court. Frequently, the royal household would have journeyed on a circuit around its territories moving from manor to manor exploiting their resources. It is possible that with the bishop-houses we have something similar in operation, with a series of key estates, one in each cantref, for the support of the bishop. However, it is clear from the Llandaf charters that major ecclesiastical sites could be the recipients of extensive gifts of lands and food renders, across large areas of land, and certainly more extensive than one estate per cantref. A more likely alternative is that these bishop houses are the remains of a system, which had one bishop for each cantref. It is probable that the cantrefs were in origin *tud* (small kingdoms) which each had their own bishop. This arrangement parallels the structure in Ireland, where each *túath* (kingdom/people) also had its own bishop (*ibid.*). It is probable that a similar situation was being replicated in Dyfed. This appears to be confirmed by a reference made by Aldhelm (*c.*639–709), Abbot of Malmesbury, in a letter to Geraint of Dumnonia, in which he refers to the 'sacerdotes of the Demetae' (i.e. Dyfed) (*Aldhelm*). Again, in this case, *sacerdotes* appears to imply 'bishops'. Thus, whilst the evidence is undoubtedly sparse and difficult to interpret, it appears that in both north-west and south-west Wales there was a multiplicity of relatively small dioceses, probably co-terminous with cantrefs or their early equivalent.

This contrasts with the pattern in south and south-east Wales where the network of bishops is likely to have been more dispersed (Davies 2003). The best-attested early bishop is Dyfrig. Although later closely associated with the territory of Ergyng in south-west Herefordshire, this link is likely to have been late and related to the attempt by the diocese of Llandaf to assert its primacy in the region (Davies 2002). He first appears in the eighth-century *Vita Samsonis*, which places his floruit in the late fifth or early sixth century AD, and links him to the monastery of Llantwit Major. He was active as far west as Caldey Island (Davies 2003, 10). This suggests his area of jurisdiction may have covered much of Glamorgan and Carmarthenshire, and it has been suggested that his seat was situated at the Roman town of Caerwent (ibid).

Another important episcopal centre in the south was Llandeilo Fawr in the valley of the river Tywi upstream from Carmarthen, although it is not clear precisely when it first took this role. One of the bishop-houses of Dyfed was located at *Llan Teulydawc* (most likely the Priory of St John and St Teulyddog, Carmarthen) downstream from Llandeilo (James 2007). It is possible that it only became the seat of a bishop following the eclipse of *Llan Teulydawc*, possibly in the seventh or eighth century. It was certainly the home of a bishop by the ninth century, when *Nobis episcopus Teiliau* is recorded in one of the ninth marginal inscriptions in the Lichfield Gospel.

Whilst the evidence is patchy and difficult to interpret it is probable that the diocesan network in Wales grew in the fifth and sixth centuries, extending from the sub-Roman sees based in former Roman towns (Fig 84). It is possible to suggest tentatively that the density of bishops in the south-west and north-west was greater than in the east of the country, with bishops associated with individual cantrefs, rather than larger territorial structures. Due to the lack of urban centres in the west, it is likely that they were based within monasteries, although distinct from the post of abbot; a similar pattern appears to have prevailed in Ireland (Sharpe 1984).

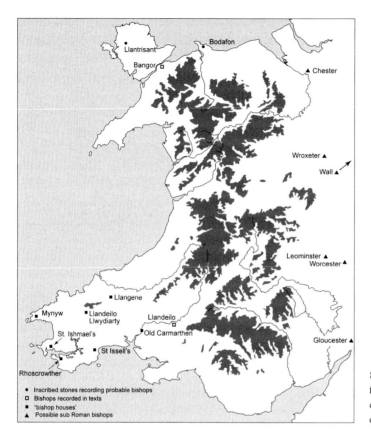

84 Locations of probable fifth- to seventh-century dioceses in Wales. (Map drawn by Yvonne Beadnell)

However, this should not be taken to imply a hard contrast between a church in the west that was firmly monastic as opposed to an urban church in the east. In the west, as noted above, one of the bishop houses, *Llan Teulydawc*, was probably associated with the Roman town at Carmarthen, whilst there is clear evidence for significant monastic sites in the east of Wales. We know, for example, from the *Vita Samsonis* that there was a monastery at Llantwit Major from the sixth century and archaeological evidence suggests that Llandough was an ecclesiastical centre from the fifth century (Holbrook and Thomas 2006). Whether located in former Roman towns or in rural monastic sites, the diocesan network was part of a wider distribution of monastic sites across Wales.

Bede's record of the Battle of Chester in the early seventh century attests to a large monastery at Bangor-on-Dee. Other monastic sites emerge through the epigraphic material. The two stones from Capel Anelog, near Aberdaron on the Llŷn peninsula record the burials of the priests Veracius and Senacius, the latter buried 'with a multitude of his brothers' (*77, 78*). It is possible that some sites which were later important monastic sites, but which have produced Group 1 stones may also have earlier origins (e.g. Merthyr Mawr in Glamorgan; St Dogmaels and Nevern in Pembrokeshire; Llandeilo Fawr in Carmarthan; Llanddewi brefi in Cardiganshire). It is also probable that many of the other major monasteries that emerged in the historical record in the eighth century onwards may also have been founded in this earlier period, but the silence of the historical record and the limited evidence from the archaeology and epigraphic material make this hard to prove. Nonetheless, it is probable that the overall distribution of ecclesiastical sites was relatively limited; even at its densest probably no more than one major church in each cantref or equivalent territorial unit.

It is certain that there was no extensive pastoral provision in these early centuries of Christianity; this can be seen most clearly through the burial evidence. The Group 1 stones are rarely associated with sites that later become churches, they carry little explicit Christian iconography and there is little reference to the belief in the epigraphic formulae used. However, the members of the religious communities themselves would have been buried within formally defined Christian cemeteries. The cemetery population from Llandough includes women and children; it is possible that they belonged to groups of individuals who were in some form of client or dependant relationship with the monastery, perhaps parallel to the Irish 'paramonastic' *manaig* (Etchingham 2006). It is probable that there was some limited preaching and sacramental provision; an early sixth-century letter to two Breton priests, Louocat and Catihern, makes mention of portable altars, which reminds us that the construction of a formal church need not be necessary for the celebration of the Eucharist (Howlett 1995, 69). Nonetheless, there is certainly no indication of any formalised network of mother churches, let alone a parochial system, this early.

Virtually nothing is known about the physical structure and layout of these earliest ecclesiastical centres. The only site that has produced any datable evidence for religious activity at this date, apart from the presence of carved stones, is Llandough, and even here it is limited to burial evidence. The archaeological evidence for structures or churches is entirely lacking. On analogy with Anglo-Saxon England and early medieval Ireland, one would expect such key monastic sites to be located within large enclosures, usually, but not always, curvilinear. This is supported by the probable later boundaries of key sites with early origins, such as Llandough. Even this must be treated with caution, as ecclesiastical boundaries were not static and could move over time (Petts 2002a; Petts and McOmish 2008).

It is possible to draw some general conclusions about the location of these early monastic sites within their physical and social landscapes. Riverine or coastal locations are common; Llandough lies above the river Ely near the coast, Llandeilo on the Tywi, Bangor (Clywd) is on the Dee, whilst St Davids, Bangor, Llantwit Major and Capel Anelog are close to the coast. This seems to indicate the importance of good access and communication. They are all also located in proximity to good agricultural land. These early foundations are not remote hermitages, but ideally placed for ease of transport and access to plentiful economic resources. Many other major ecclesiastical sites of later date, such as Margam and Merthyr Mawr, Tywyn, Meifod, Glasbury and Llanbadarn Fawr are also similarly located. This broad pattern is paralleled in south-west England, where key early monastic sites were also commonly located in valley bottoms and often close to major rivers or the coast (Blair 1992; Turner 2006, 40-48).

The central location of important ecclesiastical sites appears to be replicated with reference to their socio-political context. This can be seen most clearly at Llandough, which was constructed just over 2km from the fortified hillfort of Dinas Powys, occupied from the fifth to seventh centuries, and through which the Mediterranean imported ceramics found at

Llandough were probably redistributed (Knight 2006; Alcock 1963). Bodafon, the site of the stone recording *sacerdos* Sanctinus is close to Deganwy, a refortified hillfort which has produced early medieval imports (*83*; Alcock 1967). Llantwit Major lies close to the major court or *llys* of the kings of Glamorgan at Llysworney, although the latter site has not produced any evidence for particularly early (fifth–seventh century) activity (Richards 1960). Intriguingly, both Llandough and Llantwit Major lie close to the sites of Roman villas. It has been suggested that the monasteries grew out of late Roman house churches centred on the villa, but there is no solid evidence to substantiate such suggestions (Knight 2006).

The process by which these monastic sites were founded is unclear. For a long time, the main model for this earliest phase of conversion and missionary activity was drawn from two sources, the twelfth century hagiographic material and the evidence for church dedications (e.g. Bowen 1954; Chadwick 1954; Zimmer 1902; see Wooding 2007b). This model proposed that there was no continuity from the Romano-British church in this period, with Christianity in the west being introduced by Gaulish missionaries (Radford 1966; 1971). The thesis proposed that these holy men moved through along the Atlantic seaways spreading Christianity. Subsequent Insular converts then continued the missionary activity by founding new monasteries, which often formed confederations based around devotion to a founding father.

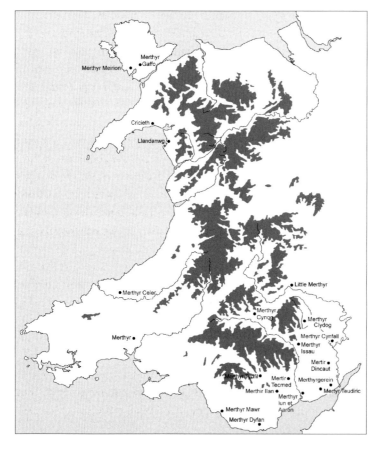

85 Location of known *merthyr* sites in Wales. (Map drawn by Yvonne Beadnell)

The argument for the non-British origin of these missionaries was buttressed by the presence of Mediterranean imported potteries in these areas; crucially one of the greatest assemblages of this material was at the coastal site of Tintagel (Cornwall) which was long interpreted as a monastic site (it is now subsequently generally accepted as a secular power centre) (e.g. Radford 1971). The perceived parallels between the British early medieval epigraphic traditions and similar material from west and southern France was also a key plank in the argument for a southern Gaulish source for the reintroduced faith. However, it has now become clear that there is no simple relationship between the distribution of the imported wares and the spread of Christianity, and that they in fact come from a much wider range of sources over a longer period of time than was originally appreciated. A greater understanding of the epigraphic material has also demonstrated that although there are parallels between Insular British and continental epigraphic traditions, these are not specific to southern Gaul (Wooding 2007b, 214-8). We no longer need to look abroad for the earliest phases of missionary activity in western and northern Wales. Whilst, there were undoubtedly contacts between Wales, Gaul and the wider Late Antique Mediterranean world in this period, it need not be adduced as the key or only conduit through which Christianity reached the non-Romanised areas of the country. It is more likely that Christianity arrived in two ways, both directly from the south and east of Wales – areas likely to already have had a network of diocese and monasteries – and perhaps also via Ireland, which was itself undergoing the process of conversion and had close physical and political contacts with south-west Wales in particular.

The arguments for the subsequent phase of site foundation was based on narratives in the saints' lives and buttressed by the distribution of churches dedicated to particular saints. However, it is now clear that the use of this hagiographic material in a positivist way to write a narrative of the spread of Christianity is not a valid approach to these documents. There is now a far better appreciation of the manner in which churches came to be dedicated to a particular saint (see Jones 2008). The distribution of particular dedications is unlikely to reflect the actual activity of the named individual. Instead sites might receive a dedication to a particular saint for a range of reasons. It might show that a newly established site was a daughter house of the home community of the saint; alternatively a saint might become the patron saint of a dynasty or kingdom and thus be actively promoted. For example, dedications to Tysilio are common in Powys; this does not reflect the movements of the saint himself, but rather than fact that he became associated with the kingdom at a later date, and his cult was nurtured by the royal lines in this area through the development of his cult centre at Meifod and patronage of sites dedicated to him.

Links between key saints and particular groups of churches were also created through the hagiographical material and other documentary resources. For example, traditional readings of the Book of Llandaf have led to the association of the sixth-century historical figure of Dyfrig (Dubricius) with the churches of Ergyng region in south-east Herefordshire. However, it has more recently been suggested by John Reuben Davies that this link was in fact propagated by the Bishops of Llandaf (Davies 2003, 80-4). It is only in the Book that he is associated with Ergyng region; earlier references suggest his main area of activity was further west. It appears that his cult had been resurrected by Llandaf and moved eastwards to allow the *familia* to demonstrate links with this contentious border region, where both the bishopric of St Davids and *Clas Cynidr* were also probably vying to cultivate their sphere of influence.

With the lack of stratigraphically secure and firmly dated archaeological evidence and the difficulty in using documentary evidence, it is problematic to construct an alternative narrative for the conversion of western and northern Wales. One final source of information that may offer a little light is the place-name evidence. In general, Welsh place-names are not as well studied as English place-names. Nonetheless there is a stratum of names related to ecclesiastical places that have Latin rather than Welsh or English origins (Roberts 1992). Apart from the unique use of the Latin word *basilica* as a place-name element forming the name of the parish Basaleg in Monmouthshire, the two key Latin borrowings were 'merthyr' from *martyrium* and 'eglwys' from *ecclesia* (church). It is most likely that *martyrium* in this context implies 'a place possessing the physical remains of a martyr which acquired the sense of a church, or a cemetery, holding the remains of a named saint or martyr (Thomas 1971, 89).

Names using this term are found across Wales in both areas of probable continuity of Christianity from the Roman period, such as Merthyr Mawr, Merthyr Dyfan and Merthyr Tydfil (all in Glamorgan), Merthyr Cynog (Breconshire), but also crucially in areas in the north and west of the country, for example Merthyr Meirion (now Llanfeirian) and Merthyr Caffo (now Llangaffo) in Anglesey. The shrine of the martyrs Julian and Aaron at Caerleon, mentioned by Gildas, appears in the Llandaf charters as Merthyr Julii and Aaron (Fig 85). 'Eglwys' names are also found across Wales; including the west (Eglwys Cain, now Llangain, Carmarthenshire), the north-west (Eglwys Ail, now Llangadwaladr in Angelsey; Heneglwys, Anglesey) and the north-east (Eglwys-rhos, Clwyd). The Latin origin of these names and the fact that they are often subsequently replaced by names using '*llan*' suggest that they belong to an early stratum of ecclesiastical place-names in Wales. Both '*merthyr*' and '*eglwys*' names are usually found with a personal name (Roberts 1992). If we accept the early date of these names, it suggests the presence of early ecclesiastical sites associated with the graves of important holy individuals. To this limited extent we can see that the earliest ecclesiastical sites may have been founded by these holy men. However, it is noticeable that the figures associated with these *merthyr* sites rarely become the figures of more extensive cult devotion and subsequent church dedications.

In conclusion, our model of conversion in the west and north of Wales must remain a simple one. It is probable that the role of individual holy men was key in establishing new monasteries, which on their death and burial became a centre of a limited devotional cult. The foundation of these sites would have been constrained by the socio-political contours of local society, as suggested by the probable presence of a bishop for each *tud*. This arrangement contrasts with the process in the south and east of Wales, where Christianity was more likely to have shown direct continuity from the Roman period, and was probably structured on the remains of the Roman urban infrastructure, with relatively large dioceses, which can be broadly equated to the *civitas* and *pagus* structure of late Roman Britain. Within this diocesan structure, based on a Roman predecessor, there was nonetheless a spread of monastic sites, founded by key early churchmen. Across the country, the wider evidence of a strong relationship between the church and local elites is shown by the frequent pairing of ecclesiastical sites with secular power centres.

'THERE IS A CHURCH OF WHICH IT IS VERY PLEASING TO UTTER': THE CHURCH IN WALES AD 700–1000

If the earliest years of the early medieval church in Wales are difficult to interpret due to the intransigence of the historical and archaeological record, its contours become easier to discern from the eighth century onwards. The documentary record increases rapidly and the nature and quantity of the surviving archaeological data improves. The changing nature of this evidential base is itself a consequence of profound transitions in the structure of the Christian church and its associated activities in this period. The eighth to eleventh centuries saw the Church transform itself both as a religious body and a social and economic power.

Bishops

The diocesan organisation of Wales continued to change and develop into the eighth century (Fig 86). In the north-west, Bangor appears to have consolidated its position as key bishopric for Gwynedd. It is not clear whether any subsidiary bishops were in place. The *Annales Cambriae* provides an obit for Elfoddw of AD 809. He is described as '*archiepiscopus in Guenedote regione*' (Archbishop in the region of Gwynedd). This suggests he may have had suffragans within the

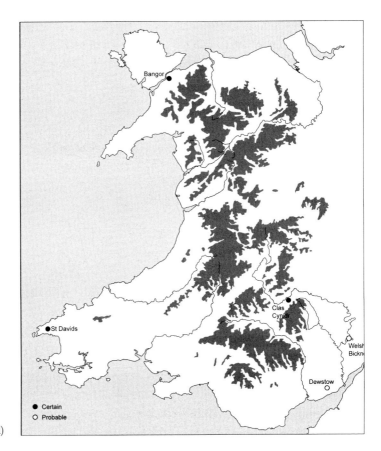

86 Location of probable eighth- to tenth-century dioceses in Wales. (Map drawn by Yvonne Beadnell)

kingdom, though nothing is known of their identity or location. It is possible that metropolitan status was simply claimed as mark of prestige, with little practical consequence, although the *Annales Cambriae* also records that Elfoddw was responsible for the acceptance of the Roman method for calculating Easter in AD 768, so he appears to have had a leading role in the Welsh church in this period. It is possible his metropolitan status in practice extended beyond the borders of Gwynedd and included bishops in the north-east of Wales and elsewhere.

Consolidation also appears to have occurred in the south-west. The prime position of St Davids was confirmed. The *Annales Cambriae* provide a more or less complete list of the bishops of St David from the ninth century; the putative bishoprics sited on the 'bishop-houses' of Dyfed were transformed and lost any episcopal status they may have had. St Davids also appears to have had metropolitan status, as Asser, Bishop of Sherbourne, but formerly a monk of St Davids, refers to Nobis, a relative of his, as *archiepiscopus* (*Life of King Alfred*). It is possible he had jurisdiction over much of south-west Wales including Ceredigion and Ystrad Tywi (Davies 2007a, 297). The claims of precedence over Llanbadarn Fawr and Llandeilo Fawr in the eleventh-century *Vita S Davidi* suggests that at some point they had come under the purview of St Davids, although the latter ultimately ended up as part of the diocese of Llandaf in the twelfth century (James 2007, 181).

In the south-east of Wales a number of additional bishops appear briefly in the historical record. A list of bishops of a site called *Clas Cynidr* was found in a fourteenth-century manuscript in France (Fleuriot 1976). The last name Tryferyn, who it records left for Hereford, is probably the same as the Tramerin recorded by the chronicle of John of Worcester as being a bishop acting for Bishop Aethelstan of Hereford, dying in 1055 (John of Worcester *Chronicle*; Davies 2007b, 301). The precise location of *Clas Cynidr* is uncertain, but is conventionally accepted as Glasbury.

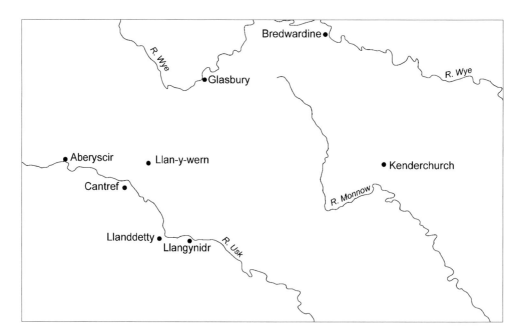

87 *Clas Cynidr* and its environs. (Map drawn by Yvonne Beadnell)

A GUADAN SACERDOS is recorded as erecting the cross for the souls of Ninid and Gurhi at Llanddetty (Breconshire) (Redknap and Lewis 2007). Llandetty is only a few miles upstream along the Usk from Llangynidr, which on the basis of its name is likely to have been a dependant of *Clas Cynidr*. Guadan may be the same individual as Gueman, the third bishop on the *Clas Cynidr* list, and potentially the same figure who appears in one of the Llandaf charters when granted Llanfihangel Tal-y-Llyn, which is also only a few miles from Llanddetty (Davies 2007b) (Fig 87).

Other dioceses which appear briefly in the historical record include one for Archenfield, the rump of the former kingdom of Ergyng in south-west Herefordshire. The Anglo-Saxon Chronicle records the capture of Cyfeiliog *biscop on Ircingafelda* (ASC sa.914); the same event is recorded by John of Worcester. It is not clear from these entries precisely where this bishop had his seat. One possibility is that he was located at Welsh Bicknor, which is recorded in one of the Llandaf charters as an *episcopalis locus* (72a) (echoing the use of the term used to describe the bishop-houses of Dyfed (Charles-Edwards 1971). Another Llandaf charter (165) records the gift of land to a bishop Comereg; in another charter an individual of the same name is recorded as the abbot of *Mochros* (Moccas, Herefordshire) hinting perhaps at another bishopric based there (Davies 1979, 103). The *Brut Y Tywysogion* also records the death of the bishop of the men of Gwent (sa. 983), which may have been the same bishopric as that located at Dewstow (Monmouthshire) and is mentioned in an early eleventh-century Anglo-Saxon charter which gave land '*ad episcopalem sedem qui dicitur Deowiesstow*' (Sawyer 1968, *913*), although the name Dewstow was also used to refer to St Davids (Owen and Morgan 2007, 431).

The reason for this apparent multiplicity of short-lived bishoprics in this relatively small part of Wales is uncertain. One answer may be its border location in an area increasingly subject to political and military pressure from the burgeoning Anglo-Saxon kingdoms. In these difficult circumstances it is perhaps not surprising to see the movement of bishops in response to actual and perceived threats. It is also important to remember that not all bishops may have had direct territorial or diocesan responsibilities. One of the Llandaf charters demands that the abbot of Llancarfan should be worthy of episcopal honour, implying that this may be as much an honorary marker of status as a specific administrative role (LL 243; Davies 2003, 15–16).

It is the increasing power of the neighbouring Anglo-Saxon kingdoms from the seventh century onwards that is probably also responsible for the decline of the putative earlier British bishoprics centred on Roman towns. In some cases, such as Worcester, the Anglo-Saxon successor diocese was situated in the same town, if not necessarily the same ecclesiastical establishment (Bassett 1992). In other cases, however, there does appear to have been a more pronounced rupture. The successor to the probable British diocese at Wall (*Letocetum*) is likely to have been Lichfield about three miles to the north; whilst a possible British diocese at Leominster shifted to Hereford (Blair 2001).

The Rise of the Monasteria

It is probably not until the eighth or even ninth century that Wales finally developed an extensive network of ecclesiastical sites that provides something resembling a comprehensive coverage of the country. At this point in time these religious centres overwhelmingly took the form of monasteries. A term commonly used to describe these early Welsh monastic sites is the Welsh word *clas* (pl. *clasau*). Trying to reach a precise definition of a *clas* is a difficult one. There are never any explicit definitions of what constitutes a *clas*, instead an understanding has to be derived from often oblique references to *clasau* and *claswyr* (the men of the *clas*). The linguistic origin of the term is relatively clear; it comes from the Latin *classis* meaning a gathering or group of people. In Wales it came to mean more specifically a group of clerics. This emphasises the fundamentally corporate nature of the *clas*. It is not always clear whether the *claswyr* followed a formal monastic order or whether they were more properly to be characterised as canons or secular clergy. Gerald of Wales, admittedly a strong supporter of the monastic reform movement, called the clerics at St Davids '*glaswir*, that is, ecclesiastical men … without any order or rule' (*Gir Camb Op*). When he highlights the lack of any rule, it is more likely that he is noting that they do not follow the reformed rule of Benedict or one of its variations. Indeed much of the documentary evidence for the *clasau* comes from the very period when they were being reformed and reorganised, either into regular monasteries or collegiate churches. One suspects that in the period before the eleventh century the precise distinction between secular canons and monastic orders was not important in practice. As John Blair noted when writing about pre-Viking Anglo-Saxon minsters, the form of religious life in these ecclesiastical establishments would have been 'essentially eclectic and inclusive in character' (Blair 2005, 180).

Rather than becoming entwined in terminological niceties it is perhaps more useful to think about defining these communities in terms of their organisation and activities. Indeed, it is the communal nature of these bodies that is fundamental; they were structured around a group of clergy, some of whom may or may not have been priests. The documentary evidence both contemporary (such as the *Life of St Samson*, vs 1.8) and of a later date is consistent in describing the *monasteria* as being headed by an abbot. Abbots also regularly appear in the Llandaf charters, e.g LL 140 (Davies 1978, 125-6) and are attested in the epigraphic material (e.g. Llantwit Major; G65). However, other terminology for the head of the *monasteria* was also in use; *princeps* is attested in the Llandaf charters (e.g. LL145) as is *magister* (e.g. 127b), which also appears in the *Life of Samson* (vs 7). Bishops were also clearly based within monasteries. As the name suggests, the bishops of *Clas Cynidr* were based in a *clas* and Gerald of Wales comments noted above are a clear statement that the bishop at St Davids was situated within a *clas*, confirming the statement in the *Historia Gruffudd cab Kenan* that he was met by 'the *clas* of the Lord Dewi' (*clas er argluyd Dewi*) (Evans 1977, 13).

Another key aspect of the *clas* was not just that they were corporate bodies but that this aspect extended to the way in which economic resources were received, held and passed on. The Welsh law codes give us some insight into this process. The fines for breaching sanctuary were meant to be paid to the abbot and other members of the community (Pryce 1993, 184; Jenkins 2000, 41), whilst the property of an abbot was meant to be inherited by the *clas* (Owen 1841, II.10). Finally, there is clear evidence from the historical sources, that there was a hierarchy of ecclesiastical sites in Wales in this period. Later writers distinguished between important (and usually older) churches and lesser (and newer) churches; these are the 'the greater churches to whom antiquity allows greater reverence' (*Description* 1.18) and the 'major churches' bequeathed money by Gruffudd ap Cynan. The Welsh laws also distinguish between a 'mother church' and other churches (Jenkins 2000, 41, 135).

Thus, broadly speaking, the major ecclesiastical sites of Wales in the eighth to the twelfth century should be understood as corporate mother churches with extensive territorial responsibilities. Defined in this way, it is easy to see the similarities between the *clas* and the Anglo-Saxon minster. In fact, the same term *monasterium* is widely used in the documentary material from early medieval Wales and Anglo-Saxon England, whereas the term *clas* is a relatively late one. Huw Pryce's proposal that the term *clas* not be used when writing about the pre-Norman Welsh church, replacing it with the more neutral (and contemporary) *monasterium* has much to recommend it (Pryce 1992b, 54). John Blair's working definition of a minster, 'a complex ecclesiastical settlement which is headed by an abbess, abbot or man in priest's orders; which contains nuns, monks, priests or laity in a variety of possible combinations, and is united to a greater or lesser extent by their liturgy and devotions; which may perform or supervise pastoral care to the laity, perhaps receiving dues and exerting parochial authority; and which sometimes act as a bishop's set, while not depending for its existence or importance on that function', would clearly suffice easily to define the Welsh *clasau/monasteria*, and emphasises the broad homology between the Welsh and English church in this period (Blair 2005, 3).

The similarity between Welsh and Anglo-Saxon *monasteria* also extends to the methodological challenges involved in identifying them in the historic and archaeological record (Blair 1985; Evans 1992; Pryce 1992b). Obviously there are the churches that are explicitly named as *clasau* or *monasteria* in the historical evidence, but these are relatively few and far between, and identify only a relatively small number of establishments. There is also some supplementary historical evidence that can be adduced to support the identification of a site as a *monasteria*, such as its later survival as a portionary or collegiate church, an extensive recorded area of sanctuary (*noddfa*) or place-name evidence. However, the paucity of documentary evidence means that inevitably there is a need to also bring the archaeological material into play. Whilst individually it is difficult to point to one overriding diagnostic factor that would securely define the presence of a *monasteria*, there are a bundle of factors that cumulatively point towards the location of such sites. These factors include evidence for a cult centres based around a patron saint, particularly the presence of a *capel/eglwys y bedd* or other forms of subsidiary churches within a single churchyard, documentary or material evidence for a relic at the site, and the presence of monumental stone carving from the site (particularly Group 3 stones). Such a *kriterien bundel* approach was taken by the Cadw Early Medieval Ecclesiastical Sites Project, and whilst there is inevitably a level of subjectivity with this, it is a useful way of exploring the issue (e.g. Ludlow 2003; Evans 2003).

Monasteria: A Brief Regional Overview (Fig 88)

Whilst the Llandaf charters indicate the presence of many ecclesiastical sites across the south and south-east of Wales between the seventh and twelfth century, it is not always easy to define their relative status. The simple mention of a place by the charters cannot be used alone to identify the site as a *monasteria*, rather than say, a dependent church or a private chapel. However, by bringing in a range of additional evidence it is possible to put forward a

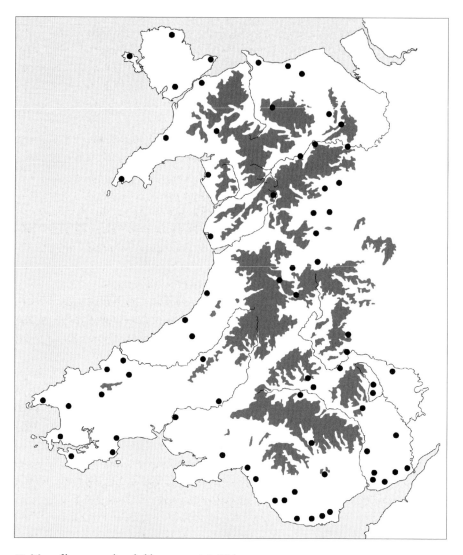

88 Map of known and probable *monasteria* in Wales

number of other sites as probable examples. In Gwent, Caerwent is one of the best-attested examples; the monastery of St Tatheus was located within the town and the artefactual record clearly indicates the presence of significant early medieval activity at the site (Knight 1998). A fragment of a tenth or eleventh-century disc-headed cross-slab found in the churchyard of St Stephen and St Tatheus seems to confirm that this church was probably the focus of early medieval ecclesiastical activity in the town (MN2). St Arvan's has also produced a Group 3 carved stone, very similar to that from Caerwent. Furthermore, it is also the site of an unusual concentration of early medieval metalwork, some of which appears to be ecclesiastical in origin (MN5; Redknap 2007). Two stone have come from near Caerleon, one from the church and one from nearby Bulmore (MN1, MN3). Bulmore was probably the site of the shrine of the martyrs Julius and Aaron mentioned by Gildas (Knight 2001a). It was also probably the site of a *capel y bedd* (see Knight 2004). In addition to these sites which have produced some archaeological and historical evidence of the status of a *monasteria*, one should add a number of sites which have Merthyr place-names, including Merthir Dincaut (Dingestow), Merthir Tecmed (Llandegfedd), Mertyr Teudiric (Mathern), Merthyrgerein (Merthyr Geryn) and Merthyr Iun et Aaron (St Julian's).

In Glamorgan, the best attested *monasteria* are Llancarfan, Llantwit Major and Llandough (Knight 2005). Llancarfan, a cult centre of Cadog, appears in the *Vita Cadoci*, and was once the home of a reliquary containing the relics of Cadog (Knight 1984, 369-70). Llantwit Major was a cult centre for Illtud that is mentioned in the *Vita Samsonsis* and the later *Vita Illtudi*. Llandough is linked to Docdwy, though he has no vita; it has also produced evidence for a substantial fifth–eleventh century cemetery (Holbrook and Thomas 2005). All three have also produced sculpture marking the importance of these sites in the tenth and eleventh centuries (G35, G42, G63-71). The *Brut y Twysogion* also records the destruction of Llantwit Major and Llancarfan by the Vikings in raids in the later tenth century.

Llandaf was clearly a significant centre; though it did not assume diocesan status until relatively late, the presence of sculpture, including part of a decorated pillar cross of late ninth–early tenth century date, indicate earlier activity at the site (Davies 2002, 13-18; G36-40). Some clearly important sites do not, however, appear in the documentary record in the early medieval period. Ewenny, Llan-gan, Margam and Merthyr Mawr have important collections of Group 3 stones indicating that they were sites of some status (G18-26, G43-6, G78-84, G98-110). The merthyr name at the latter site is an additional argument for its status as a *monasteria*; the Teilo dedication of the church is likely to be a later rededication reflecting the growth in importance of Llancarfan. Other possible *monasteria* in Glamorgan include Llangyfelach and Baglan. At Llangyfelach an associated place-name suggests it was a *clas*, and it was recorded in Rhygyfarch's *Life of David* as 'Monasterium Langemelach', where it was noted that important relics of the saint, including his staff, tunic and altar were kept. It is also a site that has produced important sculpture (G49-51). Baglan was the cult centre of the eponymous saint, and housed an major relic, the head of Baglan's crozier; it too has produced sculpture (G4-6). Finally, possible early foundations are indicated by merthyr placenames at Merthyr Tydfil, Eglwysilan (Merthir Ilan) and Merthyr Dyfan.

In Dyfed, the 'bishop-houses' were probably all important *monasteria* by the eighth century (Charles-Edwards 1971). However, other important ecclesiastical sites probably operated within the interstices of the 'bishop-houses'. In Carmarthenshire, a key foundation was Llandeilo Fawr which stood on the River Tywi, which was the base of a bishopric (see above; Strange 2002) and is also the site of a ninth-century cross-head and a cross-slab of similar date (Edwards 2007). Further west, in Pembrokeshire, additional *monasteria*, included Nevern, the cult centre of St Brynach. Early inscribed stones indicate a probable fifth or sixth-century origin of the site, but the *Vita* and the presence of later sculpture, including an elaborate late tenth or early eleventh-century cross, demonstrate the continued significance of this site (Edwards). There is also Penally, close to the important secular sites at Longbury Bank and Tenby, which has tenth-century sculpture and also appears in the Llandaf charters (Campbell and Lane 1993; Edwards 2007). Other probable *monasteria*, identifiable only through the presence of sculpture include St Dogmael's, where an inscribed stone suggests an early foundation date for the site (Edwards 2007) and St Edrin's, which has parts of at least five cross-carved stones (ibid). At Clydai, the likely existence of a *capel y bedd* (known as *Eglwys trisaint*) and several early inscribed stones, one with a later cross added in the seventh or eighth century, demonstrates the probable site of another *monasterium* (Owen 1896; Edwards 2007).

In Cardiganshire, the dominant *monasterium* was clearly Llanbadarn-Fawr (Evans 1992; Kirby 1994). It was probably the seat of a bishop, but it is best known as the home of the influential clerical dynasty of Sulien (d. 1091) and his sons, Rhygyfarch (d. 1099), Ieuan (d. 1137) and Daniel (d. 1127). Llanbadarn was the focus of the cult of St Padarn and its most important relic was Padarn's crozier. It is also the site of two pieces of ninth or tenth-century sculpture, including a 'hammer-head' cross showing both Scandinavian and Irish stylistic influences (Edwards 2007). Llanddewibrefi was in later periods a portionary church, and is recorded in the Rhygyfarch's *Life of St David*. It is also the site of an important collection of sculpture, including a stone recording the death of one Idnert during a raid on the site (Edwards 2007) and a number of cross-inscribed stones (ibid). Although lacking documentary testimony, other probable *monasteria* can be recognised by the presence of Group 2 and Group 3 stones, such as Llanddewi Aber-arth (Edwards 2007) and Silian (ibid).

In Breconshire, there are few sites which it is possible to identify with certainty as *monasteria* from the documentary evidence. *Clas Cynidr*, which on the basis of the place-name and the presence of bishops in the later first millennium, was clearly of great importance. However, its precise location is unclear; it is most likely to be Glasbury, which as the place-name suggests was probably a *clas* site, though it could also have been at Kenderchurch (Herefordshire). The two early medieval Welsh texts known as *De Situ Brecheniauc* and *Cognacio Brychan*, written in or near Brecon, were probably written by the late tenth century, despite only surviving as post-Conquest versions. They mention several churches connected to the burial places of the dynasty of the semi-mythic king Brychan (Petts 2007). They record that the grave of Rein, son of Brychan, was at Llandyfaelog Fach, a site that has produced tenth-century sculpture (Redknap and Lewis 2007). The grave of Kennauc was linked to Merthyr Cynog, the name of which also suggests an early origin, whilst Annlauch's grave was located at Llanspyddid, which has produced a carved-stone cross (Redknap and Lewis 2007). Another reference to the burial site of a king of Brycheiniog is also known, a charter granting *Lann Cors* to Llandaf in which King Awst of Brycheiniog (fl. first half of the eighth century) makes reference to Llangors as the proposed burial place of himself and his sons. Patrishow was recorded in the Llandaf charters at Merthyr Issui and is the site of an *eglwys y bedd* associated with St Ishaw. Overall, in Breconshire, the evidence for the distribution of *monasteria* is noticeably less extensive than in Dyfed, Glamorgan and Gwent. This is probably primarily due to the lesser extent of documentary evidence; the region is on the edge of the area covered by the Llandaf charters. The quantity of sculpture is also less; it is unlikely that this is due to the lack of important sites in the county and probably reflects differing patterns of investment in sculpture.

East of Brycheiniog, in the kingdom of Ergyng in south-west Herefordshire, there is no shortage of evidence for early ecclesiastical sites. A number of sites appear in the Llandaf charters, whilst churches in the region are also recorded in the section of the Book of Llandaf, which records sites in Ergyng where Herewald, Bishop of Llandaf (d.1104), exercised his episcopal rights. However, it is less easy to establish a sense of hierarchy amongst these churches. Whilst Dyfrig's connection with the area is likely to be due to the diocese of Llandaf's territorial claims in the area, the close association of Dyfrig with Moccas and the possible presence of a bishop based there (see above) makes it a candidate as an early *monasterium*. Also appearing in the Llandaf charters as Merthir Clitauc, the church at Clodock is home to an inscribed stone burial slab from the tenth or eleventh century (Redknap and Lewis 2007). A cluster of early sculpture is also known from the church at Llanveynoe in the Olchon Valley, indicating activity there in the later first millennium (Redknap and Lewis 2007).

In Radnorshire and Montgomeryshire, both the documentary and archaeological (particularly sculptural) record are extremely sparse. It is possible to identify only three possible sites in Radnorshire as potential *monasteria*. At Glascwm, its place-name suggests it may once have been a *clas*, and was home to Bangu, a handbell linked to St David. At Llowes there is a wheel-cross slab of probable tenth or eleventh-century date (Redknap and Lewis 2007). It is possible that St Harmon was also an important earlier site; one of the townships within the parish is named Clas, perhaps indicating the church had this status. It too was home to a major relic, St Curig's crozier (Journey 1.1). In Montgomeryshire, the dominant site is Meifod. Its superior status is amply recorded; it appears as one of the major churches left money by Gruffudd ap Cynan and it is the subject of the praise poem *Canu Tysilio*, which amply records its regional significance as the main cult centre of Tysilio. It sits in an extensive churchyard, and, at one point, at least three churches stood at the site. Llanrhaeadr-ym-Mochnant houses a tenth-century cross and parts of a Romanesque shrine, similar to that from Pennant Melangell (Nash-Williams 1950), and was the mother church of much of the commote of Mochnant within which it lay (Palmer 1886). This suggests it must have been of some significance in the later first millennium. Evidence for the other *monasteria* in the county is more circumstantial. Llansilin was a collegiate church and the chief church in the commote of Cynllaith. Other possible *monasteria* include Llangurig, which was associated with the term clas as a place-name as late as the sixteenth century, with tenants recorded as '*classwyre*' (Evans 1992). Llandinam was a *clas* and still had an abbot in the thirteenth century and remained a portionary church until the sixteenth century (ibid; Palmer 1886). Llanfair Caerinion was also recorded as a portionary church and Kerry was a collegiate church in the thirteenth century; potentially both sites may have been important in the later first millennium, but direct evidence is largely lacking.

In Denbighshire, Llangollen was a major site. It was home to a shrine to Collen; a *capel y bedd* probably once stood to the west of the current church and fragments of another stone Romanesque shrine are built into the eastern wall of the vestry. In the thirteenth century it was also recorded as the mother church of Wrexham, Ruabon, Chirk, Llansantffraid and Llandegla (Thomas 1911, 282). Other possible *monasteria* include Llanynis, which was a portionary church (Evans 1992, 39; Pryce 1993, 185-6), Llanelwy (St Asaph) was recorded as a *clas* (Davies 1991, 183), and Llanarmon-yn-Iâl, which was probably the Llanarmon to which Gruffudd ap Cynan left money.

Further west, although in a relatively remote location, Gwytherin was probably once also an important site, and was the cult centre for St Gwenfrewi, and home to a shrine containing relics of the saint. There were two churches within the original churchyard, and an abbot was recorded there as late as 1334 (Pryce 1993). Abergele was the mother church of Betws and Llangystenyn, and was probably the site of a *capel y bedd*. Llandrillo yn Rhos, formerly known as Dinerth, was left money by Gruffudd ap Cynan, and was probably the cult centre of Trillo; it was also a portionary church (Palmer 1886, 194).

In Caernarvonshire, Bangor was the most important *monasterium* and the seat of a key bishopric. The other major *monasterium* was undoubtedly Clynnog Fawr, which was the cult centre of Beuno and the site of an *eglwys y bedd*, which probably contained the saint's relics. A rare early medieval sundial is also known from the site, and was probably used to mark out the ecclesiastical day by the clergy at the site (Fig 89) (Nash-Williams *85* 1950). Clynnog was the target of Viking raids in 988. It was also a focus for royal patronage; Gruffudd ap Cynan left it money and there is some evidence that it received land grants in the later first millennium (Ellis 1838; Davies 1982, 271). The site was later a portionary church and the mother church of Llanwnda, Llanfaglan, Llangeinwen, Llangaffo and Llangelynin. On the Llŷn peninsula Aberdaron was also an important site connected to the monastery on Bardsey, though it may have been relocated from an earlier site at nearby Capel Anelog, which has produced early inscribed stones indicating the presence of a monastery (Nash-Williams 1950, *77, 78*). Penmachno is likely also to have been a small *monasteria*. Although most of the early inscribed stones in the church were not found in the immediate locality, until the seventeenth century there were two churches (St Tudclyd and Enclydwyn's).

On Anglesey, Penmon was clearly a site of considerable importance, its collection of carved stones, its close relation to the small monastic site on Ynys Seiriol and its major early stone church all indicate its status (Nash-Williams 1950, *37-8*). Caer Gybi, located within a Roman fort was a cult centre for Cybi and a *capel y bedd*, associated with the saint, lies within the enclosure; it was also a portionary church and had chapelries at Bodedern, Bodwrog and Llandrygarn (Palmer 1886, 177-8). Both sites were left money by Gruffudd ap Cynan; they also suffered Viking raids. There is also a *capel y bedd* at Llaneilian, on the north-east coast of Anglesey, which may indicate it was an important early cult site, though the evidence for a particularly early date for this is equivocal. A reference to an abbot (*abadaeth*) in the thirteenth century suggests it may have been a *clas* (Carr 1982). The only possible merthyr site on the island is 'Merthyr Caffo' which is mentioned in one of the lives of St Cybi; the location of this site is uncertain, though it may well be Llangaffo. Llangaffo does however appear to have been a daughter church of Clynnog Fawr on the mainland (Edwards 1986, 28; Palmer 1886, 191).

Finally we come to Merioneth, where the dominant *monasteria* was Tywyn. This church appeared in the twelfth-century praise poem by Llywelyn Fardd I. The church was the cult centre of Cadfan, and the poem records a number of relics associated with the saint, including an altar, a gospel book and a crosier. These may have been housed in the small chapel, Capel Cadfan, which once stood in the north-west corner of the churchyard. Its ravaging by Vikings is recorded. The site has also produced early sculpture, including the 'Cadfan stone', with its early Welsh inscription dating perhaps to the ninth century (Nash-Williams 1950, *287*) and a pre-Conquest sundial (Thomas 1989). The church was mother church to a number of churches within the commote of Ystumanner, including Llanfihangel-y-Pennant

89 Sundial at Clynnog Fawr. (Author's photograph)

and Pennal, and its parochia may once have covered much of the cantref of Merioneth (Pryce 2001). However, Tywyn was probably not the only *monasteria* in Merioneth. The church at Corwen, dedicated to Mael and Sulien, has produced pre-Conquest sculpture and was recorded as a portionary church (Nash-Williams 1950, *274-6*; Pryce 2001). It was also probably originally the mother church for the commote of Edeirnion. Upstream of Corwen, and also in the valley of the Dee, lay Llanfor, which as seen in the previous chapter, had early medieval origins and was possibly the mother church of Penllyn (ibid). On the coast, the church of Llandanwg was the mother church of neighbouring Llanfair and Llanbedr whose dedications suggest twelfth century foundation; Llandanwg itself has produced early medieval sculpture (Nash-Williams 1950, *279-80*). The final possible *monasteria* in this area is Llanymawddwy, the mother church for the commote of Mawddwy, and potentially the cult centre of Tydecho, although the direct evidence for the early medieval origin of this site is limited (Pryce 2001, 296).

This survey of possible eighth to eleventh-century *monasteria* in Wales has of necessity been brief and subjective. Hopefully, however, it has highlighted the range of evidence that can be produced to argue for the monastic status of these early medieval churches. It can also be seen that there is immense regional variation in their distribution. The density of possible sites is highest in the south particularly the south-west, with fewer identified sites in the north, central Wales and the Marches. The range of evidence also varies geographically, in the south documentary evidence is at its most extensive, with the Llandaf charters and the passage on the 'bishop houses' of Dyfed providing extremely useful pointers to key sites; much of the hagiographic material also comes from this area.

However, in these areas, there is also a noticeably higher intensity of eighth to eleventh-century sculpture. This contrasts strongly with central Wales and the Marches, where stone sculpture is far rarer. For example, despite clearly being a major cult centre, Meifod has only produced one carved stone, and the possible *monasteria* in Radnorshire only one fragment of carved stone between them. Thus it is important to be extremely careful in interpreting the modern geographical distribution of *monasteria*; areas of greater density are likely to be primarily areas of better evidence, whether historical or archaeological. Nonetheless, there may well be some regional differences, and in general, the density of sites appears to be greater in the lower lying areas, where it was easier to produce the agricultural surplus to support the *monasteria* and the elites who acted as their patrons. It is also necessary to be aware that within the term *monasteria* there was undoubtedly a wide range of variation in terms of size and function. In north-west Wales, for example, churches such as Bangor and Tywyn were of a different order in terms of wealth and influence to small establishments, such as Penmachno or Llandanwg. This variation was undoubtedly a factor of differing patterns of patronage and support by secular lords. Sites also show chronological variation, and it is unlikely that a map of *monasteria* in 800 would be identical to one of such sites in 1100. The power and importance of such sites would have risen and fallen over time, reacting to the ebb and flow of secular and ecclesiastical politics. For example, although mentioned by Bede as a major monastic site in the early seventh century, Bangor on Dee appears to have diminished in importance rapidly after the battle of Chester. Equally, Llandaf only emerged as a key diocesan seat in the south of Wales in the eleventh century. A great number of small *monasteria* are ultimately likely to be difficult to recognise directly either archaeologically or historically. The many small churches which retain unique dedications to Welsh saints may have been extremely small and poorly resourced *monasteria*, which due to lack of wealth or political bad luck failed to develop into more significant ecclesiastical centres. For example, Llanpumsaint, which had a *capel y bedd* ultimately failed to achieve even parochial status and was a dependant chapel of Abergwili.

Smaller Ecclesiastical Sites

In this discussion of *monasteria* it is important to remember that these sites were not the only ones in the ecclesiastical hierarchy. There was also a range of other churches during this period, including daughter houses founded by *monasteria*, hermitages and places of retreat. Identifying these is again largely a question of working with very uneven evidence. In Glamorgan, for example, eighth to eleventh-century sculpture is found at a number of sites, which are unlikely ever to have been *monasteria*. Laleston has produced two fine cross heads (G31-2). Gerald of Wales records that monks from Margam Abbey destroyed this site, probably as part of the process of the new Cistercian community at Margam taking over the site as a grange (William 1990); it is probable that the relationship between the two sites was a long one, and that Laleston originated as a daughter house of Margam in the late tenth or early eleventh century. A fragment of a recumbent slab with cross is known from Flatholm (G11), which was probably a hermitage connected with Cadog's foundation at Llancarfan (*VSC* 18). The saint's life also mentions a number of other sites, such as Barry Island, Llanmaes and Mamhilad, none of which have produced any early medieval sculpture (*vsc* 18). These dependent churches would be completely invisible if it had not been for the survival of Cadog's *Vita*. Dependant or daughter houses need not have been at a great distance from their mother churches; the clusters of sculpture from Margam at Cwrt-y-Defaid and Eglwys Nynnid are under a mile from Margam Abbey itself, suggesting that major *monasteria* may have had a penumbra of lesser ecclesiastical sites in the immediate locality (Redknap and Lewis 2007). It is possible that in some cases *monasteria* could build up interests in a particular region leading to the establishment of a series of dependant establishments in the same area. For example, *Clas Cynidr* on the basis of evidence from the Llandaf charters, epigraphic evidence and church dedications (see above), appears to have built up a series of dependant houses along the upper course of the Usk between Llangynidr and Aberyscir (Fig 87).

A differing pattern can be seen in Ergyng, where in addition to the probable major sites at Clodock, Moccas and Llanveynoe, material from the Book of Llandaf indicates that there were a series of other church sites in the region. It is possible that some had origins as daughter churches of the local *monasteria*, but there is no evidence of such a dependant relationship. It may be that these sites, recorded by chance in the Llandaf charters, represent a class of very small local churches, which only came into a relationship with a major *monasteria* after their establishment. The Llandaf charters also remind us that subsidiary estates and churches could be at some distance from their mother churches. This may also lead to the intermingling of lesser sites with differing ecclesiastical loyalties; for example, Kenderchurch, presumably a daughter church of *Clas Cynidr*, lies in the heartland of Ergyng.

A particular interpretative problem is presented by the large number of sites across Wales where eighth to eleventh century activity is known only through the presence of cross-inscribed (Group 2) stones. Are these indicative of an early church at the site or simply a cemetery? The relatively small number that have produced both early inscribed stones and these cross-inscribed stones suggests that there is a real shift in cemetery location around this period, moving away from the old family burial grounds marked by the Group 1 inscribed stones and towards new sites, which on the basis of the cross-incised stones appear to be more explicitly identified as Christian (Lewis 1976, 185). It seems unlikely that these new burial grounds were immediately provided with a church or even a formal boundary; in the terminology of Charles Thomas, these are 'undeveloped' cemeteries (Thomas 1971). However, this must remain a probability rather than a certainty, and the secure evidential base for the provision of churches at such sites is limited (primarily the excavated site at Capel Maelog; Britnell 1990). It remains to be seen how representative this site is of wider developments across Wales. If, nonetheless, we accept this model, then we can start to get a better idea of how Christianity developed at this period. We can postulate a network of *monasteria* providing some element of pastoral care, and certainly acting as a cult centre for devotional activity by clergy and lay people. Any pastoral activity at the *monasteria* does not seemingly extend to burial, which is probably only available at these sites for the members of the community itself, and potentially patrons, clients and tenants. Instead, for the majority of the population burial is provided for in these small, undeveloped cemeteries, presumably based on kinship groups. In the valley of the Gwaun in Pembrokeshire, there are a series of these probable cemeteries marked by cross-incised stones at sites, which later acquired churches (Llanllawer; Llanychaer; Llanychlwydog and Pontaen) (P32–5, P48–9, P51–4, P86–7). It is possible that the carved pillar depicting a crucifix from Llanychaer may not be a grave-marker and instead represent a focus of worship before the establishment of a church at a later date (P49).

THE CHURCH AND POWER: LAND AND LITERACY

The spread of the *monasteria* between the eighth and tenth centuries was not just simply a religious phenomenon. It was a period that saw a renegotiation of the relationship between the Church and secular authorities. Whilst much of the population may have been buried in the 'undeveloped cemeteries', the elites began to be buried at *monasteria*, seemingly as an expression of their privileged social position. One of the charters appended to the end of the *Vita S. Cadoci* and probably dateable to around the eighth century recorded that 'Conbelin gave the land called Lisdin Borrion for the traffic of the heavenly kingdom together with his own body to God and saint Cadog' (*VSC* 66), similar arrangements are also recorded in the Llandaf charters (e.g. LL 221). The evidence for the burial of kings and nobility is also expressed increasingly in the sculptural record. The Houelt recorded on a stone from Llantwit Major is probably Hywel ap Rhys, King of Glwysing, who died in 886 (G63; BYT sa.885), and whether the King Juthahel recorded on another stone from the same site was Iudhail, King of Gwent, (d. 848) or not, he is still clearly an important secular figure of power (G65).

As the church increasingly provided ideological support for the ruling dynasties through providing burial and presumably other ritual support, the nobility also provided more practical support for the church by the provision of land and other economic resources and freeing them from a range of legal obligations and rights through the establishments of privileges and liberties, such as the *Braint Teilo* (Davies 1974–6). Relationships between the church and rulers were not however always an easy; the church and secular rulers could come into conflict. The ravaging of churches by Welsh rulers was not unusual (e.g. BYT 978). Many of the Llandaf charters appear to record the donation of land as expiation of violation of church property or sanctuary (e.g. LL125a, 217). This reflects a wider pattern found across Britain with secular elites increasingly placing the powerful church communities under pressure (e.g. Blair 2005, 323–29). Wealthy in land, it must have been tempting for kings to attempt to exploit them as an economic resource, particularly as the Welsh system of partible inheritance meant that it was difficult for individual dynasties to develop extensive estates; this contrasted with the 'undying' nature of ecclesiastical bodies which allowed them to develop and consolidate land holdings over the long term.

One of the key ways in which the positive and negative relationships between the church and secular powers could be articulated and negotiated was through the written word. This was a period in which the use of documents for such purposes expanded. This is not to suggest that literacy was absent in the fifth to seventh centuries. The church was obviously a literate body, with the celebration of the liturgy intimately linked to the use of key religious texts, but there is reason to think that there may have been a continuation of lay literacy from the late Roman period, particularly in the more Romanised areas of south-east Wales. This is most likely to have occurred in a legal context. It is often assumed that in the fifth century Roman property law fell out of use to be replaced by customary laws of land-tenure. However, Thomas Charles-Edwards has noted that the Welsh legal concept of *priodor* may show the influence of Roman law (Charles-Edwards 1993, 132), and Wendy Davies places the charter-tradition of Western Britain and Ireland in the context of a continuation of Late Roman Vulgar Law rather than native Irish or Welsh law (1982, 274-5). Similarities included the use of formulae with echoes of imperial rescripts and continental formularies and the attention paid to the recording of witnesses (275). Davies also notes that some aspects of the 'Celtic' charters have parallels in early patristic writings (277). She argues that the practice of using charters to record land transfers developed in sub-Roman Britain in the fifth century in a firmly ecclesiastical context: 'The most intelligible context for the early developments of the practice would then lie on the one hand in the attempts of bishops to secure endowments and register them with their city councils, as required by the state, and on the other in the records ensuring, in the spirit of the exhortation in the *Liber Pontificalis*, to note everything' (ibid). However, it is noticeable that the only two styli known from the fifth–seventh century in Wales and Western Britain come from secular elite sites: Cadbury Congresbury, Somerset (Rahtz et al. 1992) and Dinas Powys, Glamorgan (Alcock 1963); similar objects are also known from early secular contexts in Ireland (Ó Ríordáin 1949).

However, *by* the eighth century it appears that the control of literacy was more securely embedded in an ecclesiastical context. Obviously many clerics within the church would have been literate to a greater or lesser degree, and major ecclesiastical sites may well have produced liturgical manuscripts, such as the Chad Gospels and the Hereford Gospels. We also recognise the increased use of texts by the church in co-operation with the elites to control and administer secular affairs. This is most explicit in the growth of the use of charters and the related use of gospel books to record similar arrangements. The Chad Gospels are the best example of a gospel book being used to contain charter related material, and contains a series of marginal inscriptions, most of which closely resemble charters. (Jenkins and Owens 1983). Although this is the best known example, there are a series of other instance of gospel books from broadly Insular contexts which contain charter material. Whilst undoubtedly some of these charters recorded the donation of land and renders to ecclesiastical foundations, others, such as the 'Surrexit' memorandum (Chad 2) dating to the ninth century from the Chad Gospels, are records of the settlement of land disputes between two lay individuals and deposited with the community of St Teilo and placed in the Gospel book (Jenkins and Owen 1983; Jenkins and Owen 1984; Jenkins 1994). The use of a gospel book to record the settlement of secular disputes can also be seen in the Hereford Gospel (Gameson 2002).

Material clearly directly derived from charters also appears in some hagiographical material, most explicitly in the *Life of St Cadog*, in which the last 15 chapters are essentially charters which have been appended directly to the *Vita*, sometimes supplemented with a little narrative context. One of these charters records that 'Bronnoguid, the son of Febric, gave the half part of the land, Idraclis, to God and the monastery of saint Cadog for his soul, and that his name might be written in the book of Cadog at Nantcarfan' (*VSC* 5). It is probable that this book was the gospel whose authorship was attributed to Gildas (*VSC* 34). It is likely that the Book of St Beuno (*Liber sancti Beugnobi*), a gospel book known to have been at Clynnog Fawr as late as the sixteenth century also contained similar charter material; quotes from these charters were included in a privilege of Edward IV (Davies 2003, 144). Whilst known elsewhere, the use of Gospel books as cartularies appears earliest and most widely within an Insular context. Other examples include the Book of Kells, the Book of Durrow, the Book of Deer and the Bodmin Gospel (Price 2003). Dafydd Jenkins has suggested that the practice had its origin in western Britain or Ireland (Jenkins 1994; Davies 1998).

Charters need not necessarily only be recorded within the margins of gospel books, they could often have a far more material record, such as inscribed grave-slabs, of which three are known from Wales at Merthyr Mawr and Ogmore in Glamorgan and Llanllŷr in Merioneth. There is a possible recorded example from Stoke near Hartland, Devon (Davies 1998), and an eighth-century example is also known from Kilnasaggart (County Armagh). The inscriptions used on these stones were clearly drawn from the charter tradition: '*in grefium in proprium usque in diem iudicii*'; '*dedit Arthmail agrum Deo et Gliguis … et episcopo*' (Davies 1982b).

The expansion of the use of charters and gospel books to record tributary arrangements and land transfers is likely to have flowered due to the increasing expansion of *monasteria* from the eighth century. In a society where most land was held in common, with rights to land primarily passed down through kin groups, the growth of the church and the associated desire to transfer land and other rights to it formed a challenge in finding acceptable ways and forms by which land could be alienated. Not surprisingly, the charter, with its emphasis on recording the witnesses of the transaction was a helpful way in which land could be passed to the corporate body of a church in a valid way. It is likely that in areas which had previously been dominated by customary, and probably oral, legal systems, with no existing tradition of the alienation of land, that the legal protocols of the charter system may have needed to be backed up by the threat of force. Hence it is not surprising that initially the earliest grants appear to have been made by kings, though rapidly the practice of making charters appears to have spread through the ranks of the nobility (Davies 1978). Once the practice and principal of land alienation became established, land could be passed between private individuals, and inevitably these transfers were also recorded in a similar way.

The Impact of the Vikings

Wales, as most of northern Europe during the ninth and tenth century, experienced the impact of the Vikings (Redknap 2000). They first began to raid Wales in the mid-ninth century killing King Cygen of Powys, and attacking Anglesey (*BYT* SA 852); raiding continued across Wales with the Vikings overwintering in Dyfed in 878 and suffering a major defeat at Buttington, near Welshpool (Montgomery) (*ASC* sa.894). At the turn of the tenth century, Vikings expelled from Dublin temporarily settled in Anglesey, before moving onwards to Chester. The burgeoning trade links between the Viking dominated cities of Chester and Dublin subsequently led to more peaceable relations.

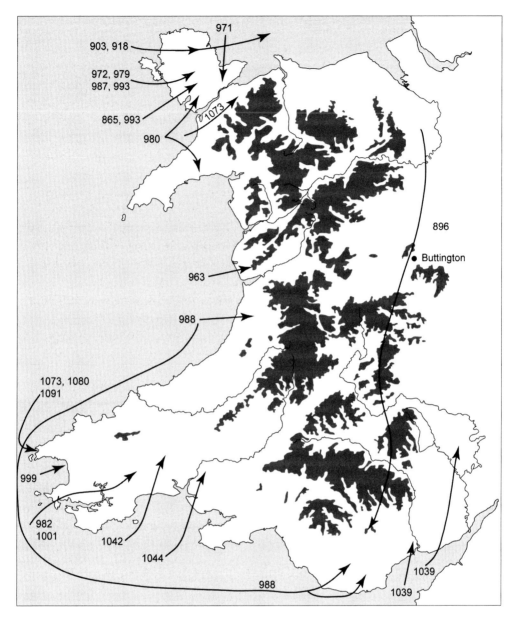

90 Map of Viking raids on Wales. (Map drawn by Yvonne Beadnell)

There was a sudden resumption of raiding after 950, which saw many *monasteria* targeted. A final phase of raiding occurred in the later eleventh century with some Vikings from Ireland fighting in alliance with Anglo-Saxon and Welsh parties and the ruling Scandinavian dynasty in England. They worked with Cnut to plunder Glamorgan (*VSC* 40) and Gruffudd ap Llywelyn to sack Hereford in 1055 (*ASC* 1055), whilst Gruffudd ap Cynan – who had some Scandinavian ancestry himself – was able to win the Battle of Mynydd Carn in 1081 with the help of a fleet partially manned by Hiberno-Norse and provided for him by Diarmait Uí Briain, King of Dublin. Hiberno-Norse fleets were used by Welsh rulers as late as 1138 to fight the Normans in Ceredigion. Whilst most Viking activity appears to have been primarily military in nature, either short term raiding or acting in concert with other factions to provide military support, there is little evidence for settlement. Never extensive in nature, Viking settlement in Wales is likely to have been most significant in Anglesey (Etchingham 2007; Redknap 2005). The *Historia Gruffudd vab Kenan* records that Ólaf Sihtricsson built a stronghold called 'Bon y Dom' on the island, possibly identifiable with the promontory fort at Castell Porth Tefadog (Longley 1991), whilst excavations by Mark Redknap at Llanbedr Goch have revealed a probable Viking farmstead or trading site, clearly in close contact with the wider Hiberno-Norse world (Redknap 2004b).

In England the Viking raids and settlement have often been seen as having a profound impact on the network of minsters that comprised the Anglo-Saxon church, with large ecclesiastical estates being dismantled and the churches and monasteries themselves being damaged or destroyed, extensive pillaging of treasuries and destruction of libraries. This view is increasingly being challenged, but it is clear that in some parts of England, the Vikings significantly affected the church (Blair 2005 292-5). The impact of the Vikings on the church in Wales was of a different order to that in England. Churches were certainly targeted for raids: the annals are a litany of Viking raids on important monasteries (Fig 90). The monks of Llancarfan took the shrine of Cadog and other relics from the monastery and sheltered at Mammelliat, although they were not safe even there and in the conflict one Viking broke a 'gilded wing' from the reliquary (*VSC* 40). One wonders how much of the 'Irish' ecclesiastical metalwork found in Viking graves in Scandinavia in fact derived from Welsh contexts. It is difficult to assess the long term impact of this raiding. It is unlikely that St Davids would have been raided 11 times between 967 and 1091 if there had not been something sufficiently valuable enough to worth raiding. All the ecclesiastical sites recorded as suffering Viking raids, such as Penmon, Clynnog Fawr, Llantwit Major and Llancarfan, all survived to become important centres once the raids ceased.

The lack of extensive Viking settlement may have helped the Welsh church weather the short-term impact of the raiding, although the Viking era may have caused longer-term structural problems in the socio-political organisation of the country (Davies 1990). The relatively temporary effects of a raid were easier to survive than the more permanent challenges of the expropriation of land and estates.

Viking impact, however, can be seen on the sculptural repertoire. There is only one certain example of a Viking 'hogback', a form of funerary sculpture that has been called a 'Viking colonial monument' (Lang 1984). The incomplete and idiosyncratic example from Llanddewi Aber-arth is outside the areas of greatest Viking activity in Wales (CD7). Closer to the known contact zone with the Vikings, a stone from Bangor (Caern.) does have some broad resemblances to hogbacks, but is probably only loosely related (Nash-Williams 1950, *80*). However, this form of monument is rare in Ireland too, with only one example known (Castledermot, County Kildare; Lang 1974). It is not surprising that in Wales, where most Viking activity was primarily Hiberno-Norse, that there are so few examples.

However, the Hiberno-Norse influence on monument form can be seen. The cross from St Edrin's (Pembrokeshire) shows strong parallels with similar stones from County Dublin and County Wicklow (Edwards 2007a), whilst the ringed-heads crosses are known from many Welsh sites including Carew, Penally (Pembrokeshire) Coychurch, Llantwit Major and Margam (Glamorgan) (P9, P82; G16, 63, 79) is found across the Danelaw and again have links ultimately with the Hiberno-Norse world. Viking influence is not just recognisable in the range of forms used, it is also apparent in the decoration itself. The best examples are on a group of stones from North Wales and Cheshire (Bryn Mawr, Anglesey; Disserth, Meliden and Whitford, Denbighshire) (Edwards 1999). It can also be seen in the type of interlace on stones from St Davids, Nevern and Carew (Pembrokeshire) (Edwards 2007). These artistic influences demonstrate Wales' position within a broader Hiberno-Norse milieu, in which elements of design were being freely borrowed and developed across the Irish Sea zone and beyond towards the western and northern Isles. Nevertheless, there is a clear difference between Wales and other areas, particularly the Danelaw. In areas of England that saw definite Scandinavian settlement the converted Viking elites appear to have adopted the Anglo-Saxon minsters for burials; this can be recognised through the clusters of distinctive stone monuments at minsters showing recognisable Scandinavian design elements and forms wedded to pre-existing trends in Anglo-Saxon sculpture (Lang 1978). Good examples include the clusters of Anglo-Scandinavian sculptures including hogbacks and crosses found in Northern England, at sites such as Gainford, Sockburn and Brompton. The number of monuments from each site that the community comprised not just individuals of Anglo-Scandinavian origin utilising these sites, but groups perhaps linked by ties of lordship or kinship. In Wales the situation is different. Whilst examples of Viking-influenced sculpture are known, there is no replication of the clustering that one might expect to find if groups of Viking settlers were exercising the opportunity to use Welsh *monasteria* for burial. This is probably because Viking settlement was never extensive and limited to isolated examples; putative political suzerainty in areas such as Anglesey need not have led to the plantation of a new stratum of lordship. In any case such periods of possible Viking control were probably relatively short term, with little time for the elites to become embedded into local society.

'WITH CHURCHES AND DEDICATIONS LIKE THE HEAVEN WITH STARS': THE CHURCH IN WALES AD 1000–1300

The Rise of the Parish

In Anglo-Saxon England the phase of Viking re-use of minster churches dated to the late ninth to mid-tenth century, after which the development of local churchyards is likely to have led to the minsters ceding their role as focal burial sites to the cemeteries linked to local churches (Blair 2005, 321). This creation of a new strata of churches, subordinate to the *monasteria*, and often linked to the elites, was to become the basis of the parochial system which came to dominate the ecclesiastical landscape of England, leading to the end of the system of *monasteria* which had hitherto formed the infrastructure of the Saxon church. This process of the replacement, usurpation and bypassing of monastic houses with regional responsibilities by churches and chapels with more local jurisdictions and loyalties was a phenomenon that spread widely across Europe in the later first millennium (Zadora-Rio 2003; Wood 2006). Whilst this trend was found at an international scale, the precise details and trajectories of this process varied widely, and Wales is no exception to this rule.

The rise of the parochial system in Wales can be seen occurring at the same time as the increased patronage of local churches. This is similar to the pattern in England in the tenth and eleventh centuries, where John Blair has argued that the foundations of the parochial system were laid in the increasing 'privatisation' of pre-existing religious foci (Blair 1996). Whilst the two phenomena are related, the link is not necessarily a direct one. A private chapel or church need not have the wider pastoral responsibilities of a parish church. Features that defined a parish include the shift of pastoral responsibilities and crucially, their associated incomes, from mother churches to local churches. The key pastoral responsibilities included the obligation to bury the dead and baptise newborns. The important incomes accrued at a local level included the payment of tithes and burial fees. The detailed documentary evidence for the formation of parishes in Wales is limited. The Norwich taxation of 1254 and the taxation of Pope Nicholas IV in 1291 show that by the end of the thirteenth century, the parochial system was well established (Pryce 2001). They provide little further information though about this process beyond a broad *terminus ante quem*.

It is probable that the major *monasteria* became increasingly interested in providing pastoral care to local communities, both in response to the wider European move towards the integration of the population within the church, but also to prevent potential lucrative sources of income being hived off into the pockets of others. This pastoral care is likely to have been provided through the network of daughter churches that most major *monasteria* had by now acquired. For example, it is clear from the Book of Llandaf that many parts of south-east Wales, such as Gwent and Ergyng were relatively well covered by a network of churches dependant on Llandaf or its predecessors. Elsewhere, Meifod was the mother church of Llanfair Caereinion, Guilsfield, Welshpool and Alberbury (Shropshire), whilst Llanbadarn Fawr had over 20 daughter houses. There is some regional patterning to be found; mother churches with larger numbers of daughter churches tend to be found in the north and west of Wales, which reflects the tendency for parishes in these areas to have more townships (Sylvester 1967). This pattern of parishes with large numbers of townships is not just a feature of these parts of Wales, but reflects a wider distinction between the north and west and the south and east of England and Wales, with large parishes being found in a wide band running from Cardiganshire through Cheshire to Lancashire and Northumberland. The reasons for this pattern may be manifold, but undoubtedly reflect both the variations in the topography (highland versus lowland) and differing patterns of manorialisation and lordship following the Norman Conquest.

Not surprisingly, there is a broad link between the manorialisation of areas of Wales settled by the Normans, particularly in the south-west and south, and the creation of parishes. Many of these new, and often small, parishes were spatially coterminous with these new manors. The formation of parishes was not, however, exclusively a Norman prerogative; parochial networks became established under the native rulers too. It is probable that princely initiative was important in this process. It is likely that as in the Norman areas of Wales, these new parishes were linked to secular land structures. Thomas Charles-Edwards has argued that they were based on the boundaries of pre-existing *maenorydd* (Charles-Edwards 1993, 445-6). Colin Gresham, however, suggested a greater level of princely initiative, arguing on the basis of the similarity in boundaries of the townships found in the Aberconwy and Cymer charters with the boundaries of the parochial network in the same area, that both may have been laid out by the kings of Gwynedd (Gresham 1987; Pryce 2001, 258-9). He argued that this had been completed by the 1170s, although some problems with the precise chronology of this material have now been recognised (Insley 1999).

One way of recognising the spread of parishes is through the distribution of fonts, as baptism was one of the key pastoral functions devolved to parish churches. The present of a font is a *de facto* indicator of parochial status. There was a rapid flowering of fonts across Wales in the twelfth century. The group of distinctive carved fonts from Anglesey using interlace may indicate the royal patronage of Gruffudd ap Cynan (d.1137) or his son Owain Gwynedd (d.1170); it is noticeable that the font from Newborough is in a church adjacent to the royal *llys* at Rhosyr (see above). This might seemingly confirm Gresham's broad hypothesis that the spread of parishes in native Wales was a princely initiative. However, the widespread appearance of fonts at local churches across Wales is more likely to indicate a change in lower-level secular patronage with investment by local elites rather than royalty. This seems to be the case at Patrishow,

91 An aerial view of the *llys* at Rhosyr (Anglesey) and the associated church (top left). (© GAT)

where an inscription on the font appears to record its donation by a certain Genillin, who is probably the Genyllyn, son of Rhys Goch born about 1070, suggesting a late eleventh or early twelfth-century date (B43). It is likely that the font was a donation to the church at the time of its reconsecration by Herewald, Bishop of Llandaf (LL 279), which seems to record the establishment of a network of parishes across Herefordshire at this time.

In general though, it is difficult to distinguish the formalised process of establishing territorial parishes with their key pastoral responsibilities from a wider process of increased privatisation and local investment in churches in the eleventh and twelfth centuries. One of the key dynamics behind the process was the tension between the bishops and the nobility who sought more influence and control over the ecclesiastical sites within their territory. Whilst the provision of economic support and the threat of physical violence allowed the Welsh rulers to exert indirect power over *monasteria,* there was a search for more direct ways of controlling churches. One way in which this might have been exercised was through retaining churches as private property. A number of charters from the Book of Llandaf refer to the donation of churches to monasteries by kings and other lay men, which may suggest that they were in private hands up until that point (e.g. LL73a, 199a, 231; Davies 1978). It is not clear whether this implies that lay individuals had founded these churches. It is possible that this reflects powerful laymen exerting direct influence over pre-existing establishments and re-allocating land from one church to another for political reasons, perhaps paralleling Alfred's gifting of the minsters of Congresbury and Banwell to Asser (*Asser* c.81; Blair 2005, 324-5). However, it is clear from one or two examples that in some cases laymen were attempting to exercise their rights of presentment (the authority to appoint priests to the church). A charter claiming to date from the mid-eighth century records Cuchein donating land to bishop Guodloiu along with Gwynwal and his family to serve it (LL168); this is a rare exception, and evidence for the lay control over the appointment of clergy at this early date is rare.

In general, evidence for direct secular intervention in the establishment of churches does not begin until the eleventh century. It finds its most powerful and explicit expression in the biography of Gruffudd ap Cynan, who died in 1137, which records of his reign 'now people began to found churches … Gruffudd also built large churches next to his palaces, which he built and established beautifully, sparing no expense' (*VGFC* 33). Whilst there is an undoubtedly rhetorical dimension to this passage, which is an encomium to his reign, it does appear to attest to the establishment of proprietary churches by the king and other laypersons. The creation of these churches can be recognised on the ground in the spread of twelfth-century stone churches across Anglesey (see Chapter Three). At Rhosyr, one of the *llysoedd* (courts) of the kings of Gwynedd, the church of St Peter's which lies to the north of the main site in a separate enclosure, may be one of these royal foundations (Fig 91).

There is other evidence for the foundation of churches by secular initiative. At Llanfihangel-y-Traethu a pillar stone dating to *c.*1150 reads 'Here is the tomb of Wleder, the mother of Odeleu, who first built this church in the time of King Owain' (Fig 21). It is also possible that individuals mentioned in church names may also be their founders. The most secure example is probably that of Betws Gwerful Goch (Denbighshire) founded by

Gwerful Goch, daughter of Cynan ab Owain Gwynedd around the turn of the thirteenth century (Roberts 1991; Bartrum 1963–4, 103). Other examples of *Betws* place-names with the probable founders' names include Betws Beldrws (Cardiganshire), Betws Cedewain (Monmouthshire) and Betws Leucu (Cardiganshire). Almost all examples of churches with the place-name Betws are dependant chapels, and it may be that they were established by individuals attempting to create their own private churches within an already developed parochial or quasi-parochial network. It is also quite possible that many of the *Llan* place-names with otherwise unattested personal names record the name of the patron or founder, rather than otherwise unrecorded saints as is sometimes assumed.

In general, the eleventh and twelfth centuries saw a significant increase in investment and new patterns of patronage in churches by the secular elite. These can be recognised in several ways. There appears to be a genuine transformation in the nature of churches themselves, with a transition from primarily wooden architecture to a tradition based on building in stone. The lack of a pre-Norman stone church tradition in Wales is highly distinctive and it is only in the twelfth century that stone churches begin to become common. It is perhaps not surprising that the best evidence for early stone churches comes from the parts of Wales that saw early Norman settlement, particularly the south-west and south-east. Elsewhere, though, it is probable that many churches built in the twelfth century were not new foundations, but the consolidation of pre-existing field cemeteries. The best example of this is at Capel Maelog, probably constructed in the twelfth century on a site which had already seen simple burial activity, then had subsequently been enclosed by a ditch (Britnell 1991). It is likely that by the end of the twelfth century, all simple field cemeteries had been converted, either into parish churches or dependent chapels. The crucial factor is the recognition that this process saw the culmination of a struggle for control over burial between the church and kinship groups.

It is not just the use of stone fabric that is significant in gaining a better understanding of the process of local patronage, privatisation and parish formation. Although the evidential base is small, it is noticeable that the few pre-Conquest wooden churches known were significantly smaller than their stone successors; this can be seen clearly at Llanelen and Burry Holmes. It is possible that this may reflect the changing function of these churches. The small, early wooden churches are too confined to have contained anything but a very small congregation. The increased size of the structure may indicate the need for greater space to accommodate growing congregations, though even these larger churches were still, relatively small in size. There may be some significance in the change from single cell structures to bicameral churches; it has been suggested that the presence of a chancel was indicative of a pastoral and thus parochial role (e.g. O'Keefe 2006). However, in Wales many parish churches never developed an eastern compartment, with the difference between the chancel and the nave being marked simply by a screen. In this way it may partly reflect the situation in Ireland, where large single-cell structures were common (Ó Carragáin 2006).

Monasteria

Despite the growth of parish and proprietary churches from the tenth century onwards, the pre-existing *monasteria* continued to be important in the ecclesiastical geography of the

Welsh church. However, these churches underwent a variety of developments, and whilst most *monasteria* survived this period of rapid change, it was usually because they had undergone some form of transformation of form or function.

It was perhaps the tenth and eleventh centuries that saw the *monasteria* reach their apogee. They were consolidating their economic and social power through the accumulation of land grants and incomes derived through pilgrimage. Larger and more powerful communities increasingly assumed a dominant role over lesser churches in their sphere of influence. These may have been donated directly to them by local nobles, as is seen throughout the Llandaf charters, or they may have founded what were daughter houses and granges. Some, such as Meifod, also became the focus for royal patronage and developed as dynastic burial grounds. Others, such as Llanbadarn Fawr and Llancarfan became notable centres of learning. It is these powerful houses with their relics, altars and influential patronage that were celebrated in poems such as *Canu Cadfan*, *Canu Tysilio* and *Canu Dewi*. These all make reference to the liberality and hospitality of these churches, and as has been noted 'the boundary between the secular and the ecclesiastical seemed to have become hopelessly blurred in the native Welsh church' (Davies 1991, 176). This is captured clearly in Gerald of Wales's description of the appearance of the lay abbot of Llanbadarn and his retinue arriving to celebrate a feast day armed with long spears (*Journey* 2.5). An absence of celibacy and the hereditary and communal nature of membership of many ecclesiastical communities doubtless aggravated this perceived drift to secularism. Combined with the Welsh practice of partitive inheritance, secular interests in churches multiplied (Davies 1991, 176-77; Evans 1992). Gerald noted 'A Welsh church has as many incumbents and sharers in the living as there are important families resident in the parish' (*Journey* 2.6).

From the twelfth century onwards a key way in which the former *monasteria* might develop was by being converted into houses of the reformed monastic orders that dominated the western European church at this time. Whilst the members of the *monasteria* undoubtedly followed a broadly codified monastic discipline, the rules are likely to have been local and developed organically. The spread of the reformed Benedictine rule began in England in the later tenth century thanks to the advocacy of Bishops Dunstan, Aethelwold and Oswald. However, there is no evidence of the adoption of the rule by any Welsh houses before the twelfth century, though it is not inconceivable that monasteries may have taken to the rule due to local initiative. It is noticeable that one of the key factors in the success of the Benedictine reforms in England had been the royal sponsorship provided by King Eadgar (943–75). It is doubtful whether any Welsh kings in the later tenth or eleventh centuries had the political power or indeed interest to encourage reform at anything beyond a very local level. By the twelfth century, however, the impact of the reform movement was being felt in Wales. Some *monasteria* were reformed and allocated to the new Orders; Bardsey, Penmon and Beddgelert became Augustinian houses, demonstrating a preference for the Augustinians in north Wales (Davies 1987, 196). In the south-east the 'bishop-houses' at Carmarthen and St Dogmaels fell under the control of the Augustinians and Tironians respectively.

A final possible trajectory for *monasteria* was demotion and privatisation. A good example of this is Patrishow. Its early *merthyr* place-name and the presence of an *eglwys-y-bedd* suggest that it was originally a small *monasteria* and a cult centre for St Ishaw. However, by the late eleventh century it appears to have become a proprietary church. It is possible that its consecration by Herewald marked its formal transition from corporate monastic site to proprietary church (see above). This kind of process parallels similar patterns known from Anglo-Saxon England, which saw minsters devolving into private ownership, such as the former minster of Kirkdale (North Yorkshire) where an inscription records how the new owner 'bought St Gregory's minster when it was completely broken and fallen and he had it newly built from the ground' (Blair 2005, 359).

The Impact of the Normans

The Normans loom large in discussions of the changes in the Welsh church in the eleventh and twelfth centuries. It is important to be cautious in laying the responsibility for all the changes in the Welsh church at the door of the incoming French. It is easy to characterise this period as one in which an aggressive Norman church imposes reform and reorganisation on a passive Welsh church, which had hitherto been isolated from the wider developments in western Christendom. This would be far from the truth. Whilst the impact of a powerful new political dynasty in England, the establishment of aggressive marcher lords and significant settlement in some areas of Wales by Norman knights undoubtedly had an impact on the Welsh church, it was not the causative factor behind the changes it was undergoing (Lieberman 2007; Davies 1987, 172-212). Rather they acted as a catalyst, hastening processes already underway. However, this is not to suggest that the Normans had no effect on the Welsh church. They certainly stimulated and accelerated the spread of the reformed monastic orders, though it is important not to forget that the native rulers of Wales promoted many of these foundations. The Cistercians appear to have achieved a special place in the loyalties of the native Welsh rulers (Robinson 2006).

The majority of Cistercian houses were either native foundations or within native territory. These included Whitland (1140), Strata Florida (1164), Strata Marcella (1170), Cwm-hir (1176), Llantarnam (1179), Llanllŷr (1180), Aberconwy (1186), Cymer (1199) and Valle Crucis (1201). It is notable that a number of these monasteries appear to have been located on sites that may already have had an earlier church on them. A cross-carved stone of eighth or ninth-century date is known from Strata Florida (CD1) and a stone recording a land grant is known from Llanllŷr (ibid). The foundation charter of Valle Crucis refers to the village Llanegwestl, which was cleared to allow the construction of the monastery; the place-name suggests the presence of a church at the site (Pryce 2005, 500). However, in all these cases there is nothing to suggest that the earlier religious sites were of particular status. It is possible that the founders of the Cistercian houses were deliberately avoiding refounding or reforming powerful and entrenched native ecclesiastical communities, and instead opting to work from a clean slate. It is interesting to note that the Cistercian foundations which certainly were pre-existing native *monasteria*, such as Margam and probably Neath, were both founded by Anglo-Norman lords, who perhaps had a vested interest in making connections to existing power-structures within their territories.

The creation of new political borders also led to pressure being exerted on the dioceses of Wales. A Norman bishop was imposed on St Davids in 1115 and Bangor in 1120. The diocese of St Asaph was probably an entirely new foundation when the first Norman bishop was appointed in 1145, whilst the diocese of Llandaf emerged in the eleventh century. The new Norman appointments were unambiguous declarations of intent that the Welsh church should come under the jurisdiction of Canterbury. There was also reform of the *clas* churches, which were home to the Welsh bishops, with the establishment of cathedral chapters and associated prebends (e.g. Pearson 2000–1). The diocesan hierarchy was further enhanced with the creation of archdeacons and deaneries (Davies 1991, 185), which can be seen even in North Wales in the Valuation of Norwich (1254) and the *Taxatio Ecclesiastica* (1291) (Pryce 2001, 255–6).

The need for bishops to justify and buttress their existing secular and spiritual territorial claims had a number of consequences. Crucially, we see what was, in practice, a rediscovery of the importance of history. The flowering of hagiography at this time reflects a new attempt by ecclesiastical communities to certify and validate their claims by appealing to the testimony of the past, particularly the imprimatur of a long-established link with an important saint. The need to provide documentary support for claims to jurisdiction was felt by both native and Norman churches. It was, of course, the newly created Norman diocese of Llandaf that produced the *Liber Landauensis* as a dossier in support of its territorial integrity and ecclesiastical jurisdiction (Davies 2007a).

The increased importance of making links to saints is also reflected in a rash of relics being discovered, translated or provided with a new shrine. Bishop Urban oversaw the translation of the relics of St Dyfrig and St Elgar from Bardsey Island to the church at Llandaf. It is clear that whilst the Norman ecclesiastical hierarchy had some qualms about the un-reformed nature of the Welsh church, they had no such compunction about adopting native Welsh saints. Winefride's relics were removed from Gwytherin by the monks of Shrewsbury in 1137 seemingly in order to provide their monastery with some relics of their own. According to Robert of Shrewsbury their Prior bemoaned that 'they frequently lamented to each other that they had a great need of some relics of the saints, and with all their efforts applied their minds to acquiring some' (Robert of Shrewsbury quoted in Bartlett 1999). This revival in the 'discovery' and movement of saints' relics occurs at the same time as a change in the way in which relics were presented within churches. Nancy Edwards has noted that in Wales, it is not until the eleventh or twelfth century that corporeal relics began to be placed in above ground reliquaries. Previously, holy tombs appear to have been elaborated by the construction of burial chapels around them. The bodies themselves were raised up and placed in more elaborate shrines. This process is seen most clearly at Pennant Melangell, the other sites with similar carved stone shrines in Powys. At St Woolos Newport, a possession of Gloucester Priory, it appears that the relics of Gwynllyw were provided with a fine new Romanesque chapel; presumably this, too, coincided with the elevation of the saint's relics (Knight and Wood 2006).

Church, Kinship and Land

From the tenth to twelfth century, a new form of land holding, *tir cyfrif* (reckon land), was beginning to develop in northern Wales. Rather than emphasising inheritance through membership of a kinship, it emphasised inheritance through membership of a townland (Charles-Edwards 1993 400-407). It is probable that *tir cyfrif* was imposed from above by the powerful kings of Gwynedd to facilitate the payment of royal dues (ibid 433-4). One consequence of this change in landholding was that, for bondsmen, land was no longer reallocated following the death of a member of a kinship; instead sharing took place when a son reached his majority. Thus, for those of lower status the intimate link between land and inheritance on one hand and death and its commemoration on the other was broken. In many ways this is reflected in the move away from the family burial grounds of the earlier periods to church-controlled enclosed cemeteries and parochial churchyards. The growth of the parish meant that the relationship between the individual and their church became defined by residence rather than kinship. This move from structuring of society through space and territory, rather than kinship and personal relationships reflects wider transitions in early second millennium Europe linked to the rise of feudalism (Dodgshon 1987, 126-30).

The development of direct control over burial by the church and the rise of the parish may well have acted to reduce the importance of kinship, as a key form of creating socal identity, particularly for those of lower status. Charles-Edwards has suggested that kinship was less important for lower-status individuals in both Wales and Ireland. (Charles-Edwards 1997, 413-78). Nonetheless, whilst forms of landholding such as *tir cyfrif* led to a territorialisation of community for those of lesser status, kinship remained a crucial structuring element in the upper levels of society. The fact that the parish churches were most likely built and supported by local elites is a reminder that in many ways they were exercising increased influence over the church at a local level. For the lords of native Wales and the Norman marches, land and status continued to be inherited through the family line. At this time, we see the expressions of status reflected in the new forms of burial monument, such as effigies and other forms of monumental sculpture. These reflect a new drive by the elites to perpetuate and re-assert their own importance, and that of their lineages, within their local churches. This goes hand in hand with the use of more distinctively 'Norman' monument types, such as carved recumbant burial monuments and effigies which engage with a wider pan-Norman tradition of funerary sculpture.

CROSS CURRENTS: THE WELSH CHURCH IN ITS WIDER CONTEXT

Throughout this book, whether looking at church construction, the use of relics or the development of the Christian burial rite, the focus has been on showing that the church in early medieval Wales was not isolated or unique. The Welsh church, of course, had its own distinct history; unlike the Anglo-Saxon church it developed from an earlier stratum of Roman Christianity, and it did not accept the Roman Easter until the eighth century. However, it is wrong to have a simplistic model of the church in Wales as remote from and uninfluenced by, the Anglo-Saxon church.

From the late eighth century there was clear interaction between the Anglo-Saxon church and the Welsh church. This inter-relationship can be seen in many ways. Alfred would hardly have sought out Asser to act as Bishop of Sherbourne if there were hostile relationships between the Anglo-Saxon and British churches; this political act shows that the court of Wessex had a detailed knowledge of the people and personalities of St Davids. It is probable that Anglo-Saxon churchmen also took up positions in the Welsh church if the names of Wilfred and Ælfric in the bishop list of *Clas Cynidr* are an indicator (Fleuriot 1976). It is not surprising that along the Anglo-Welsh border we see many indicators of Anglo-Saxon influence, whether in the choice of a distinctive Mercian cross type at the Pillar of Eliseg or the hints of Anglo-Saxon linear planning in the arrangement of *eglwys y bedd* at Pennant Melangell and Patrishow. Anglo-Saxon names appear on 'Welsh' sculpture, such as Siwerd son of Vulmer, recorded on a stone from Llangors (Redknap and Lewis 2007). The fact that it has been so difficult to identify the precise origin of the Chad Gospels and the Hereford Gospels shows that, whilst one appears to have originated to the west of Offa's Dyke and one to the east, they belong to the same manuscript tradition.

Equally, whilst the church had close links with Ireland, it would be erroneous to maintain an artificial construct of a distinct 'Celtic' church. There are certainly borrowings from Ireland, such as the use of ogham in the fifth and sixth centuries, though even this is more likely to have been borrowed in a secular context. There is also undoubted Irish influence in the sculptural tradition of Wales (Edwards 2007). Nonetheless, in emphasising the debts to Ireland, it is easy to miss the many areas where there is no influence. The Irish tradition of high crosses, for example, has no convincing Welsh analogues. Most conspicuous though is the fact that despite the presence of vibrant traditions of stone church architecture in contemporary Ireland and England, stone churches were not built in Wales until the eleventh century at the very earliest. They would certainly have been familiar with the building traditions of Ireland and England. Arguments that the Welsh church was too poor to build stone churches remain unconvincing. One is reminded of the call by Nechtan, king of the Picts to Ceolfrid to ask for architects to build a stone church in the Roman style (*EH* 4.21); a clear demonstration of how, in the early medieval world, the material used in the construction of a church could be laden with symbolic importance.

The complexity of the meaning behind particular classes of object can be seen in the distribution of Irish enamelled metalwork, which is surprisingly mainly found in the borders between Wales and Mercia, rather than the traditional Hiberno-Welsh contact zones of Anglesey and Dyfed. Is this simply a chance distribution or does it reflect a distinct area of circulation of Irish style metalwork? It is noticeable that the construction of the only crannog in Wales, a typically Irish building form, is at Llangors. This suggests that notions of Irish identity were being constructed and manipulated in this part of Wales, perhaps linked to a perceived or real Irish origin for earlier royal dynasties. A final example of the creativity and complexity of Welsh religious practice can be found further north in Powys, where the construction of elaborate Romanesque stone shrines at a series of churches, including, Pennant Melangell, Llanrhaeadr-ym-Mochnant and Llangollen, suggest a unique and localised response to the political threats imposed by the burgeoning Norman marcher lords. But if these shrines, primarily to native Welsh saints, are an indigenous reaction to the changing political complexion of this part of Powys, then it is expressed in a new material vocabulary drawing on models from beyond England and looking wider to France, the home of the Normans.

The presence of these distinct, national and local, expressions of religious practice do not make the Welsh church any different from any of the other developed churches of western Christendom. The churches of France, Germany or Anglo-Saxon England all show a variety of responses to the diverse political and social landscapes in which they were situated. At a wider level furthermore, the churches of northern Europe follow a similar trajectory, moving from loose networks of monastic establishments, sometimes structured on a pre-existing framework of Roman towns, to large mother churches (minsters/*monasteria*) covering large territories which are often co-terminous with secular administrative structures. These mother churches are encroached upon by an increasing number of privatised churches (*eigenkirchen*/ estate churches) developed by the secular aristocracy, which ultimately form the basis for the establishment of a fully developed parochial system that characterises the church of the high medieval period. This book has shown that the Welsh church conforms to this broader pattern, and should be understood as part of the mainstream of early medieval Christianity in Europe and not as an isolated and idiosyncratic backwater.

BIBLIOGRAPHY

AC   *Archaeologia Cambrensis*
AJ   *Archaeological Journal*
AnJ   *Antiquaries Journal*
BBCS   *Bulletin of the Board of Celtic Studies*
CA   *Church Archaeology*
CMCS   *Cambridge/CMSC*
MA   *Medieval Archaeology*
PRIA   *Proceedings of the Royal Irish Academy*
SC   *Studia Celtica*
TAAFC   *Transactions of the Anglesey Antiquarian and Field Club*

Ahronson, K.W., Gillies and F. Hunter. 2004. 'Early Christian activity at Scottish cave sites' *CA* 7/8/9

Aitchison N.B. 1994. *Armagh and the royal centres in early medieval Ireland* Woodbridge

Aitchison, N.B. 2006. *Forteviot* Stroud

Alcock, E., 1992. 'Burials and cemeteries in Scotland' in Edwards, N. and Lane, A. (eds) 1992

Alcock, L. 1963. *Dinas Powys* Cardiff

Alcock, L, 1967. 'Excavations at Degannwy Castle, Caernarvonshire, 1961–6' *AJ* 124

Aldhelm – Aldhelm: The Prose Works (trans M. Lapidge and M. Herren) Cambridge

Alexander, J. and Binski, P. (eds) 1987. *Age of Chivalry* London

Allen, J.R. 1891. 'A medieval thurible found at Penmaen in Gower' *AC* 8

Allen, J.R. 1898. 'Metal bowls of the late Celtic and Anglo-Saxon periods' *Archaeologia* 56

The Anglo-Saxon Chronicle (ed and trans M. Swanton) London

Anon, 1848. 'Archaeological intelligence' *AJ* 5

Anon 1859. 'Proceedings at the Meetings of the Archaeological Institute' *AJ* 16

Anon, 1859. 'Cardigan meeting' *AC* 5

Anon, 1912. 'Report of the 65th annual meeting held at Abergele' *AC* (6th series) 12

Arnold, C.J. 1998. "Excavations at Ty Newydd, Ynys Enlli (Bardsey Island), Gwynedd' *AC* 147

Arnold, C.J. and Davies, J. 2000. *Roman and early medieval Wales* Stroud

Asser's Life of Alfred (trans Keynes, S. and Lapidge, M.) 1983 *Alfred the Great* Harmondsworth

Atherton, M. 2002. 'Introduction' in Atherton, M. (ed) 2002

Atherton, M. (ed) 2002. *Celts and Christians* Cardiff

Backhouse, J., D.H. Turner and L. Webster (eds) 1984. *The Golden Age of Anglo-Saxon Art* London

Badger, A.B. and Grew, F. 1925. 'The Chapel traditionally attributed to St Patrick, Whitesand Bay, Pembrokeshire' *AC* 82

Badham, S. 1999.' Medieval minor effigial monuments in West & South Wales' *Church Monuments* 14

Baily, R. 1974. 'The Anglo-Saxon metalwork from Hexham' in D.P. Kirby (ed) *Saint Wilfrid at Hexham* Newcastle

Bammesberger, A. and Wollman, A. (eds) 1990. *Britain 400–600: Language and History* Heidelberg

Barford, P., Owen, W.G. and Britnell, W.J. 1986. 'Iron spearhead and javelin from Four Crosses, Llandysilio, Powys' *MA* 30

Baring-Gould, S. and Fisher, J. 1907–15. *The lives of the British saints* London

Barker, K. 1984. 'Sherborne in Dorset: an early ecclesiastical settlement and its estate' *AASAH3*

Barnwell, E.L. 1872. 'Wooden font, Efenechtyd Church' *AC* (4th series) 3

Barnwell, P. 2004. 'The laity, the clergy and the Divine presence' *JBAA* 157

Barrowman, R., Batey, C. and Morris, C.D. 2007. *Excavations at Tintagel Castle, Cornwall, 1990–1999* London

Bartlett, R. 1999. 'Cults of Irish, Welsh and Scottish saints in twelfth-century England' in Smith, B. (ed) 1999. *Britain and Ireland, 900–1300* Cambridge

Bartlett, R. 2006. *Gerald of Wales* troud

Bassett, S. 1985. 'A probable Mercian royal mausoleum at Winchcombe, Gloucestershire' *AnJ* 65

Bassett, S. 1991. 'Churches in Worcester before and after the conversion of the Anglo-Saxons' *AnJ* 69

Bassett, S 1992a. 'Church and diocese in the West Midlands: the transition from British to Anglo-Saxon control' in J. Blair and R. Sharpe (eds) 1992

Bassett, S. 1992b. 'Medieval ecclesiastical organisation in the vicinity of Wroxeter and its British antecedents' *JBAA* 135

Beckwith, J. 1972 *Ivory carvings in early medieval England* London

Bennett, G. 1838. *The pedestrian's guide through North Wales*, London

Biddle, M. 1986. 'Archaeology, architecture and the cult of saints in Anglo-Saxon England' in L.A.S. Butler and R.K. Morris (eds) 1986. *The Anglo-Saxon Church*, York, 1–31

Bieler, L. 1979. *The Patrician texts in the Book of Armagh* Dublin

Bischoff, B. 1990. *Latin Palaeography* Cambridge

Blair, J. 1985. 'Secular minster churches in Domesday Book' in P. Sawyer (ed), *Domesday Book* London

Blair, J. and Sharpe, R. (eds) 1992. *Pastoral Care Before the Parish*, Leicester

Blair, J. 1995. 'Ecclesiastical organisation and pastoral care in Anglo-Saxon England' *Early Medieval Europe* 4

Blair J, 1996. 'Churches in the early English landscape: social and cultural contexts', in J Blair and C Pyrah (eds) 1996

Blair, J. 2001. 'The Anglo-Saxon Church in Herefordshire: Four Themes' in Leominster History Study Group (ed) *The Early Church in Herefordshire* Leominster

Blair, J. 2005. *The Church in Anglo-Saxon Society* Oxford

Blair, J. and C Pyrah (eds) 1996. *Church Archaeology*, York

Blindheim, M. 1984. 'A house-shaped Irish-Scots reliquary in Bologna' *Acta Archaeologia* 55

Boake, E.J. 1926. 'Report on the excavation of the Chapel of St Justinian, St Davids' *AC* 81

Boon, G. 1972. *Isca; The Roman legionary fortress at Caerleon,* Cardiff

Boon, G. 1992. 'The early church in Gwent 1.The Romano-British Church' *Monmouthshire Antiquary* 8

Borg, A. 1985. 'The Gloucester candlestick' in T. Heslop and V. Sekules (eds) *Medieval Art and Architecture at Gloucester and Tewkesbury* London

Bourke, C. 1980. 'Early Irish hand-bells' *Journal of the Royal Society of Antiquaries of Ireland* 110

Bowen, E. and Gresham, C. 1967. *History of Merioneth. Vol I,* Cardiff

Boyle, S.D. 1991. 'Survey and excavation at Towyn y Capel, Trearddur Bay' *TAAFC*

Boyer, R. 1981. 'An attempt to define the typology of medieval hagiography' in H. Bekker-Nelson (ed) *Hagiography and Medieval Literature* Odense

Bowen, E. 1954. *The Settlements of the Celtic Saints* Cardiff

Bowen, E. 1969. *Saints, seaways and settlements in the Celtic lands* Cardiff

Bradley, R. 1990. *The passage of arms* Cambridge

Bradley, R. 1993. *Altering the Earth* Edinburgh

Bradley, R. 2000. *An archaeology of natural places* London

Bradley, J. 1994. 'The Monastic Town of Clonmacnoise' *Clonmacnoise Studies* 1, Dublin, 42–55

Brady, N. 1997. '*De Oratorio; Hisperica Famina* and church building' *Peritia* 11

Bradley, I. 1999. *Celtic Christianity: making myths and chasing dreams* Edinburgh

Brassil, K.S, Owen, W.G. and Britnell, W.J. 1991. 'Prehistoric and early medieval cemeteries at Tandderwen, near Denbigh, Clwyd' *AJ* 148

Brenan, J. 1991. *Hanging-bowls and their contexts* Oxford, BAR 220

Briggs, C.S. 1997, *An Inventory of the Ancient Monuments in Brecknock (Brycheiniog), The Prehistoric and Roman Monuments, Part i: Later Prehistoric Monuments and Unenclosed Settlements to 1000 AD* Stroud

Brinley Jones, R, 2004 'Llwyd, Humphrey (1527–1568)', *Oxford Dictionary of National Biography*, Oxford [http://www.oxforddnb.com.voyager.chester.ac.uk/view/article/16867, accessed 5 July 2007]

Britnell, W.J. 1990. 'Capel Maeolog, Llandrindon Wells, Powys: Excavation 1984-1987' *MA* 34

Britnell, W.J. 1994a. 'The boundaries of the parish of Pennant Melangell' *Montgomeryshire Collections* 82

Britnell, W.J. 1994b. 'Excavation and Recording at Pennant Melangell Church,' *Montgomeryshire Collections* 82

Bromwich, R. 2006. (ed and trans) *Trioedd Ynys Prydein: The Welsh Triads,* (3rd Edition) Cardiff

Brook, D. 1985/6. 'The early Christian church in Gwent' *Monmouthshire Antiquary* 13

Brooke, C. 1986. *The Church and the Welsh Border in the Central Middle Ages* Woodbridge

Brown, D. 1982. *The Lichfield Gospels* London

Bruce-Mitford, R. 2005. *A Corpus of Late Celtic Hanging Bowls* Oxford

Bullough, D. 1983. 'Burial, Community and Belief in the Early Medieval West' in P. Wormald (ed) 1983 *Ideal and Reality in Frankish and Anglo-Saxon Society.* Oxford

Burnham, B. and Wacher, J. 1990. *The Small Towns of Roman Britain* London

Burnham, B. 1993. 'Sites explored in Roman Britain: Wales' *Britannia* 24

Butler, L.A.S. 1971. 'Medieval ecclesiastical architecture in Glamorgan and Gower' in T.B. Pugh (ed) *Glamorgan County History* III Cardiff

Butler, L. 1996. 'The medieval church on the Isle of Man *c*1200–1600' in Blair, J. and Pyrah, C. (eds) 1996

Butler, L. and Graham-Campbell, J. 1990.' A lost reliquary casket from Gwytherin, North Wales' *AnJ* 70

Bryant, R. 1980. 'Excavations at St Mary De Lode, Gloucester 1978–1979' *Glevenis* 14

BYT – Brut y Tywysogion or The Chronicle of the Princes, Peniarth MS. 20 Version, (transl. Thomas Jones), Cardiff

Cameron, K. 1968. 'Eccles in place-names' in M.W. Barley and R.P.C. Hanson (eds) *Christianity in Britain* Leicester

Campbell, E. 1988. 'The Post-Roman Pottery' in Edwards, N. and Lane, A. (eds) 1988

Campbell, E. 1991. *Imported Goods in Early Medieval Celtic West* PhD thesis, University of Wales

Campbell, E. 1996. 'The early medieval pottery' in Wilkinson, P. 1996. 'Excavations at Hen Gastell, Briton Ferry, West Glamorgan, 1991–92' *MA* 39

Campbell, E. 1997. 'The Dark Age Ceramics' in Hill, P. (ed) 1997. *Whithorn and St Ninian*, Stroud

Campbell, E. 2007. *Continental and Mediterranean imports to Atlantic Britain and Ireland AD400–800*). York

Campbell, E. and Macdonald, P. 1993. 'Excavations at Caerwent Vicarage Orchard Garden 1973: an extra-mural post-Roman Cemetery' *AC* 142

Carr, A.D. 1982. *Medieval Anglesey* Llangefni

Cartwright, J. (ed) 2003. *Celtic Hagiography and Saint's Cults* Cardiff

CB – Cognacio Brychan/ Family of Brychan in Wade-Evans, A. (ed and trans) 1944. *Vitae Sanctorum Britanniae et Genealogiae* Cardiff

Chadwick, O. 1959. 'The evidence of dedications in the early history of the Welsh church' in O. Chadwick (ed) *Studies in early British history*, Cambridge

Chambers, R.A. 1987. 'The Late and Sub-Roman Cemetery at Queenford Farm, Dorchester-on-Thames, Oxon' *Oxoniensis* 52

Charles, B.G. 1947. 'The Second Book of George Owen's Description of Pembrokeshire' *National Library of Wales Journal*

Charles-Edwards, G. 2003. 'The Springmount Bog tablets: their implications for insular epigraphy and palaeography' *SC* 36

Charles-Edwards, G. 2005. 'The Palaeography of the Inscriptions' in M. Redknap and J. Lewis (eds) 2007

Charles-Edwards, T. 1970–2. 'The seven bishop houses of Dyfed' *BBCS* 24

Charles-Edwards, T. 1978. 'The authenticity of the *Gododdin*' in Bromwich, R. and R.B. Jones (eds) *Astudiaethau ar yr Hengerdd*

Charles-Edwards, T. 1989. *Writers of Wales: The Welsh Laws* Cardiff

Charles-Edwards, T. 1993. *Early Irish and Welsh Kingship* Oxford

Charles-Edwards, T. 2002. '*Érlam*: the patron-saint of an Irish church' in A. Thacker and R. Sharpe (eds) 2002.

Charles-Edwards, T. 2004. '*Gorsedd, dadl* and *llys*: assemblies and courts in medieval Wales' *in Pantos, A. and Semple, J. (eds)*

Clancy, T. 2003. 'Magpie hagiography in twelfth-century Scotland' in J. Cartwright (ed) 2003

Clarke, S. 1991. 'The origins of medieval pottery in south-east Wales' *Medieval Ceramics* 15

Clear, J.B. 1866. 'The contents of graves in St David's Cathedral' *AC* (3rd series) 12

Coe, J. 2004. 'Dating the boundary clauses in the Book of Llandaf' *CMSC* 48

Coe, J. 2002. *Placenames of the Book of Llandaf* PhD thesis, University of Wales

Cole, J.R. and Pratt, D. 1993. 'Capel Spon, Buckley, Clwyd' *AW* 33

Coleman, S. and Elsner, J. 1995. *Pilgrimage past and present in the World Religions* London

Colloms, B. 2004. 'Gould, Sabine Baring (1834–1924)', *Oxford Dictionary of National Biography*, Oxford [http://www.oxforddnb.com.voyager.chester.ac.uk/view/article/30587, accessed 7 July 2007]

Conf. – Confessio in *St. Patrick: his writings and Muirchu's Life* (ed and trans A.B.E. Hood) London

Conran, T. 1992. *Welsh Verse* Seren

Conway, G. 1997. 'Towards a cultural context for the eleventh-century Llanbadarn manuscripts' *Ceredigion* 13(1)

Coplestone-Crow, B. 1989. *Herefordshire Place-names* Oxford

Courtney, P. 1993. 'Copper alloy' in W.J. Britnell 1994. 'Excavation and recording at Pennant Melangell Church' *Montgomery Collections* 82

Courtney, P. Jones, N.W. and Britnell, W.J. 1990. 'Medieval pottery' in Britnell, W.J. 1990

Craig, D. 1997. 'The sculptured stones' in P. Hill *Whithorn and St Ninian* Stroud

Cramp, R. 1981. *The hermitage and the offshore island* London

Crankshaw, D.J. and Gillespie, A. 2006 'Parker, Matthew (1504–1575)', *Oxford Dictionary of National Biography*, Oxford [http://www.oxforddnb.com.voyager.chester.ac.uk/view/article/21327, accessed 5 July 2007]

Crew, P and S. 1997 'Geophysical Survey at Llanfor, Merioneth 1997' *AW* 37, 13, 20

Crummy, N., Crummy, P. and Crossan, C. 1993. *Colchester archaeological report. 9,* Colchester

Cuissard, C. 1883. 'Vie de Saint Paul de Léon de Bretagne' *Revue Celtique* 5

Dark, K.R. 1992. 'Epigraphic, art-historical and historical approaches to the chronology of Class I inscribed stones' in Edwards, N. and Lane, A. (eds) 1992

Dark, K.R. 1993. 'St Patrick's *uillula*' in D. Dumville (ed) 1993. *St Patrick AD493–1993*, Woodbridge

Dark, K.R. 1994. *Civitas to Kingdom* Leicester

Dark, K.R. and Dark, S.P. 1996. 'New archaeological and palynological evidence for a sub-Roman reoccupation of Hadrian's Wall' *Archaeologia Aeliana* (5th series) 25

Davidson, A. 2001. 'Parish churches' in J. and L. Beverley Smith (eds) 2001

Davidson, A.F. and J.E., Owen-John, H. and Toft, L.A. 1988. 'Excavations at the sand covered medieval settlement at Rhossili, West Glamorgan' *BBCS* 34

Davies, J.R. 1998. '"The Book of Llandaf: a twelfth-century perspective' *Anglo-Norman Studies* 21

Davies, J.R. 2002. 'The saints of South Wales and the Welsh Church' in Thacker, A. and Sharpe, R. (eds) 2002

Davies, J.R. 2003. *The Book of Llandaf: Norman Church in Wales* Woodbridge

Davies, J.R. 2007a. 'Some observations on the "Nero", "Digby" and "Vespasian" recensions of *Vita S. David* in J. Wyn Evans and J. Woodings (eds) 2007

Davies, J.R. 2007b. 'The archbishopric of St Davids and the bishops of *Clas Cynidr*' in J.W. Evans and J. Wooding (eds) 2007

Davies, R.R. 1991. *Conquest, coexistence and change* Oxford

Davies, R.R. 1997. *The revolt of Owain Glynd r* Oxford

Davies, S. (ed and trans) 2007. *The Mabinogion* Oxford

Davies, T. 2006. 'Llanfor and the Upper Dee Valley: An early medieval landscape study' *MSRG Annual Report* 21

Davies, W. 1974–6 'Braint Teilo *BBCS* 26

Davies, W. 1978. *An early Welsh microcosm* London

Davies, W. 1979. *The Llandaf Charters* Aberystwyth

Davies, W. 1982a. *Wales in the early Middle Ages* Leicester

Davies, W. 1982b. 'The Latin charter tradition in Western Britain, Brittany and Ireland in the Early Medieval Period' in Dumville et. al. 1982

Davies, W. 1992. 'The myth of the Celtic church' in Edwards, N. and Lane, A. 1992

Davies, W. 1998. 'Charter-writing and its used in early medieval Celtic societies' in Pryce, H. (ed) 1998

Davies, W. 2004. 'Looking backwards to the early medieval past' *Welsh Historical Review* 22/2

Davies, W., Graham-Campbell, J., Handley, M., Kershaw, M., Koch, J.T., Le Duc, G. and Lockyear, K. *The Inscriptions of Early Medieval Brittany* Aberystwyth

Davy, N. 1964. 'A Pre-Conquest Church and Baptistery at Potterne' *Wiltshire Archaeology Magazine* 59

De Excidio – The ruin of Britain, and other works Gildas (ed and trans Michael Winterbottom) London

De la Borderie, A. 1901. *Chronologie du Cartulaire de Redon* Rennes

Description – The Description of Wales Thorpe 1978

Dix, G. 1945. *The shape of the Liturgy*. Westminster

Doble, G.H. 1971. *Lives of the Welsh Saints* Cardiff

Dodgshon, R.A. 1987. *The European Past* Basingstoke

Dornier, A. 1977. 'The Anglo-Saxon monastery at Breedon-on-the-Hill, Leicestershire' in Dornier, A. 1977. *Mercian Studies* Leicester

Driscoll, S. 2004. *'The Archaeological Context of Assembly in Early Medieval Scotland'* in Pantos, A and Semple, S. (eds)

Dumville, D. 1972–74. 'Some aspects of the chronology of the *Historia Brittonum*' *BBCS* 25

Dumville, D., Whitelock, D., McKitterick, R. 1982. *Ireland in early mediaeval Europe* Cambridge

Dumville, D. 1992. *Liturgy and the Ecclesiastical History of Late Anglo-Saxon England* Woodbridge

Dumville, D. (ed and trans) *Annales Cambriae, A.D. 682–954* Cambridge

EH – Bede, Ecclesiastical History of the English People (ed and trans by L. Shirley Price) 1990, Harmondsworth

Edwards, N. 1986. 'Anglesey in the Early Middle Ages' *TAAFC*.

Edwards, N. 1994. 'Holy Wells in Wales and Early Christian Archaeology' *Source* 1 [http://people.bath. ac.uk/liskmj/living-spring/sourcearchive/ns1/ns1ne1.htm]

Edwards, N. 1995. 'Eleventh century Welsh illuminated manuscripts' in Bourke, C. (ed) 1995. *From the Isles of the North* Belfast

Edwards, N. 1996. Identifying the archaeology of the early church in Wales and Cornwall' in Blair, J. and Pyrah, C. 1996

Edwards, N. 1999. 'Viking-influenced sculpture in North Wales' *CA* 3

Edwards, N. 2001a. 'Early medieval inscribed stones and stone sculpture in Wales' *MA* 45

Edwards, N. 2001b. 'Monuments in a landscape: the early medieval sculpture of St David's' in H. Hamerow and A. Macgregor (eds) 2001

Edwards, N. 2002. 'Celtic saints in early medieval archaeology' in A. Thacker and R. Sharpe (eds) 2002

Edwards, Nancy. 2007. 'Early Medieval sculpture in south-west Wales: the Irish Sea connection'. In Moss, Rachel (ed), *Making and meaning in insular art* Dublin

Edwards, N. and Gray Hulse, T. 1994. 'A fragment of a reliquary casket from Gwytherin, North Wales' *AnJ* 72

Edwards, N. and Lane, A. 1988. *Early medieval settlements in Wales, A.D. 400–1100*, Bangor

Edwards, N. and Lane, A. 1992. *The Early Church in Wales and the West,* Oxford,

EH – Bede, *Ecclesiastical History of the English People* (ed and trans by L. Shirley-Price,), Harmondsworth

Etchingam, C. 2006. 'Pastoral provision in the first millennium: a two-tier service?' in Fitzpatrick, E. and Gillespie, R. (eds). 2006. *The parish in medieval and early modern Ireland* Dublin

Etchingham, C. 2007. 'Viking-age Gwynedd and Ireland: political relations' in Jankulak, K. and Wooding, J. (eds) 2007

Evans, D.S. 1990. *A mediaeval prince of Wales: the life of Gruffudd ap Cynan* Felinfach

Evans, E. 1905. 'Bucket from Ty'r Dewin, Caernarvonshire' *AC* 5

Evans, E. 2003. *Early medieval ecclesiastical sites in south-east Wales: Desk-based assessment* GGAT 2003/30

Evans, E., Davidson, A., Ludlow, N. and Silvester, B. 2000. 'Medieval churches in Wales' *CA* 4

Evans, G.E. 1918. 'Caldey Island' *Transactions of the Carmarthenshire Antiquarian Society and Field Club* 12

Evans, J.W. 1986. 'The early church in Denbighshire' *Denbighshire History Society Transactions* 35

Evans, J.W. 1991. 'The Reformation and St David's cathedral' *Journal of the Welsh Ecclesiastical History Society* 7

Evans, J.W. 1992. 'The survival of the *clas* as an institution in Medieval Wales' in N. Edwards and A. Lane (eds) 1992

Evans, J.W. and J. Woodings (eds) 2007. *St David of Wales* Woodbridge,

Evans, J.W. 1993. 'Meidrum: Some sidelights on the church and parish' *Carmarthenshire Antiquary* 29

Evans, J.W. 2003. 'St David and St Davids' in J. Cartwright (ed) 2003

Fanning, T. 1981. 'Excavation of an early Christian cemetery and settlement at Reask, Co. Kerry' *PRIA* 81c2

Farwell, D.E. and Molleson, T.I. 1993. *Poundbury Volume 2: The Cemeteries* Dorchester

Fawtier, R. (ed) 1912. *La Vie de saint Samson* Paris

Fenn, R.W.D. 2000. 'The character of early Christianity in Radnorshire' *Transaction of the Radnorshire Society* 70

Fenn, R.W.D. and Sinclair, J.B. 1990. 'The Christian origins of Montgomeryshire: an interpretation' *Montgomeryshire Collections* 78

Fisher, C. 1926. 'The Welsh Celtic Bells' *AC* 81 (2)

Fisher, I. 2001. *Early medieval sculpture in the West Highlands and Islands,* Edinburgh

Fitzpatrick, E. 2004. 'Royal Inauguration Mounds in Medieval Ireland' in Pantos, A and Semple, J. (eds)

Flanagan, M.T. and Green, J.A. (eds) 2005. *Charters and Charter Scholarship in Britain and Ireland* London

Fleuriot, L. 1976, 'Les éveques de la *Clas Cynidr*' *Etudes celtiques* 15

Flobert, P. (ed) *La Vie Ancienne de saint Samson de Dol* Paris

Foster, I. Ll. 1964. "Obituary' *AC* 113

Fox, C. 1926. 'A Bronze Age Barrow on Kilpaison Burrow, Rhoscrowther, Pembrokeshire' *AC* 81

Fox, C. 1939. 'The Capel Garmon Firedog' *AnJ*

France, J. (ed and trans) *Rodolfus Glaber. The Five Books of the Histories* Oxford

Frere, S.S. 1976. 'The Silchester church: the excavation by Sir Ian Richmond in 1961' *Archaeologia* 106

Fulton, H. 2001. 'Tenth-Century Wales and *Armes Prydein*' *Transactions of the Honourable Society of Cymmrodorion 2000* n.s. 7

Gailliou, P. 1989. *Les Tombes d'Armorique* Paris

Gameson, R. 2002. 'The insular gospel book at Hereford Cathedral' *Scriptorium* 56

Gardner, I. and Fisher, J. 1917. 'Some fonts of Gwent and Herefordshire' *AC* (6th series) 17

GE – The Jewel of the Church (ed and trans by J. Hagen), Brill

Gelling, M. 1992–3. 'Paganism and Christianity in the Wirral' *Journal of the English Place-name Society* 25

Gethin-Jones, E. 1979. *The Dymock School of Sculpture* Chichester

Gesta – William of Malmesbury *The deeds of the bishops of England (Gesta Pontificum Anglorum)* (ed and trans by David Preest.) Woodbridge

Gray, M. 1991. 'The last days of the shrines and chantries of Monmouthshire' *Journal of the Welsh Ecclesiastical History Society* 7

Gray, M. 1996 'Penrhys: the archaeology of a pilgrimage' *Morgannwg* 10

Gray, M. 2000. *Images of Piety* Oxford

Gray, M. 2001. 'The pilgrimage as ritual space' in A. T. Smith and A. Brookes, (eds) 2001. *Holy Ground,* Oxford

Gray Hulse, T. 1998. 'Three saints, two wells and a Welsh parish' *Source* (ns) 6, http://people.bath.ac.uk/ liskmj/living-spring/sourcearchive/ns6/ns6tgh1.htm

Gresham, C. 1939. 'The Aberconwy Charter' *AC* 94

Gresham, C. 1969. *Medieval Stone Carving in North Wales* Cardiff

Gresham, C. 1982–3. 'The Aberconwy Charter: further considerations' *BBCS* 30

Grinsell, L. V. 1982. 'The later history of Ty Illtud' *AC* 130

Grogan, E. and Eogan, G. 1987. 'Lough Gur Excavations by Seán P. Ríordáin' *PRIA* 87 C

Grosjean, P. (ed). 1956. 'Vies et miracles de S. Petroc' *Analecta Bolandiana* 74

Gruffydd, A. 1992. 'St Cybi environmental improvement scheme, Caergybi' *AW* 32

Guigon, P. 1997. *Les eglises du Haut Moyen Age en Bretagne* St Malo

Hadley, D. 2002. 'Burial Practices in Northern England in the later Anglo-Saxon period', in S. Lucy and A. Reynolds (ed) 2002. *Burial in Early Medieval England and Wales* London

Hague, D. B. 1960. 'A Medieval Church on the island of St Tudwal' *Transactions of the Caernarvonshire Historical Society* 21

Halliday, G. 1900. 'Llantwit Major Church, Glamorganshire' *AC* (5th series) 17

Hamerow, H. and MacGregor, A. (eds) 2001. *Image and Power in the Archaeology of Early Britain* Oxford

Handley, M. 2001. 'The origins of Christian commemoration in late antique Britain' *Early Medieval Europe* 10/2

Handley, M. 2001a. 'Isidore of Seville and 'Hisperic Latin' in early medieval Wales' in J. Higgit et al. (eds) 2001

Handley, M. 2003. *Death, society and culture* Oxford

Harbison, P. 1992. *High Crosses of Ireland* Bonn, Habelt

Harris, A. 2003. *Byzantium, Britain and the West* Stroud

Harvey, A. 2001. 'Problems in dating the origin of the Ogham script' in J. Higgit et al. (eds)

Haslam, R. 1979. *Buildings of Wales: Powys* Harmondsworth

Haycock, M. 2007. *Legendary poems from the Book of Taliesin* Aberystwyth

Hayes, J. 1972. 1972. *Late Roman Pottery* London

Heighway, C. and Bryant, R. 1999. *The Golden Minster* York

Hemp, W.J. and Radford, C.A.R. 1953. 'The Llanelltyd Stone' *AC* 102

Henderson, G. 1987. *From Durrow to Kells* London,

Henry, F. 1967. *Irish Art: In the Romanesque period,* London

Henken, E. 2003. 'Welsh hagiography and the nationalist impulse' in Cartwright, J. (ed) 2003

Herbert, M. 2005. 'Before charters? Property records in pre-Anglo-Norman Ireland' in Flanagan, M. and Green, J.A. (eds) 2005

Herren, M. and Brown, S. 2002. *Christ in Celtic Christianity* Woodbridge

HGVK – Evans, D.S. 1977 *Historia Gruffudd vab Kenan* Cardiff

Herity, M. 1993. 'The Tomb Shrine of the Founder Saint' in R.M. Spearman and J. Higgit, J. (eds) 1993. *The Age of Migrating Ideas* Stroud

Higgit, J., Forsyth, K. and Parsons, D. (eds) 2001. *Roman, runes and ogham* Donington

Higham, N.J. 1997. *The Convert Kings* Manchester

Hillaby, J. 2001. 'The early church in Herefordshire: Columban and Roman' in Leominster History Study Group (ed) *The Early Church in Herefordshire* Leominster

Hill J. and Swan, M. 1998. *The community, the family and the saint* Turnhout

Hiscock, N (ed) 2003. *The White Mantle of the Church* Turnhout

Holbrook, N. and Thomas, A. 2005. 'An early medieval monastic cemetery at Llandough, Glamorgan: Excavations in 1994' *MA* 49

Horne, E. 1928. 'Saxon cemetery at Camerton, Somerset' *Proceedings of the Somersetshire Archaeological and Natural History Society* 74

Howe, M. 1996. *Wales from the air* Cardiff

Howlett, D. 1995. *The Celtic Latin Tradition of Biblical Style* Dublin, Four Courts Press

Hübner, E. 1876. *Inscriptiones Britanniae Christianae* Berlin

Hudd, A.E. 1908. 'Some Roman remains from Monmouthshire' *Proceedings of the Clifton Antiquarian Club* 6

Hughes, H. 1904. 'Discoveries of graves in the Parish of Llanbedr-Goch, Anglesey' *AC* (6th series) 4

Hughes, H. 1909. 'Sword found at Gelliniog Wen, Anglesey' *AC* (6th series) 9

Hughes, H. 1924. 'An ancient burial ground at Bangor' *AC* (7th series)

Hughes, H. 1930. 'The ancient churches of Anglesey' *AC* 85

Hughes, K. 1958. 'British Museum MS Cotton Vespasian A xiv (*Vitae Sanctorum Wallensium*)' in N.K. Chadwick, K. Hughes, C. Brooke and K. Jackson (eds) *Studies in the early British Church* Cambridge

Hunwicke, J. 2002. 'Kerry and Stowe revisited' *PRIA C* 102

Huws, D. 1978. 'A Welsh manuscript of Bede's *De Natura Rerum*' *BBCS* 27(4)

Huws, D. 2002. *Medieval Welsh Manuscripts* Cardiff

Insley, C. 1999. 'Fact and fiction in thirteenth century Gwynedd: The Aberconwy charters' *SC* 33

Isaac, G. 2002. '*Gwarchan Maeldderw*: A "lost" medieval Welsh classic' *CMSC* 44

Isaac, G. 2007. '*Armes Prydain Fawr* and St David' in J. Evans and J. Wooding (eds) 2007

Jackson, K.H. 1963. *Language and History in Early Britain* Edinburgh

Jackson, K.H. 1969. *The Gododdin* Edinburgh

James, E. 1977. *The Merovingian archaeology of south-west Gaul* (2 vols) Oxford

James, H. 1987. 'Excavations at Caer, Bayvil, 1979' *AC* 136

James, H. 1992. 'Early medieval cemeteries in Wales' in Edwards, N. and Lane, A. (eds) 1992

James, H. 1993. 'Roman Carmarthen' in S. Greep (ed) 1993. *Roman Towns* York

James, H. 1993. 'The cult of St David in the Middle Ages' in Carver, M. (ed) 1993. *In Search of Cult* Woodbridge

James, H. 2007. 'The geography of the cult of St David' in J. W. Evans and J. Wooding (eds), 2007

James, J. W. (ed and trans) 1967. *Life of St David* Cardiff

Jankulak, K. 2003. 'Swine, saints and Celtic Hagiography' in J. Cartwright (ed) 2003

Jankulak, K. and Wooding, J. (eds) 2007. *Ireland and Wales in the Middle Ages*, Dublin,

Jarrett, M.G. 1969. 'Caer Gai' in Nash-Williams, V. 1969. *The Roman Frontier in Wales* Cardiff

Jenkins, D. 1994. 'From Wales to Weltenburg:' in Brieskorn, N (ed) *Vom Mittelalterlichten Recht zur neuzeitlichen rechtwissenschaft* Paderborn

Jenkins, D. 2000. *The Law of Hywel Dda* Llandysul

Jenkins, D. and Owen, M.E., 1983. 'The Welsh marginalia in the Lichfield Gospels' *CMSC* 5

Jenkins, D and Owen, M.E., 1984 'The Welsh marginalia in the Lichfield Gospels' *CMSC* 7

Jenkins, G.H. 2004 'Evans, Theophilus (1693–1767)', *Oxford Dictionary of National Biography*, Oxford [http://www.oxforddnb.com.voyager.chester.ac.uk/view/article/8980, accessed 5 July 2007]

John, T. and Rees, N. 2002. *Pilgrimage: A Welsh Perspective* Llandysul

Johns, C.N. 1956. 'Long-cist graves at Ty'n Y Felin Quarry, Llanddyfnan' *TAAFC*

Johnson, R. 2004. 'On the Dating of some Early-medieval Irish Crosiers' *MA* 44

Johnston, D. 1993. *Iolo Goch; Poems* Llandysul

Johnstone, N. 1997. 'The location of the Royal Courts of Thirteenth-Century Gywnedd' in N. Edwards (ed) 1997. *Landscape and settlement in Medieval Wales* Oxford

Jones, E. 1959. 'Rhirid Flaidd' in Ralegh Radford, C.A.R. 1958. 'Pennant Melangell: The Church and the Shrine' *AC* 108

Jones, F. 1992. *Holy wells of Wales* Cardiff

Jones, C.A. 2001. 'Old English *Fant* and its compounds in the Anglo-Saxon vocabulary of baptism' *Medieval Studies* 63

Jones, G.R.J. 1972. 'Post-Roman Wales' in H.P.R. Finberg (ed) *The Agrarian History of England and Wales* Vol. 1, Cambridge

Jones, G. 2008. *Saints in the landscape* Stroud

Jones, M. 1994. 'St Paul in the Bail, Lincoln: Britain in Europe' in K. Painter (ed) '*Churches Built in Ancient Times*' London

Jones, N.A. and Owen, M. 2003. 'Twelfth-century Welsh hagiography' in J. Cartwright (ed) 2003

Jones, T. (ed and trans) 1967. 'The Black Book of Carmarthen "Stanzas of the Graves"' *Proceedings of the British Academy* 53

Journey – *The Journey through Wales*, Thorpe 1978

Kelly, R.S., 1991. 'Ffynnon Beuno, Aberffraw', *AW* 31

Kendrick, T.D. and Senior, E. 1937. 'St Manchan's Shrine' *Archaeologia* 86

Kirby, D. 1994. 'The political development of Ceredigion c.400-1081' in Davies, J.L. and Kirby, D. (eds) *Cardiganshire County History, Vol. 1* Cardiff

Kissock, J. 1996. 'Pottery' in Schlesinger, A. and Walls, C. 1996

Kissock, J. 1997. 'God Made Nature and Men Made Towns' in N. Edwards (ed) 1997, *Landscape and Settlement in Medieval Wales* Oxford

Klar, K. and Sweetser, E. 1996. 'Reading the unreadable: "Gwarchan Maelderw" from the *Book of Aneirin*' in Klar, K. et al. (ed) 1996. *A Celtic florilegium,* Lawrence

Knight, J.K. 1981. 'Excavations at St Barruc's Chapel, Barry Island, Glamorgan' *Transactions of the Cardiff Naturalists Society* 99

Knight, J K 1984 'Sources for the early history of Mongannwg', in Savory, H.M. (ed) 1984

Knight, J.K. 1987. 'Pottery in Wales: the Pre-Norman Background' in Vyner, B. and Wrathmell, S. (ed) 1987

Knight, J.K. 1992. 'The early Christian Latin inscriptions of Britain and Gaul' in Edwards, N. and Lane, A. (eds) 1992

Knight, J. 1998. 'Late Roman and post-Roman Caerwent: some evidence from metalwork' *AC* 145, 34–66

Knight, J.K. 1999. *The End of Antiquity* Stroud

Knight, J. 2001a. 'Britain's Other Martyrs: Julius, Aaron and Alban at Caerleon' in *Alban and St Albans* London

Knight, J.K. 2001b. 'Basilicas and Barrows: the Latin Memorial stones of Wales and their archaeological context' in Higgit, J., Forsyth, K. and Parsons, D. (eds) 2001

Knight, J. 2006. 'From villa to monastery: Llandough in context' *MA* 49

Knight, J.K. 2006 and Wood, R. 'St Gwynllyw's Cathedral, Newport: the Romanesque archway' *AC* 155

La Niece, S. and Stapleton, C. 1993. 'Niello and enamel on Irish metalwork' *AnJ* 73

Lambert, J. (ed) 1996. *Transect Through Time* Lancaster

Lang, J.T. 1971. 'The Castledermot Hogback' *JRSAI* 101(2)

Lang, J.T. 1984. 'The hogback: a Viking colonial monument' *AASAH3*

Lapidge, M. 1974. 'The Welsh-Latin poetry of Sulien's family' *SC* 8–9

Latouche, R. (ed) 1911. 'Le plus ancienne vie de S. Malo' *Melanges d'histoire Cournouaille* Paris

Laws, E. 1895. 'Review of *Index to 'The Historical tour through Pembrokeshire'* by Richard Fenton' *AC* (5th series) 12

Lawlor, H.J. and Best, R.J. 1931. *The Martyrology of Tallaght* London

Lewis, B.J. 2005. *Welsh poetry and English pilgrimage: Gruffudd ap Maredudd and the Rood of Chester* Aberystwyth

Lewis, J. 1969. 'Two pewter vessels from White Castle' *Monmouthshire Antiquary* 2(3)

Lewis, J.M. 1976. 'A survey of early Christian monuments in Dyfed, west of the Taf' in Boon, G.C and Lewis, J.M. (eds) 1976, *Welsh Antiquity* Cardiff

Lieberman, M. 2008. *The March of Wales, 1067-1300* Cardiff

Lindsay, W.M. 1912. *Early Welsh Script* Oxford

Lhywd, E. 1911. *Parochialia, Part II – North Wales and South Wales* Morris, R. (ed) *AC* supplement

LL – *The Text of the Book of Llan Dâv* (ed J. Rhys and J. Evans) Oxford.

Lloyd, J.E. 2004. 'Rees, William Jenkins (1772–1855)', rev. Beti Jones, *Oxford Dictionary of National Biography,* Oxford [http://www.oxforddnb.com.voyager.chester.ac.uk/view/article/23291, accessed 7 July 2007]

Lloyd, T., Orbach, J. and Scourfield, R. 2004. *Buildings of Wales: Pembrokeshire* London

Lloyd Griffith, J. 1895. 'Ancient stone-lined graves found at Llanfaethlu' *AC* (5th series) 12

Longden, G. 2003. 'Iconoclasm, belief and memory in early medieval Wales' in H. Williams (ed) 2003. *Archaeologies of Remembrance* New York

Longley, D. 1991. 'The excavation of Castell, Porth Trefadog, a coastal promontory fort in North Wales' *MA* 35

Longley, D. 1996. 'Excavations at Bangor, Gwynedd' *AC* 144

Longley, D. 2004. 'The early medieval cemetery' in Lynch, F. and Musson, C. 2005. 'A prehistoric and early medieval complex at Llandegai, near Bangor, North Wales: excavations directed by C.H. Houlder 1966–67' *AC* 150

Lord, P. 2003. *The Visual Culture of Wales: Medieval Vision* Cardiff

Ludlow, N. 2001. '"Spiritual and temporal": church building in medieval and later Carmarthenshire' *Carmarthenshire Antiquary* 36

Lywyd, A. 1832. *A History of the Island of Mona*, Ruthin, R. Jones and Longman,

Ludlow, N. 2003a. *Cadw: Welsh Historic Monuments, eary medieval ecclesiastical sites project. Stage 2* Cambria Archaeology unpublished report no.2003/39

Ludlow, N. 2003b. 'St Cristiolus churchyard, Eglwyswrw, Pembrokeshire' *AC* 149

Macalister, R.A.S. 1945-9. *Corpus Inscriptionum Insularum Celticarum* Dublin

MacDermott, M. 1955. 'The Kells crosier' *Archaeologia* 96

MacDonald, P. 2007. *Llyn Cerrig Bach: a study of the copper alloy artefacts* Cardiff

Mango, M., Mango, C., Care Evans, A. and Hughes, M. 1989. 'A sixth century Mediterranean bucket from Bromeswell Parish, Suffolk' *Antiquity* 63

Manning, C. 1998. 'Some early masonry churches and the round tower at Clonmacnoise' *Clonmacnoise Studies* 2, Dublin

Mascetti, K. 2001. 'Presidential address: the Cambrians and the Railways' *AC* 150

Mason, D.J. 1987. 'Chester- the Canabae legionis' *Britannia* 18

Mawer, C.F. 1995. *Evidence for Christianity in Roman Britain: The Small Finds* Oxford

Mayr-Harting, H. 1992. *The coming of Christianity to Anglo-Saxon England*. London

McKenna, C. 1996. 'The hagiographic poetics of *Canu Cadfan*' in Klar, K. et al. (ed) 1996. *A Celtic florilegium*, Lawrence

McManus, D. 1991. *An Introduction to Ogom* Maynooth

Merdrignac, B. 2003. 'The process and significance of rewriting in Breton hagiography' in J. Cartwright (ed)

Michelli, P.E. 1986. 'Four Scottish crosiers and their relation to the Irish Tradition' *Proceedings of the Society of Antiquaries of Scotland* 116 (1986)

Michelli, P.E. 1988. 'Fragments of a fifth crosier from Scotland' *Proceedings of the Society of Antiquaries of Scotland* 118

Moore, D. 1998. 'Cambrian Meetings 1847-1997' *AC* 147

Morgan Evans, D. 2005. 'The origin of Powys – Christian, heretic or pagan?' *Montgomeryshire Collections* 93

Morris, C. 1983. 'The survey and excavations at Keeill Vael, Druidale in their context' in C. Fell, P. Foot, J. Graham-Campbell and R. Thompson (eds) *The Viking Age in the Isle of Man*. Isle of Man

Morris, C. 2000. *Wood and woodworking in Anglo-Scandinavian and Medieval York* York

Murphy, K. 1987. 'Excavations at Llanychlwydog Church, Dyfed' *AC* 136

Murphy, K. 1992. 'Plas Gogerddan, Dyfed' *AJ* 149

Musson, C. 1994. *Wales from the air* Cardiff

Nash-Williams, V. 1950. *The early Christian monuments of Wales*, Cardiff

Neil Baynes, E. 1935. 'Some stone-lined graves at Llanruddlad' *TAAFC*

Newman, J. 1995. *Buildings of Wales: Glamorgan* Harmondsworth

Newman, J. 2000 *The Buildings of Wales: Gwent / Monmouthshire* London

Newman, R. 1985. 'Atlantic Trading Estate, Barry' *AW* 25

Newman, R. and Parkin, L. 1986. 'Atlantic Trading Estate' *AW* 26

Nowakowski, J. and Thomas, C. 1990. *Excavations at Tintagel parish churchyard, Cornwall, Spring 1990* Truro

O'Brien, E. 1992. 'Pagan and Christian burial in Ireland during the first millennium AD: continuity and change' in Edwards, N. and Lane, A. (eds) 1992

Ó Carragáin, T. 2005. 'Regional variation in Irish pre-Romanesque architecture' *AnJ* 85

Ó Carragáin, T. 2006. 'Church building and pastoral care in early medieval Ireland' in Fitzpatrick, E. and Gillespie, R. (eds). 2006. *The parish in medieval and early modern Ireland* Dublin

Ó Floinn, R. 1994. *Irish shrines and reliquaries* Dublin

O'Keefe, T. 2003. *Romanesque Ireland* Dublin

O'Keefe, T. 2006. 'The built environment of local community worship between the late eleventh and early thirteenth centuries' in Fitzpatrick, E. and Gillespie, R. (eds). 2006. *The parish in medieval and early modern Ireland: Community, territory and building* Dublin

O'Kelly, M.J. 1958. 'Church Island near Valencia, Co. Kerry' *PRIA* 59c

Okasha, E. 1993. *Corpus of early Christian inscribed stones of south-west Britain* Leicester

Ó Ríordáin, S.P. 1949. 'Lough Gur excavations: Carraig Aille and the "Spectacles"' *PRIA* 52

Owen, A. 1841. *The Ancient laws and institutions of Wales* London

Owen, E. 1896. 'Lewis Morris's notes on some inscribed stones in Wales' *AC* (5th series) 13

Owen, H.W. and Morgan, R. 2007. *Dictionary of Place-names of Wales* Llandysul,

Owen, W. 1994. 'Medieval and post-medieval pottery' in Quinnell, H. and Blockley, M. 1994. *Excavations at Rhuddlan,* York

Padel, O. 1976–7. 'Cornish names of parish churches' *Cornish Studies* 2

Padel, O. 1977. *Cornish place-name elements* Nottingham

Pantos, A. and Semple, S.J. (eds) 2004. *Assembly Places and Practices in Medieval Europe* Dublin

Parkhouse, J. 1988. 'Excavations at Biglis, S. Glamorgan' in 1988, Robinson, D.M. 1988 *Biglis, Caldicot and Llandough* Oxford

Parsons, D. 1995. 'Early churches in Herefordshire: documentary and structural evidence' in D. Whitehead (ed) 1995. *Medieval art, architecture and archaeology at Hereford* London

Parsons, D. 1996. 'Liturgical and social aspects' in Boddington, A. 1996. *Raunds Furnells* London, English Heritage

Pearson, M. 2000-1. 'The creation of the Bangor cathedral chapter' *Welsh Historical Review* 20

Pearson, M. 2000. 'The creation and development of the St Asaph cathedral chapter 1141–1293' *CMSC* 40

Peden, A. 1981. 'Science and philosophy in Wales at the time of the Norman Conquest; A Macrobius manuscript from Llanbadarn' *CMSC* 2

Petts, D. 1998. 'Burial and gender in late and sub-Roman Britain' in C. Forcey, J. Hawthorne and R. Witcher (eds) *TRAC* 97 Oxford

Petts, D. 2001. *Burial, religion and identity in sub-Roman and early medieval Britain: AD 400–800*, PhD Thesis, University of Reading

Petts, D. 2002a. 'Burials and Boundaries in Early Medieval Western Britain'. in S. Lucy and A. Reynolds *Burial in Early Medieval England and Wales* London

Petts, D. 2002b. 'Votive Hoards in Late Roman Britain: Pagan or Christian?' in M. Carver (ed) 2002. *The Cross Goes North,* Woodbridge

Petts, D. 2003. *Christianity in Roman Britain* Stroud

Petts, D. 2004 'Early Medieval or Late Antique?: Burial in Western Britain AD410 to 600' in Collins, R. and Gerrard, J. (eds) 2004. *Debating Late Antiquity* Oxford

Petts, D. 2007. '*De Situ Brecheniauc* and *Englynion y Beddau*: Writing about burial in early medieval Wales' *ASAH* 14

Petts, D. 2009 'Thinking about the British in early medieval England' in D. Sayer and H. Williams (ed) *Festschrift volume*

Petts, D. and McOmish, J. 2008. *Fey Field, Whithorn* York [http://www.iadb.co.uk/yat/publish.htm?PUB=58]

Petts, D. and Turner, S. 2009. 'Multiple church complexes on early medieval ecclesiastical sites in Western Britain' in N. Edwards (ed) *Archaeology of Early Medieval Celtic Churches c. 400–1100* London

Phillips, D.R. 1910-15. 'The Twrog manuscript' *Journal of the Welsh Bibliographic Society* 1

Philpott, R. 1991. *Burial Practices in Roman Britain* Oxford

Pluskowski, A. G. and Patrick, P. J. 2003. 'How do you pray to God?' Fragmentation and variety in early medieval Christianity', in M. Carver (ed), *The Cross Goes North* Woodbridge

Pollock, K. 2006. *The Evolution and Role of Burial Practice in Roman Wales* Oxford

Poulin, J.-C. 1987. 'Les Dossiers de saint Samson de Dol' *Francia* 15

Price, C. 1985. 'Atlantic Trading Estate' *AW* 25

Price, C. 1986. 'Atlantic Trading Estate' *AW* 26

Price, C. 1987. 'Atlantic Trading Estate' *AW* 27

Pryce, H. 1992a. 'Ecclesiastical wealth in early medieval Wales' in Edwards, N. and Lane, A. (eds) 1992

Pryce, H 1992b. "Pastoral care in early medieval Wales', in J. Blair and R. Sharpe (eds) 1992

Pryce, H. 1993. *Native law and the church in Wales* Oxford

Pryce, H. (ed) 1998 *Literacy in Medieval Celtic Societies* Cardiff

Pryce, H. 2000a. 'The context and purpose of the earliest Welsh law books' *CMSC* 39

Pryce, H. 2000b. 'The household priest (*Offeiriad teulu*)' in Charles-Edwards, T. Owen, M. and Russell, P. *The Welsh King and his Court* Cardiff

Pryce, H. 2001. 'The Medieval Church' in J. B. Smith and Ll. B. Smith (eds) *History of Merioneth. Vol* II Cardiff

Pryce, H. 2005. 'Culture, power and the Charters of the Welsh Rulers' in Flanagan, M. and Green, J.A. (eds) 2005

Pryce, H. 2005. *The Acts of Welsh rulers, 1120–1283* Cardiff

Quensel-von Kalbern, L. 1999. 'The British Church and the Emergence of the Anglo-Saxon Kingdoms' *AASAH* 10

Radford, C.A.R. 1961. 'Presidential address' *AC* 111

Radford, C.A.R. 1963. 'The native ecclesiastical architecture of Wales c. 1100–1285' in I.L. Foster and L. Alcock (eds) *Culture and Environment* London

Radford, C.A.R. 1966. 'Cultural relations in the early Celtic world' in *Proceedings of the International Congress of Celtic Studies 1963,* Cardiff

Radford, C.A.R. 1971. 'Christian origins in Britain' *MA* 15

Radford, C.A.R. 1975. *The Early Christian Inscriptions of Dumonia* 1974 Edinburgh

Rahtz, P. 1993. *Glastonbury* London

Rahtz, P. Hirst, S. and Wright, S.M. 2000 *Cannington Cemetery* London

Ratkai, S. 2000. 'Pottery from the motte at Hen Domen' in Higham, R. and Barker, P. 2000. *Hen Domen, Montgomery* Exeter

RCAHMS 1999. *Kilmartin: prehistoric and early historic monuments,* Edinburgh

Reavill, P. and Geake, H. 2005. 'A cast copper-alloy 'architectural' censer-cover' *MA* 49

Redknap, M. 1995. 'Insular non-ferrous metalwork from Wales of the eighth to tenth century' in Bourke, C. (ed)

Redknap, M. 1998. 'On broken letters scarce remembred' in Hill, J. and Swan, M. (eds) 1998

Redknap, M. 2000. 'The medieval wooden crucifix figure from Kemeys Inferior, and its church' *Monmouthshire Antiquary* 16

Redknap, M. 2004a. 'Worship and devotion in Monmouthshire: some late medieval metalwork' *Monmouthshire Antiquary* 20

Redknap, M. 2004b. 'Viking-age settlement in Wales and the evidence from Llanbedrgoch'. *In* Hines, John; Lane, Alan; Redknap, Mark (ed), *Land, sea and home* Leeds

Redknap, M. 2005. 'Viking-age settlement in Wales: some recent advances'. *Transactions of the Honourable Society of Cymmrodorion* 12

Redknap, M. 2007. 'Crossing boundaries – Stylistic diversity and external contacts in early medieval Wales and the March' *CMSC* 53/54

Reynolds, A. 1998. 'The definition and ideology of Anglo-Saxon Execution and Cemetery sites' in De Boe, G. and Verhaeghe, F. (eds) *Death and Burial in Medieval Europe* Zellik

RCAHMW 1913. *County of Denbigh* London

RCHMW, 1917. *The County of Carmarthen* London

RCHMW, 1925. *The County of Pembroke* London

RCHMW 1937. *Anglesey* London

RCHMW 1976. *An inventory of the ancient monuments in Glamorgan. Vol. 1, Pre-Norman. Pt. 3, The early Christian period.* Cardiff

RCHMW 1991. *An inventory of the ancient monuments in Glamorgan* III, Pt1a. *Medieval Secular Monuments: The early castles from the Norman Conquest to 1217* London

Reavill, P., Leahy, L. and Geake, H. 2008. 'Irish casket fitting' *MA,* 329

Rees, A.D. 1935. 'Notes on the significance of white stones in Celtic archaeology and folk-lore with reference to recent excavations at Ffynnon Degla, Denbighshire', *BBCS*

Reimer PJ, et al. 2004 *Radiocarbon* 46

Richards, M. 1960. 'Gwrinydd, Gorfynydd and Llyswyrny', *BBCS* 18

Richardson, H. 1993. 'Remarks on the liturgical fan, flabellum or rhipidion' in R.M. Spearman and J. Higgitt (eds) *The Age of Migrating Ideas* Edinburgh

Rigoir, J. Rigoir, Y. and Meffre, J-F. 1973. 'Les sigillées palaéochretiénnes du groupe atlantique' *Gallia* 31

Ripoll, G. 1991. 'Materiales funerarios de la Hispania Visigodia' in Périn, P. (ed) 1991. *Gallo-Romains, Wisigoths et Francs en Aquitaine, Septimanie et Espagne* Rouen

Ripoll López, G 1993. 'The formation of the Visigothic Spain' in J.P. O'Neill, K. Howard *et al.* (eds) *The Art of Medieval Spain* New York

Roberts, T. 1992. Welsh ecclesiastical place-names and archaeology' in N. Edwards and A. Lane (eds) 1992

Robinson, D.M. 2006. *The Cistercians in Wales* London

Rodwell, W. and Rodwell, K. 1982. 'St Peter's Church, Barton-upon-Humber' *AnJ* 62

Romilly, Allen, J. 1899. 'Early Christian Art in Wales' *AC* 16

Russell, P. 2005. *Vita Griffini Filii Conani: the medieval Latin life of Gruffudd ap Cynan* Cardiff, University of Wales Press

Ryan, M. 1980. 'An early Christian hoard from Derrynaflan, Co. Kerry' *North Munster Antiq. Journal* 22

Ryan, M. 1989. 'Church metalwork' in S. Youngs 1989

Ryan, M. 1990. 'The formal relationships of insular early medieval eucharistic chalices' *PRIA* 90

Ryder, P. 1985. *The Medieval cross slab in Durham* Durham

Rutter, J.A. 1988. 'Saxon pottery' in Ward, S. 1988. *Excavations at Chester: 12 Watergate Street 1985* Chester

Savory, H.N. 1954/6. 'Early Iron Age discoveries on Merthyr Mawr Warren (Glam)' *BBCS* 16

Savory, H.N. 1960. 'Excavations at Dinas Emrys, Beddgelert, Caernarvonshire, 1954–6' *AC* 109

Savory, H.M. 1984. *Early Glamorgan: pre-history and early history* Cardiff

Schlesinger, A. and Walls, C. 1997. 'An Early church and medieval farmstead site: excavations at Llanelen, Gower' *AJ* 153

Scott, J.G. 1969. 'A Romanesque censer from Bearsden, Glasgow' *Glasgow Archaeological Journal.* 1

Sell, J. 1988. 'The Pottery' in Davidson, A.F. et al. 1988

Sell, S.H. 1996. *Archaeological Desk-Based Assessment, Atlantic Trading Estate Barry*, GGAT Report 96/031 (Unpublished)

Sharpe, R. 1984. 'Some problems concerning the organisation of the church in early medieval Ireland' *Peritia* 3

Sharpe, R. 2002. 'Martyrs and local saints in Late Antique Britain' in A. Thacker and R. Sharpe (eds) 2002

Sherlock, D. 1976. 'The Roman Christian silver from Biddulph' *AnJ* 56

Shoesmith, R. 1987. 'Urishay Chapel' *Transactions of the Woolhope Naturalists' Field Club* 45

Siewers, A.K. 2005. 'Writing an Icon of the Land: the *Mabinogi* as a Mystagogy of Landscape' *Peritia* 19 193–228

Sims-Williams, P. 1986. 'The visionary Celt' *CMSC* 11

Sims-Williams, P. 1990. 'Dating the transition to Neo-Brittonic' in A. Bammesberger and A. Wollman (eds) 1990

Sims-Williams, P. 1991. 'The emergence of Old Welsh, Cornish and Breton Orthography 600–800' *BBCS* 38

Sims-Williams, P. 1996. 'Edward IV's confirmation charter for Clynnog Fawr' in C. Richmond and I. Harvey (eds) 1996. *Recognitions: essays presented to Edmund Fryde.* Aberystwyth

Sims-Williams, P. 1998. 'Celtomania and Celtoscepticism' *CMSC* 36

Sims-Williams, P. 2001. 'Clas Beuno and the Four Branches of the Mabinogi' in B. Maier and S. Zimmer
(eds) 2001. *150 Jahre "Mabinogion" -Deutsch-Walisische Kulturbeziehungen*, Tübingen

Sims-Williams, P. 2003. *The Celtic inscriptions of Britain* Blackwell, Oxford

Smith, C. Roach, 1880. *Collectanea Antiqua* London

Smith, J.M.H. 1990. 'Oral and written; saints, miracles and relics in Brittany c.850–1250' *Speculum* 65

Smith, G., White, S. and Carr, A. 1999. 'A funerary and ceremonial centre at Capel Eithin, Gaerwen,
Anglesey' *TAAFC6*

Speake, G. 1989. *A Saxon bed burial on Swallowcliffe Down* London

Stallybrass, B. 1914. 'Recent Discoveries at Clynnogfawr' *AC* (6th series) 14

Stanley, W.O. 1846. 'Towyn-y-Capel and The Ruined chapel of St Bride' *AJ* 3

Stanford, S.C. 1995. 'Excavations at Meole Brace 1990 and Bromfield 1981–1991' *Transactions of the
Shropshire Archaeological Society* 70

Stephens, G.R. 1985. 'Caerleon and the martyrdom of SS. Aaron and Julius' *BBCS* 32

Stephens, M. 2007 'Hen bersoniaid llengar (*act.* 1818–1858)', *Oxford Dictionary of National Biography*, Oxford
[http://www.oxforddnb.com.voyager.chester.ac.uk/view/theme/95356, accessed 7 July 2007]

Suggett, R. 1996. 'Festivals and social structure in early modern Wales' *Past and Present* 152

Sweet, R. 2004. *Antiquaries: The Discovery of the Past in Eighteenth-century Britain*, London, Hambledon and
London

Sylvester, D. 1967, 'Parish and township in Cheshire and north-east Wales', *J. Chester Arch. Soc.* 55

Taylor, H.M. 1973. 'The position of the altar in early Anglo-Saxon churches' *AnJ* 53

Taylor, H.M. and Taylor, J. 1965. *Anglo-Saxon Architecture Vol I-III* Cambridge,

Taylor, S. 1996. 'Place-names and the early Church in eastern Scotland' in B. Crawford (ed) 1996. *Scotland in
Dark Age Britain* St Andrew's

TED'A 1987 *Els Enteraments del Parc de la Ciutat,* Tarragona

Tedeschi, C. 1995. 'Osservazioni sulla paleografia delle iscrizioni britanniche paleocristiane (V-VII sec.)'
Scrittura e Civiltà 19

Tedeschi, C. 2001.'Some observations on the Palaeography of Early Christian' in J. Higgett. (ed) 2001

Thacker, A. and Sharpe, R. (eds). 2002. *Local Saints and Local Churches in the Early Medieval West* Oxford

Thomas, A. and Holbrook, N. 1995. *Excavations at Great House Farm, Llandough,* Cirencester, Unpublished
Report

Thomas, C. 1967. 'An Early Christian cemetery and chapel on Ardwall Isle, Kirkcudbright' *MA* 11

Thomas, C. 1971. *The Early Christian Archaeology of North Britain* Oxford

Thomas, C. 1981a. *Christianity in Roman Britain* London

Thomas, C. 1981b. *Provisional List of Imported Pottery in Post-Roman Western Britain and Ireland* Redruth

Thomas, C. 1994. *And shall these mute stones speak?* Cardiff

Thomas, D R. 1911–13. *History of the diocese of St Asaph* volume 2–3

Thomas, G. 1997. *The Charters of the Abbey of Ystrad Marchell* Aberystwyth

Thomas, W 1970. 'Medieval church building in Wales' in D Moore (ed) 1970. *The Irish Sea Province in archaeology and history* Cardiff

Thomas, W.G. 1989. 'An early sundial from the Tywyn area' *AC* 138

Thorpe, L. (ed and trans) 1978. *Gerald of Wales The Journey through Wales / The Description of Wales* Harmondsworth

Thurlby, M. 1999. *The Herefordshire school of Romanesque sculpture*, Woonton Almeley

Thurlby, M. 2006. *Romanesque architecture and sculpture in Wales* Woonton Almeley,

Todd, M. 1999. 'The latest inscriptions of Roman Britain' *Durham Archaeological Journal*

Toller, H. 1977. *Roman Lead Coffins and Ossuaria in Britain* Oxford

Tyrell Green, E. 1928. *Baptismal fonts* London

Tuck, M. 2003. 'Abernant, Kemeys Inferior' *AW* 39

Turner, S. 2006. *Making a Christian Landscape* Exeter

Vince, A. 1987. 'Medieval pottery in the Welsh borderland' in Vyner, B. and Wrathmell, S. (eds) 1987

VC – Adomnán of Iona, *Life of St Columba* (ed and trans by Richard Sharpe), 1995 Harmondsworth

VGFC – Russell, P. 2005. *Vita Griffini Filii Conani: the Medieval Latin life of Gruffudd ap Cynan* Cardiff

VSB – Vita Sancti Bernachii / Life of St Brynach in Wade-Evans, A. (ed and trans) 1944. *Vitae Sanctorum Britanniae et Genealogiae* Cardiff,

VSC – Vita Sancti Cadoci/ Life of Saint Cadog in Wade-Evans, A. (ed and trans) 1944. *Vitae Sanctorum Britanniae et Genealogiae* Cardiff

VSD – Sharpe, R. and Davies, J.R. (ed and trans) 2007. 'Rhigyfarch's *Life of St David*' in J.W. Evans and J. M. Wooding (eds) 2007

VSD II – Bowen Jones, T. 1934. *The Life of St David by Geraldus Cambrensis* MA Thesis, Cardiff

VSG – Vita Sancti Gundleii/Life of Saint Gwynllyw (ed and trans) 1944. *Vitae Sanctorum Britanniae et Genealogiae* Cardiff

VS I – Vita Sancti Iltuti/ Life of St Illtud (ed and trans) 1944. *Vitae Sanctorum Britanniae et Genealogiae* Cardiff

VSK – Vita Sancti Kebii/Life of Saint Cybi (ed and trans) 1944. *Vitae Sanctorum Britanniae et Genealogiae* Cardiff

VSP – Vita Sancti Paterni/Life of Saint Padarn, (ed and trans) 1944. *Vitae Sanctorum Britanniae et Genealogiae* Cardiff

VST – Vita Sancti Tathei/Life of St Tatheus, (ed and trans) 1944. *Vitae Sanctorum Britanniae et Genealogiae* Cardiff

VSW – Vita Sancte Wenefrede/Life of St Wenefred, (ed and trans) 1944. *Vitae Sanctorum Britanniae et Genealogiae* Cardiff

Vyner, B. and Wrathmell, S. (eds) 1987. *Studies in Medieval and Later Pottery in Wales*, Cardiff

Wade-Evans, A.W. 1944. *Vitae Sanctorum Britanniae et Genealogiae* Cardiff

Ward, A. 1975. 'A radio-carbon date for the Bronze Age in south-west Wales' *Carmarthenshire Antiquarian* 11

Warner, R. 1979. 'The Clogher Yellow Layer' *Medieval Ceramics* 3

Warrilow, W., Owen, G. and Britnell, W. 1986. 'Eight ring-ditches at Four Crosses, Llandysilio, Powys, 1981–85' *Proceedings of the Prehistoric Society* 52

Watts, L. and Leech, P.J. 1996. *Henley Wood* York

Way, A. 1869. 'Alabaster reliquary found in Caldey Island, Pembrokeshire' *AC* 26

Webster, C. and Brunning, R. 2004. 'A Seventh-Century AD Cemetery at Stoneage Barton Farm, Bishop's Lydeard, Somerset' *AJ* 161

Webster, P. 2005. 'Pottery from excavations at Tomen-y-Muir' *SC* 39

Weddell, P.J. 2000. 'The excavation of a post-Roman cemetery near Kenn' *Devon Archaeological Journal* 58

West, S. and Plouviez, J. 1976. 'The Roman site at Icklingham' *East Anglian Archaeology* 3

Westwood, J.O. 1846. 'Description of the Vitialianus Ogham stone.' *AC* 1

Westwood, J.O. 1848. 'On the ancient portable handbells of the British and Irish churches.' *AC* 3

Westwood, J.O. 1876–9. *Lapidarium Walliae* Oxford

White, R.B. 1971–2. 'Excavations at Arfryn, Bodedern' *TAAFC*

White, R.B. 1985. 'Caer Gai and the giants of Penllyn' *Journal of the Merioenth Historical and Record Society* 10

White, R.B. 1986. 'The Roman fort at Caer Gai, Meirionydd' *AC* 135

Williams, D. 1990. *Atlas of Cistercian Lands in Wales* Cardiff

Williams, D. and Redknap, M. 2005. 'The early medieval pottery' in N. Holbrook and A. Thomas 2005

Williams, G. 1962. *The Welsh Church from Conquest to Reformation* Cardiff

Williams, G. 1968. 'The Unfeigned Faith and an eighteenth century pantheologia' *Numen* 15/3

Williams, G. 1979. *Religion, language and nationality in Wales* Cardiff

Williams, G. 1991. 'Poets and pilgrims in the fifteenth and sixteenth centuries' *Transactions of the Honourable Society of Cymmorodion*

Williams, G. 1997. *Wales and the Reformation* Cardiff

Williams, G. 2004 'Davies, Richard (*c.*1505–1581)', *Oxford Dictionary of National Biography*, Oxford University Press, [http://www.oxforddnb.com.voyager.chester.ac.uk/view/article/7255, accessed 5 July 2007]

Williams, G. 2007. 'The crisis of the sixteenth century' in J.W. Evans and J. Wooding 2007 (eds)

Williams, I. 1931–3. 'Marwnad Cynddylan' *BBCS* 6

Williams, I. 1972. *The beginnings of Welsh Poetry* Cardiff

Williams, I. 1980. 'An Old Welsh Poem' in R. Bromwich (ed) *The Beginnings of Welsh Poetry* Cardiff

Williams, I. (ed) and Bromwich, R. (trans) 1982. *Armes Prydein: The Prophecy of Britain* Dublin

Williams, D. and Redknap, M. 2005. 'The early medieval pottery' in Holbrook, N. and Thomas, A. 2005

Williams, W.W. 1878. 'Leaden Coffin, Rhyddgaer' *AC* (4th series) 9

Willmott, G. 1938. 'Three burial sites at Carbury, Co. Kildare' *JRSAI* 68

Wilson, D.M. 1973. 'The bowls and miscellaneous silver: form and function' in A. Small, C. Thomas and D. Wilson (eds) *St Ninian's Isle and its Treasure* Aberdeen ,106-24

Wilson, D.M. and Blunt, C.E. 1961. 'The Trewhiddle hoard' *Archaeologia* 98

Wilson, D.R 1990. 'Air-reconnaissance of Roman Wales 1969–1988' *Trivium* 25

Wilson, R J A, 2004. 'The Roman "officer's tomb" at High Rochester revisited', *Archaeologia Aeliana* (5th series) 33

Wooding, J.M. 1996. *Communication and commerce along the western sealanes* Oxford

Wooding, J.M. 2007a. 'The figure of David' in J. Wyn Evans and J. Wooding (eds) 2007

Wooding, J. 2007b. 'Island and Coastal Churches and in Medieval Wales and Ireland' in Wooding, J. and Jankulak, K. (eds) 2007

Wood, S. 2006. *The Proprietary Church in the Medieval West* Oxford

Wright, T. 1843. *Three chapters of letters relating to the suppression of monasteries,* London

Wyn Evans, J. 2007. 'Transition and survival: St David and St David's Cathedral' in J. Wyn Evans and J. Wooding (eds) 2007

Youngs, S. 1989. *Work of the Angels* London

Zadora-Rio 2003. 'The Making of Churchyards and Parish Territories in the Early-Medieval Landscape of France and England' *MA* 47

Zarnecki, G., Holland, J. and Holt, T. (eds) 1984. *English Romanesque Art* London

Zimmer, H. *The Celtic church in Britain and Ireland* London

INDEX